CALIFORNIA SURFING AND CLIMBING IN THE FIFTIES

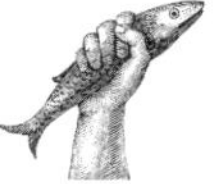

T. ADLER BOOKS, SANTA BARBARA

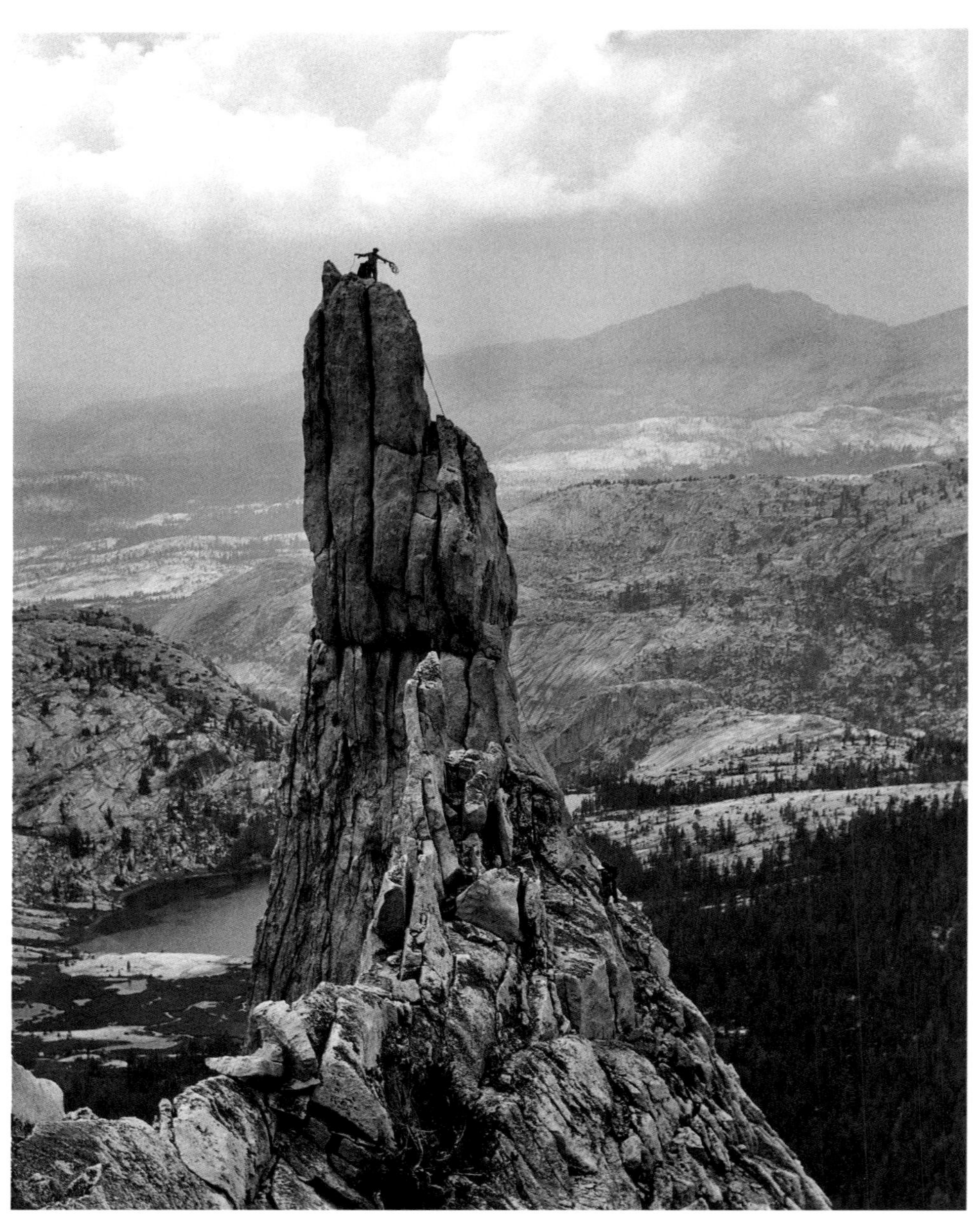

Eichorn Pinnacle, a stunning satellite of Cathedral Peak, Yosemite National Park. Photo: Bob Swift

The choice is yours to make,
time is yours to take;
some dive into the sea,
some toil upon the stone.

To live is to fly
all low and high,
so shake the dust off of your wings
and the sleep out of your eyes.

– Townes Van Zandt

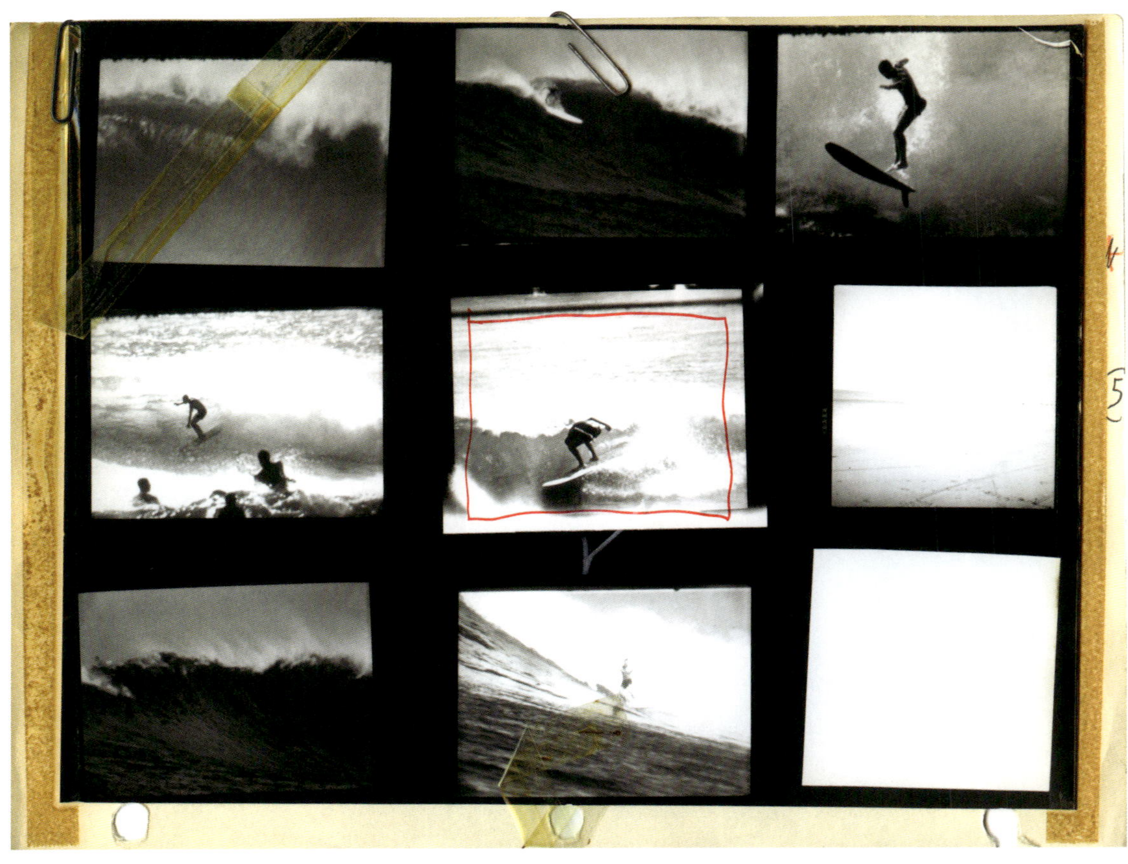

A proof sheet of John Severson's grainy 16MM frame grabs for a promo booklet called The Surfer (a year later it became Surfer magazine) produced for his 1960 film "Surf Fever". Photo © John Severson / surferart.com

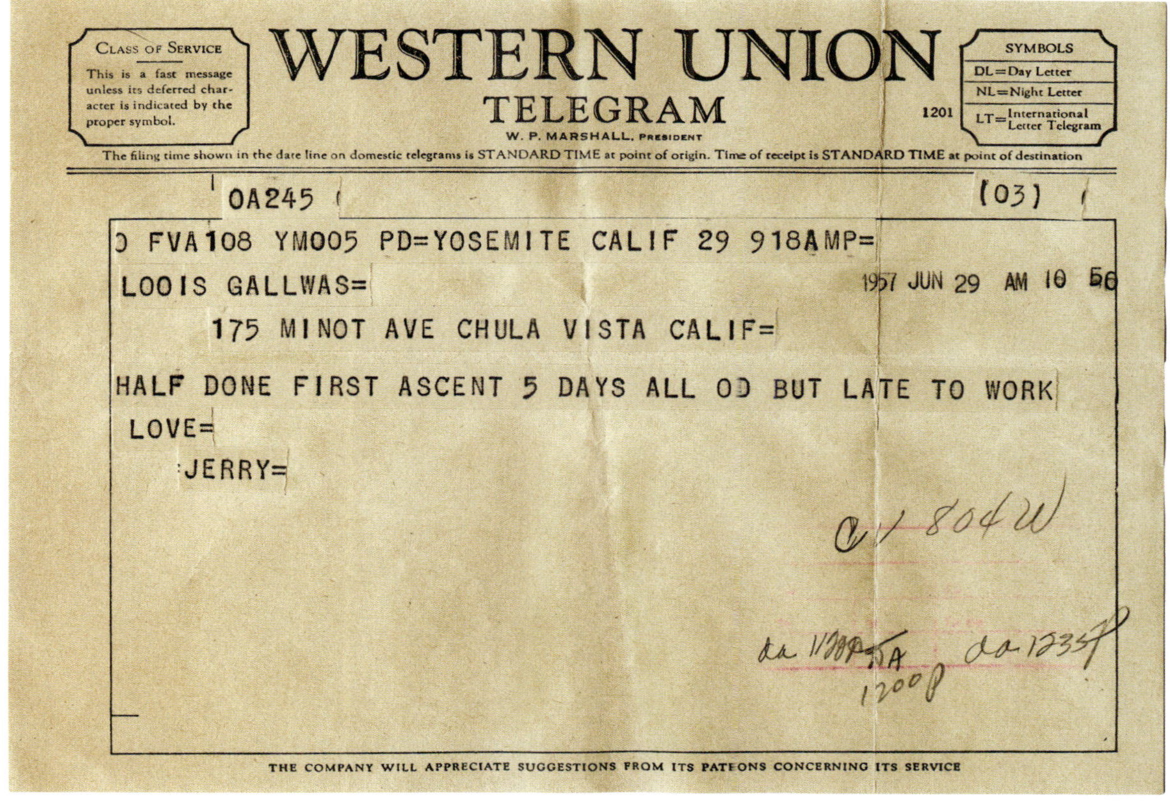

CLASS OF SERVICE
This is a fast message unless its deferred character is indicated by the proper symbol.

WESTERN UNION
TELEGRAM
W. P. MARSHALL, PRESIDENT

1201

SYMBOLS
DL=Day Letter
NL=Night Letter
LT=International Letter Telegram

The filing time shown in the date line on domestic telegrams is STANDARD TIME at point of origin. Time of receipt is STANDARD TIME at point of destination

OA245 (03)

O FVA108 YM005 PD=YOSEMITE CALIF 29 918AMP=

LOOIS GALLWAS= 1957 JUN 29 AM 10 56

175 MINOT AVE CHULA VISTA CALIF=

HALF DONE FIRST ASCENT 5 DAYS ALL OD BUT LATE TO WORK

LOVE=

JERRY=

THE COMPANY WILL APPRECIATE SUGGESTIONS FROM ITS PATRONS CONCERNING ITS SERVICE

Telegram sent by Jerry Gallwas to his mother after the first ascent of the Northwest face of Half Dome, 1957. Jerry Gallwas collection

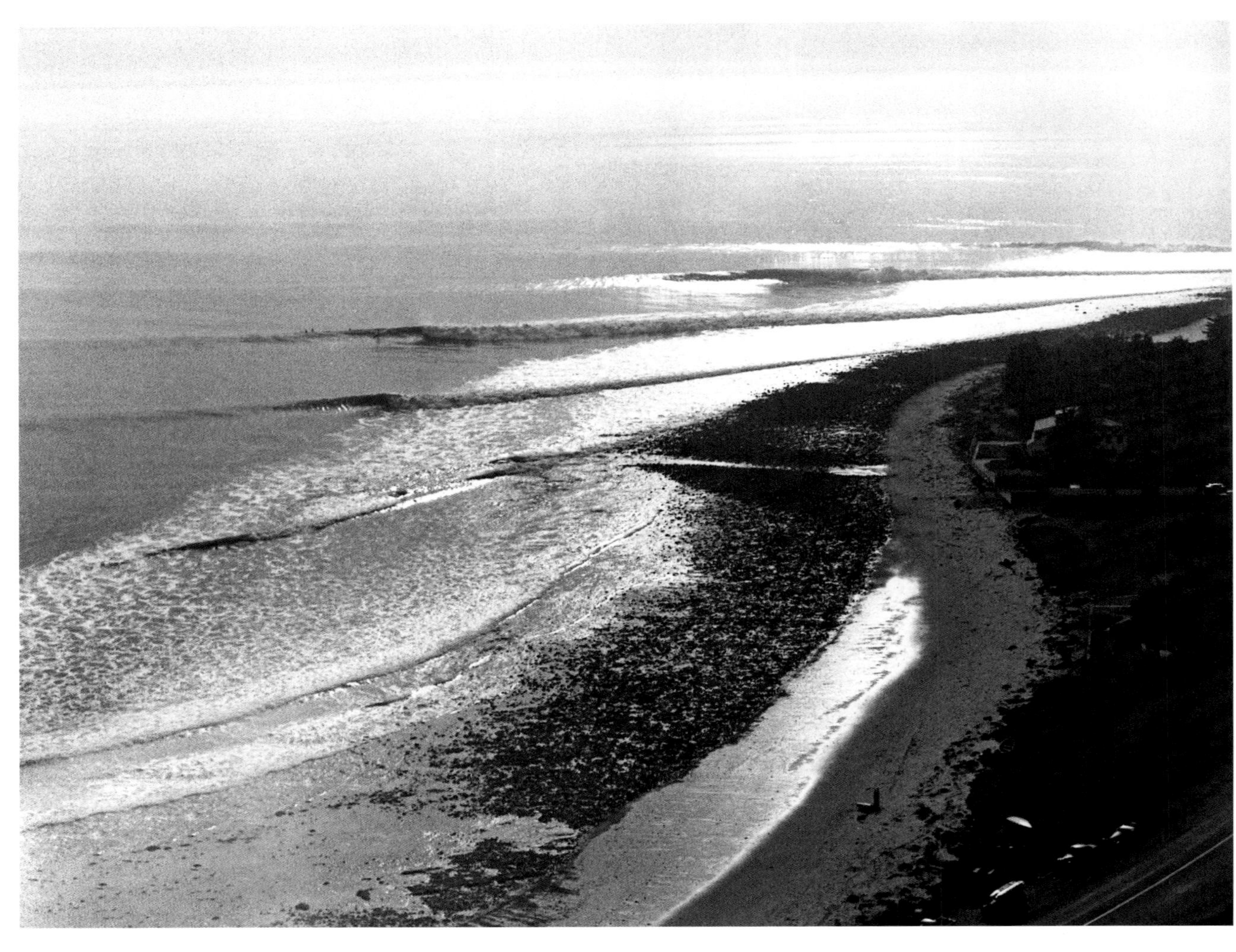

"The Queen of the Coast." Rincon's long, lined-up, second point waves pushed Joe Quigg to make the first pintails (circa-'49-'50). Such waves made an ideal test track for new ideas. Photo: Joe Quigg

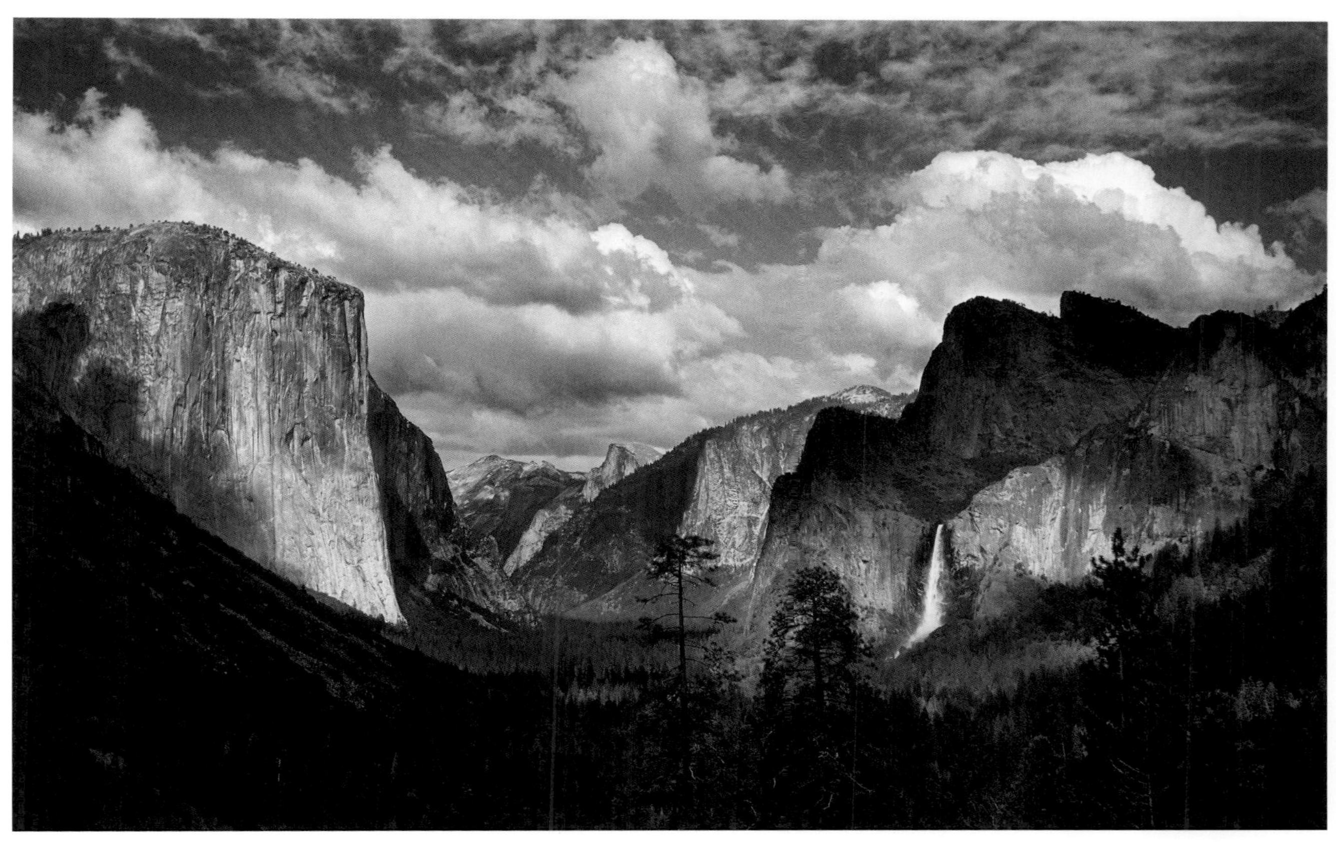

Yosemite Valley from the west, with El Capitan on the left and Bridalveil Fall on the right. Photo: Glen Denny

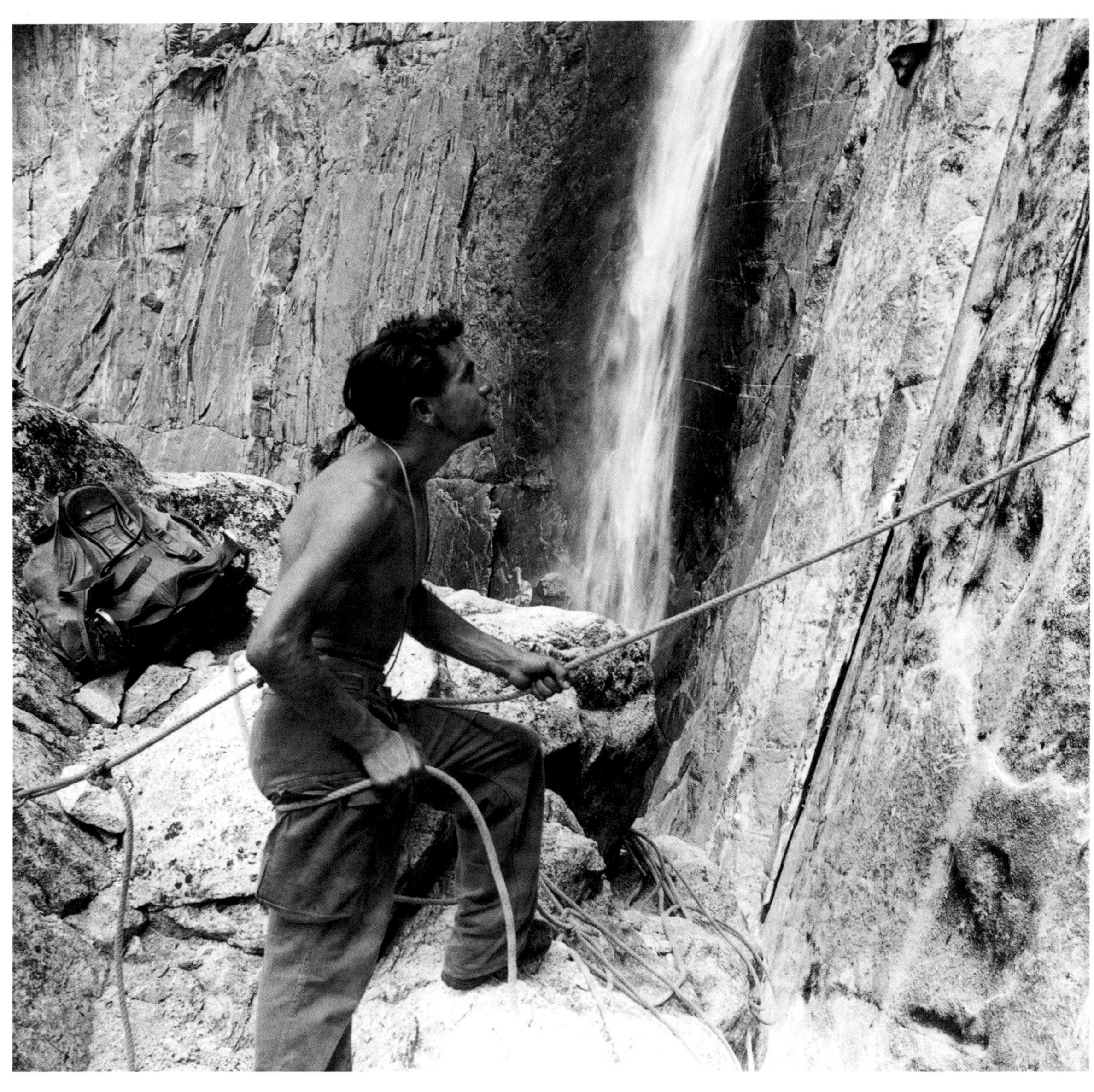

Warren Harding belaying, Yosemite Valley. Photo: Bob Swift

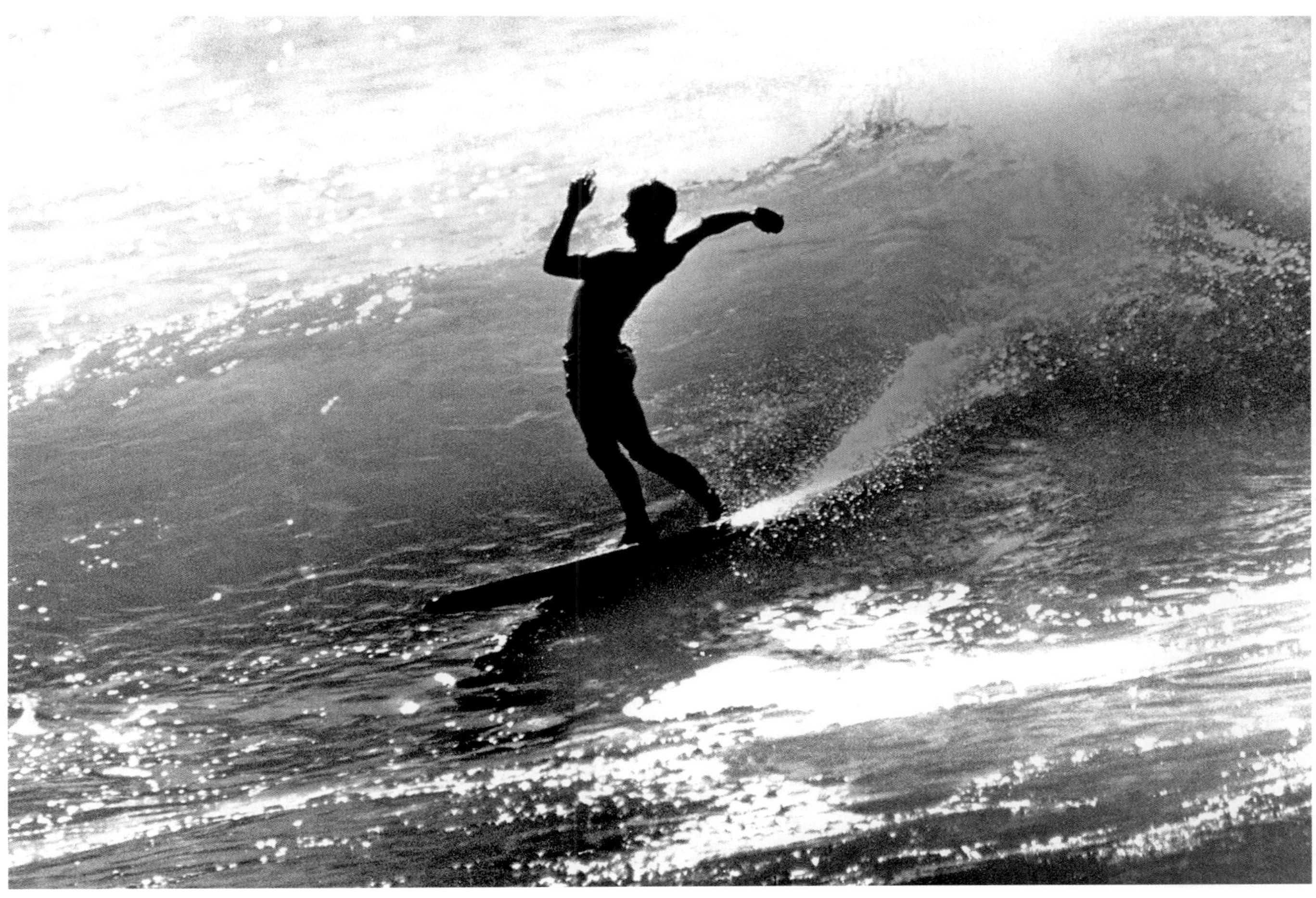

Kemp Aaberg, styling through the inside section at Rincon. An accomplished flamenco guitarist, he was the first to describe surfing as dance. This shot was taken with an 80 pound telephoto lens borrowed from Warren Miller. Photo © John Severson / surferart.com

"At either end of the social spectrum there lies a leisure class." — Eric Beck

The most exciting time in the life span of any sport or social movement is the golden age, the first dozen years or so when innovation in the equipment and technique comes fast and furious.

It's natural that the Golden State with its diverse immigrant culture, its vast natural resources, and laid-back attitude would give birth to so many sports and social revolutions.

The fifties were the easy years in California. With full employment from the Korean War, we were enjoying all the fruits of the fossil fuel culture. Gas was a quarter a gallon, used cars could be bought for twenty-five dollars, campgrounds were free, and you could easily live off the excess fat of society. Those of us in the countercultures of climbing and surfing were, as climber Pete Sinclair said, "the last free Americans."

I've been lucky to have been part of that golden age of not only surfing and climbing but also falconry, spear fishing, whitewater kayaking, and, later on, telemark skiing.

In 1954, I went down to General Veneer in Los Angeles, bought some balsa planks, and made my first surfboard. I later traded that board for a model A Ford engine. Tooling down Malibu Canyon from my home in Burbank, if I saw another surfer coming back from Malibu they would give me a thumbs-up if there was surf.

My first blacksmith shop was a chicken coop in my folks' backyard in Burbank. There's a photo of me hammering out my first pitons in 1957 and there's a surfboard in the background. I'd often climb for half of a day at Stoney Point in Chatsworth, then go up to Rincon for the evening glass after I'd freedive for lobsters and abalone on the coast between Zuma and the county line. I almost always got my limit of ten lobsters and five abalone.

A lot of my shop work was portable, so I'd cruise the coast from San Diego to Big Sur, working on the beach and riding waves when the tide and the wind were just right. During those years I figured I slept on the ground 250 days a year.

When I moved my shop to Ventura to be closer to the surf, the ultimate day was what we called a McNab: Skiing on Pine Mountain, climbing on the Sespe Wall, playing tennis, and surfing the glass-off at C Street or Rincon. Where else in the world except for New Zealand could you pull off a day like that? — Yvon Chouinard

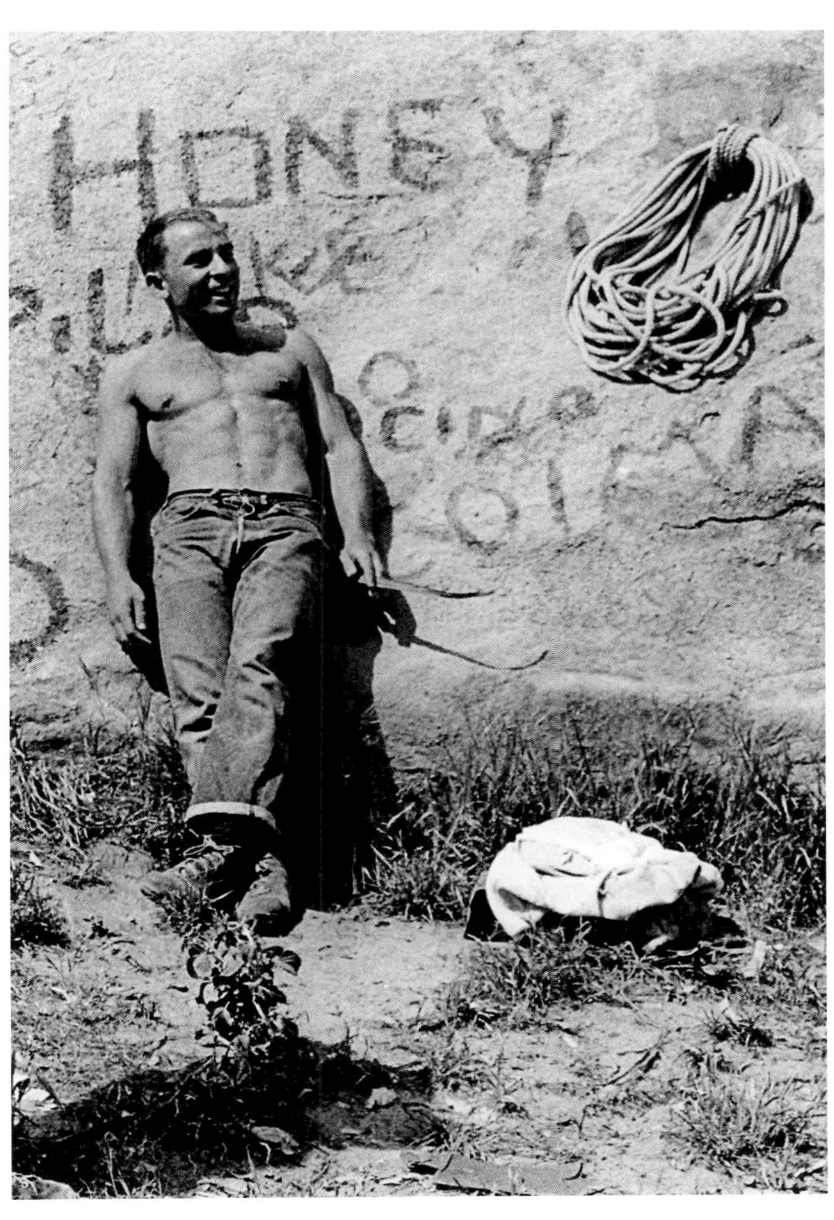

Yvon Chouinard relaxing at Stoney Point, late ’50s. Photo: Roger Cotton Brown

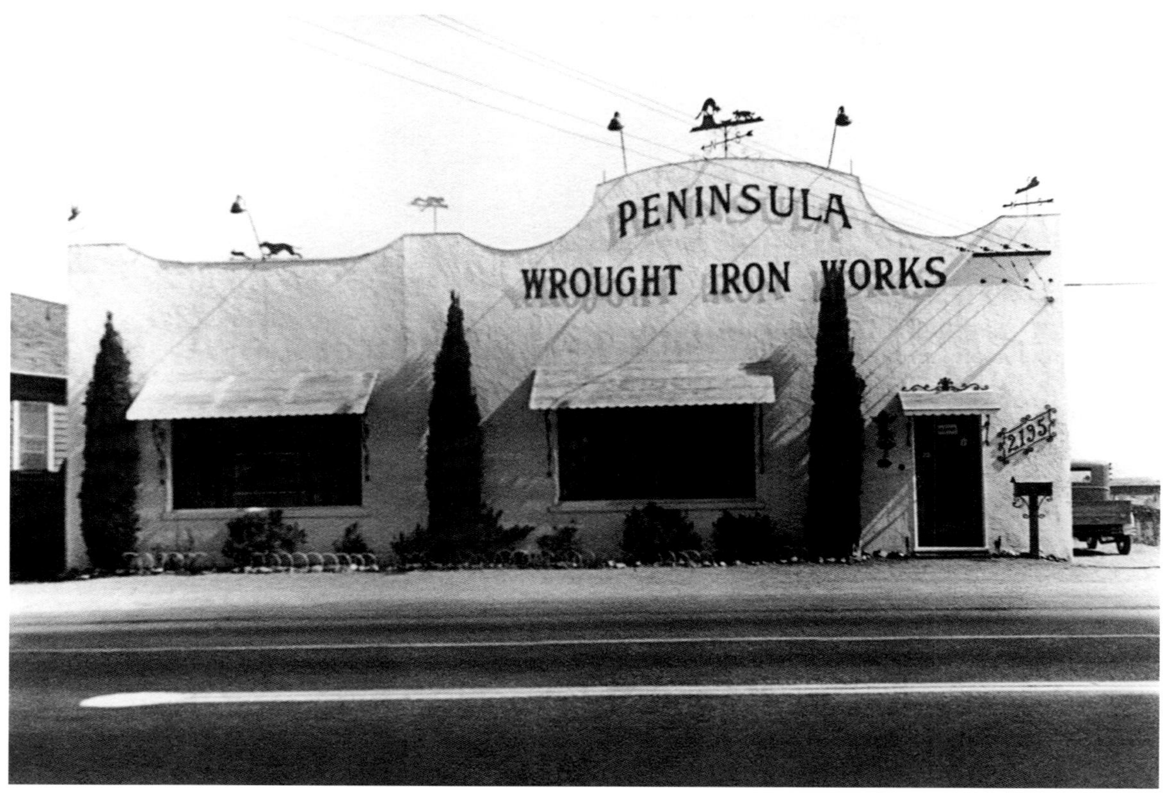

The Peninsula Wrought Iron Works, the San Mateo, California shop of famed climber John Salathé.
Photo: courtesy John Salathé Jr. / Ken Yager, Yosemite Climbing Association

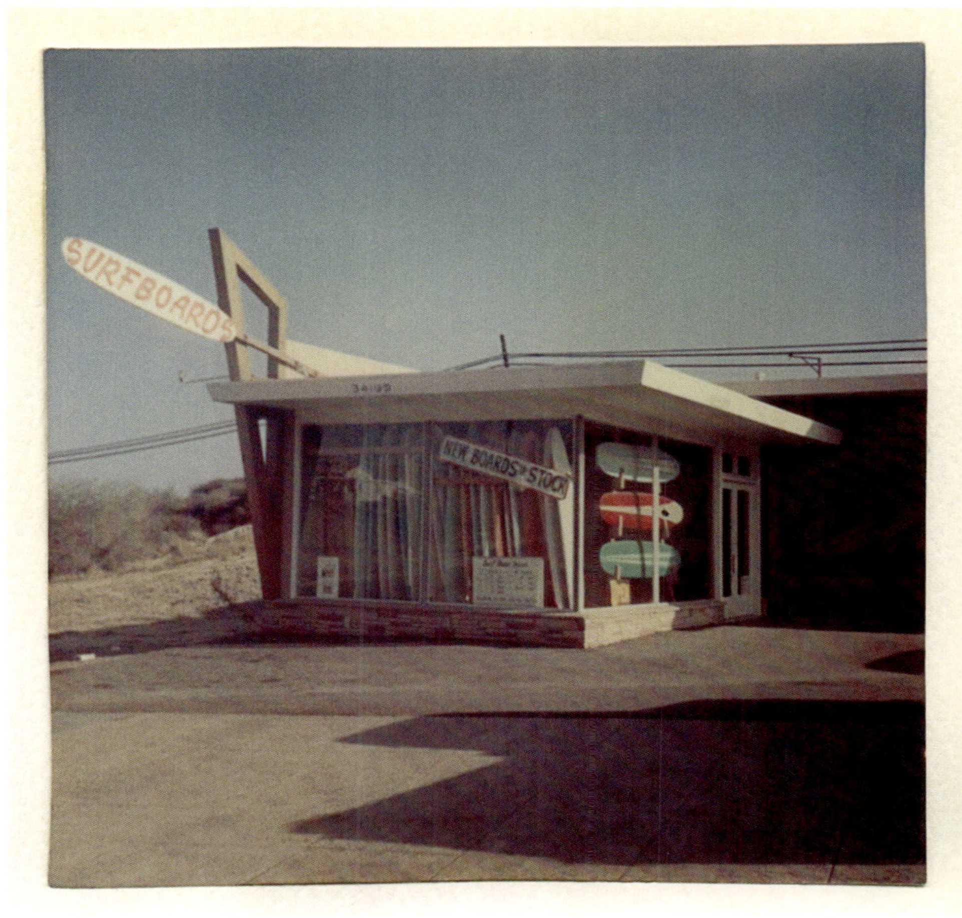

Constructed on PCH in Dana Point in 1954 with the help of his father, Hobie's was the first structure built to house surfboard manufacture and retail. Photo: Dick Metz, courtesy Hobie Alter family collection / SHACC

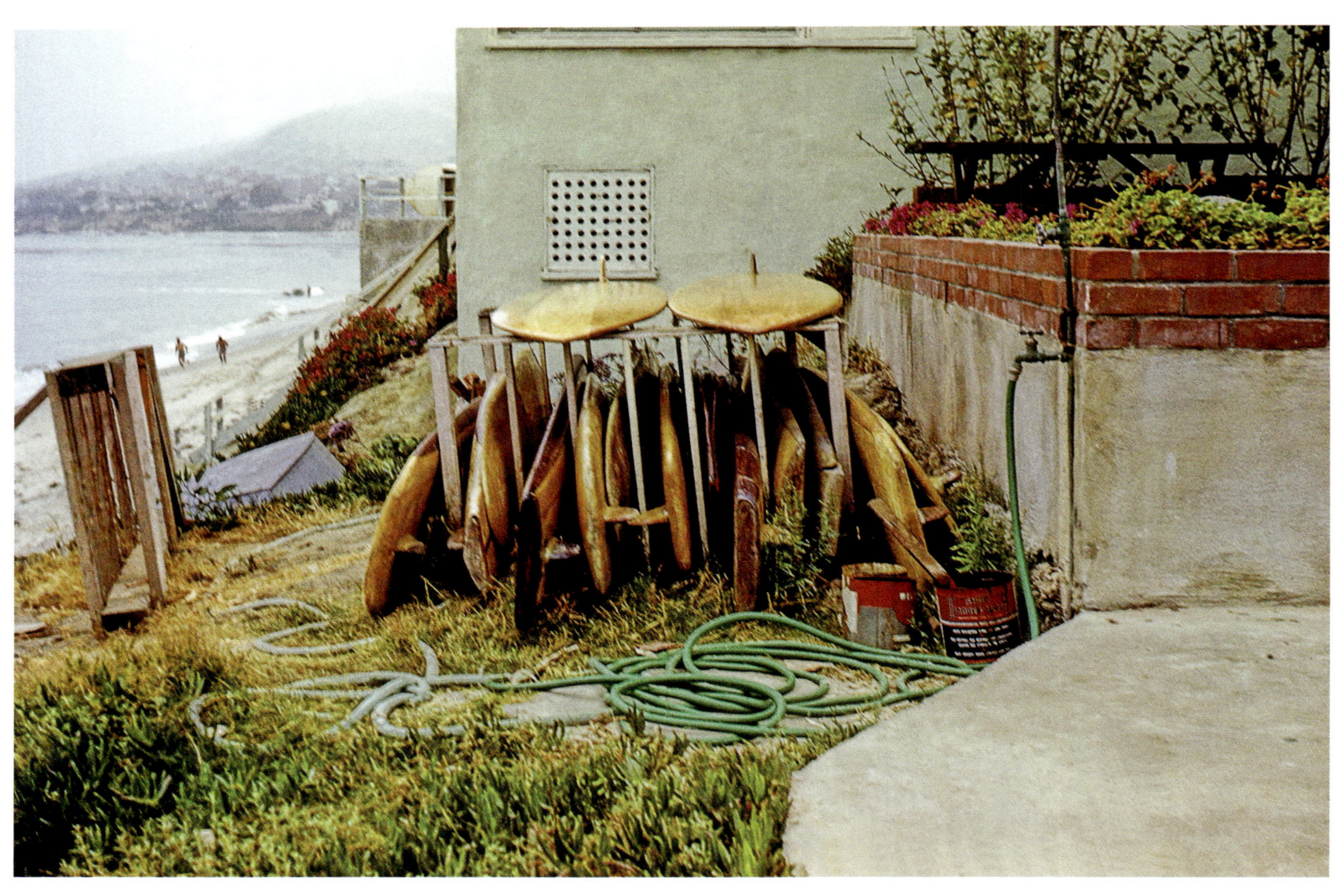

The Alter family home near the top of the Brooks Street beach stairs provided convenient board storage for the early '50s Laguna crew. Photo: Dick Metz, courtesy Hobie Alter family collection / SHACC

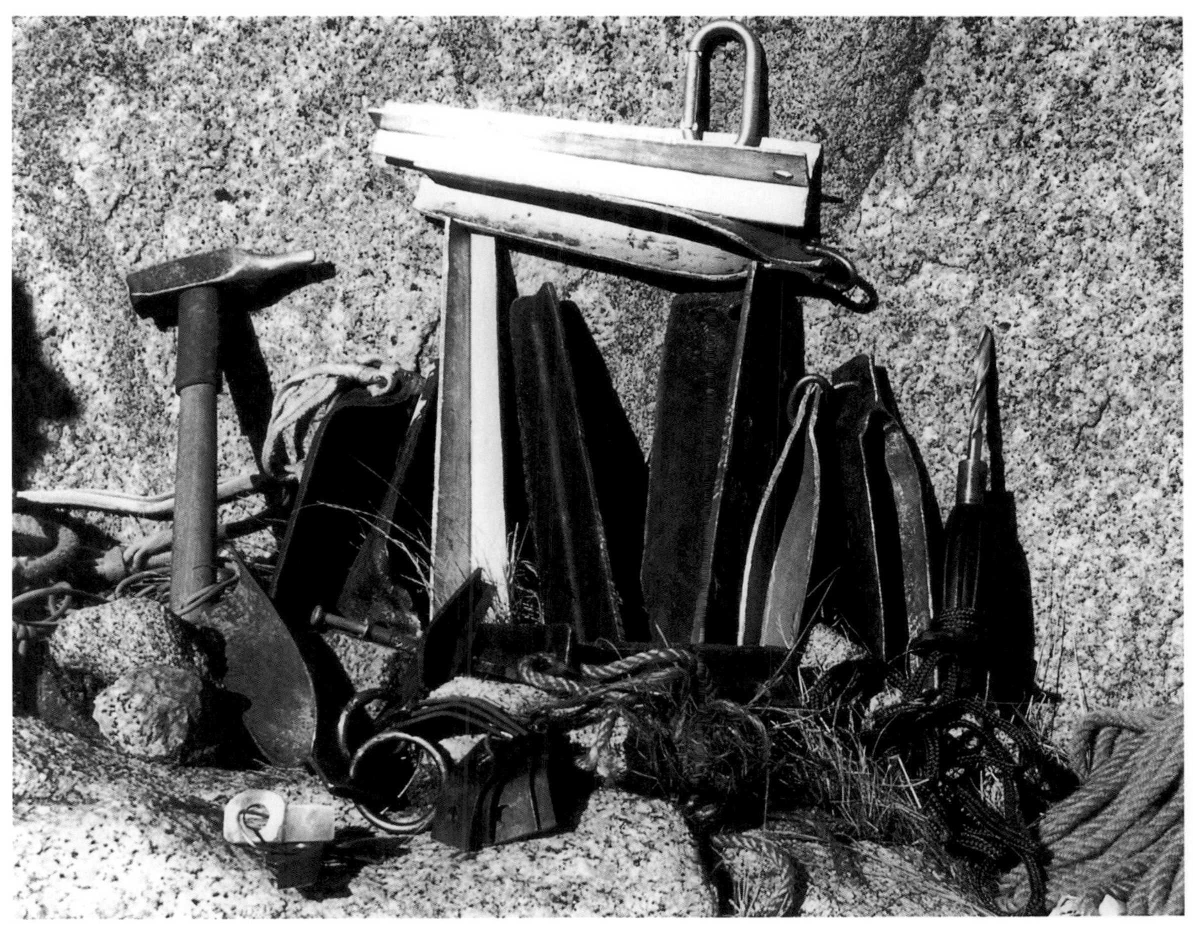

Some of the tools used on the first ascent of the face of El Capitan's Nose Route, 1958. Photo: Bill Feurer

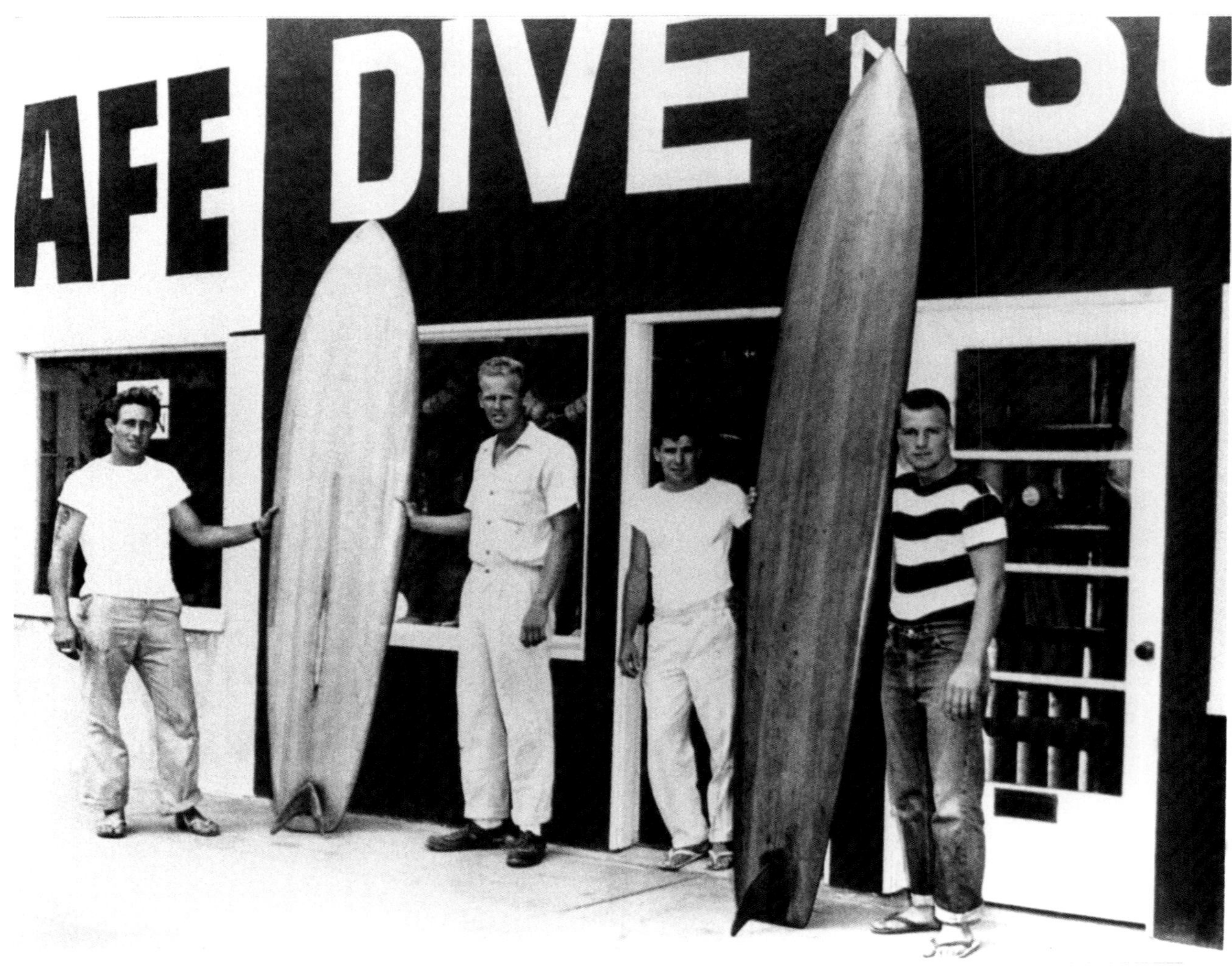

Dale Velzy, Hap Jacobs, Bill Meistrell and Bev Morgan, at Dive N' Surf in Redondo Beach, mid-50s. Ironically, all became wealthy making ocean toys and gear but Dale, whose outlandish persona inspired the surf-lifestyle industry to come. Photo: Bev Morgan collection / SHACC

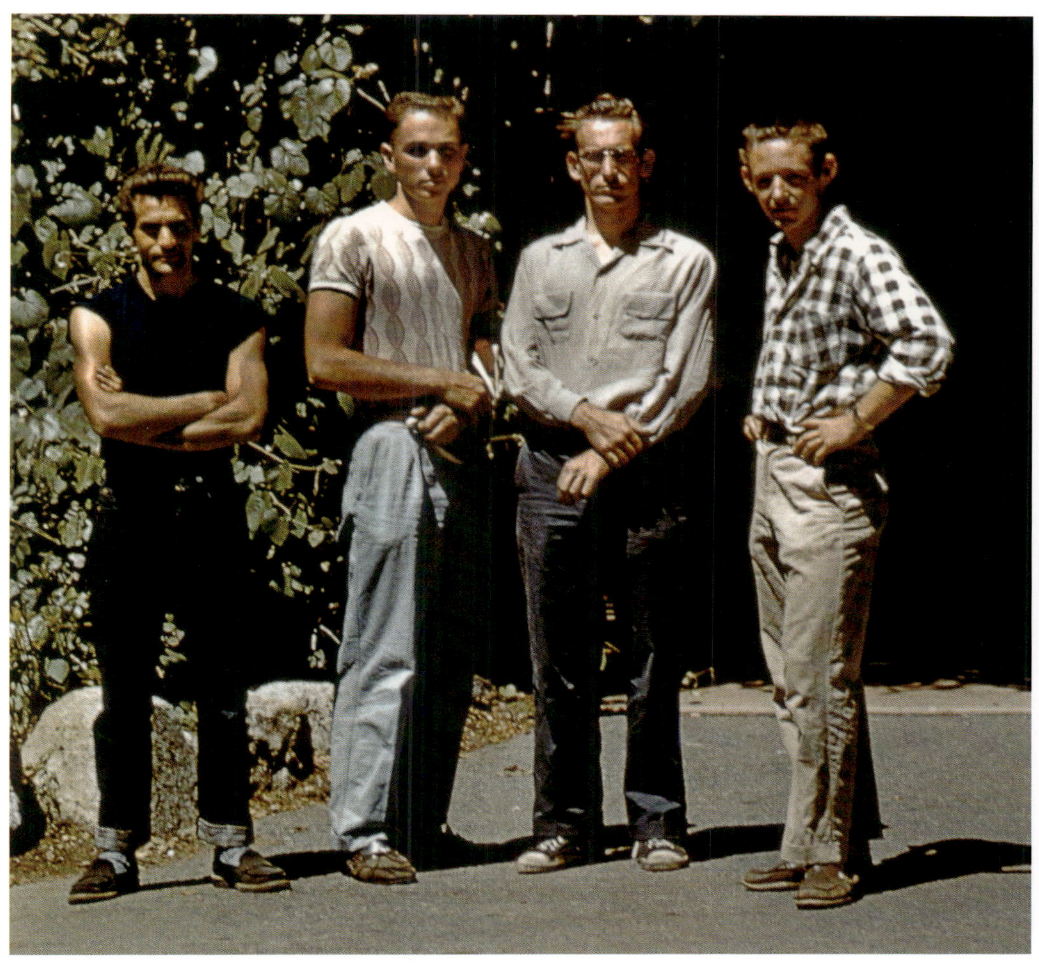

Warren Harding, Jerry Gallwas, Royal Robbins, and Don Wilson after an attempt on the Northwest face of Half Dome, 1955.
Photo: Jerry Gallwas collection

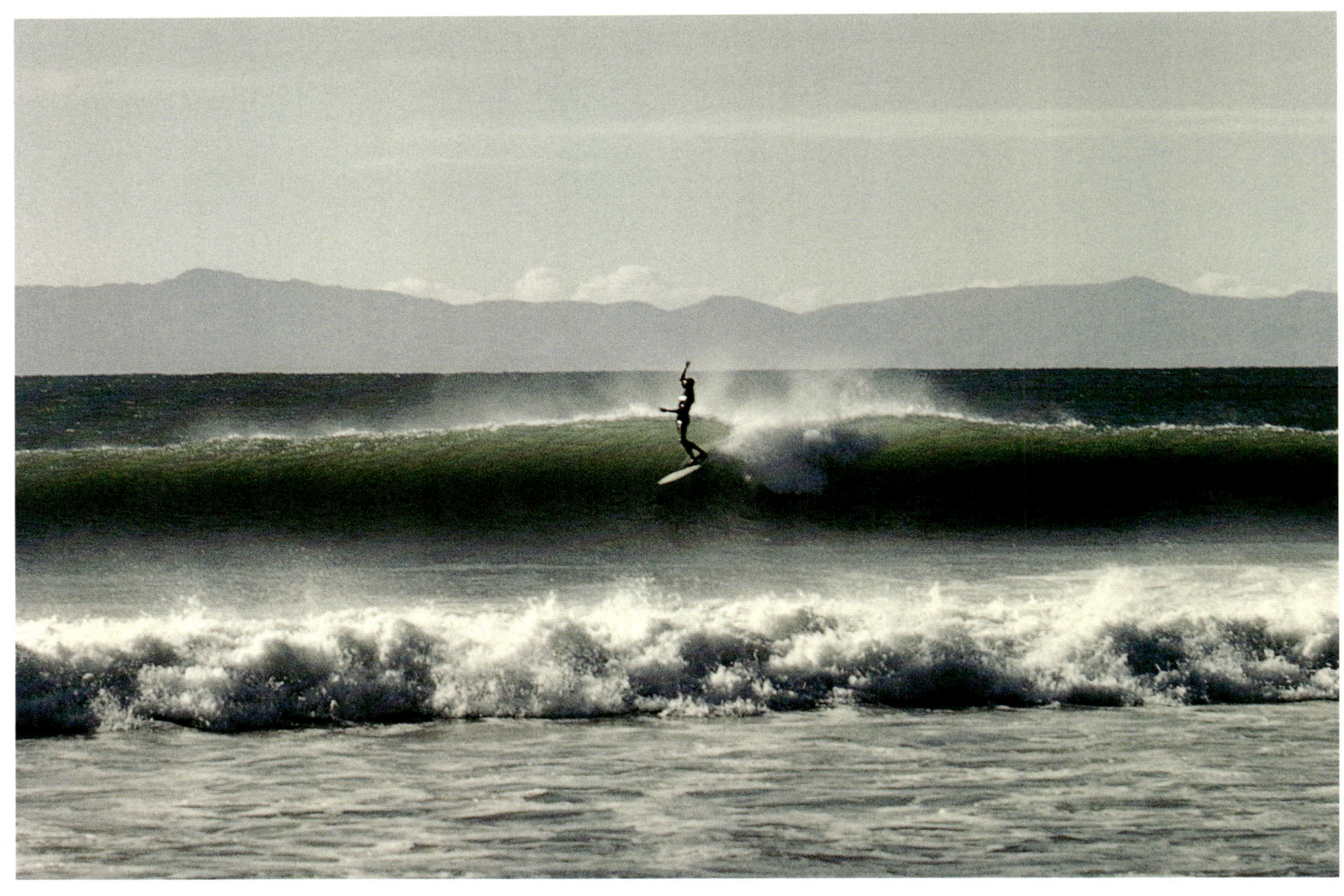

Reynolds Yater soloing at Hammonds Reef, circa-1959.
A quiet man, his elegant, minimalist surfing and the sleek surfboards he built were his statement. Photo: Dick Perry

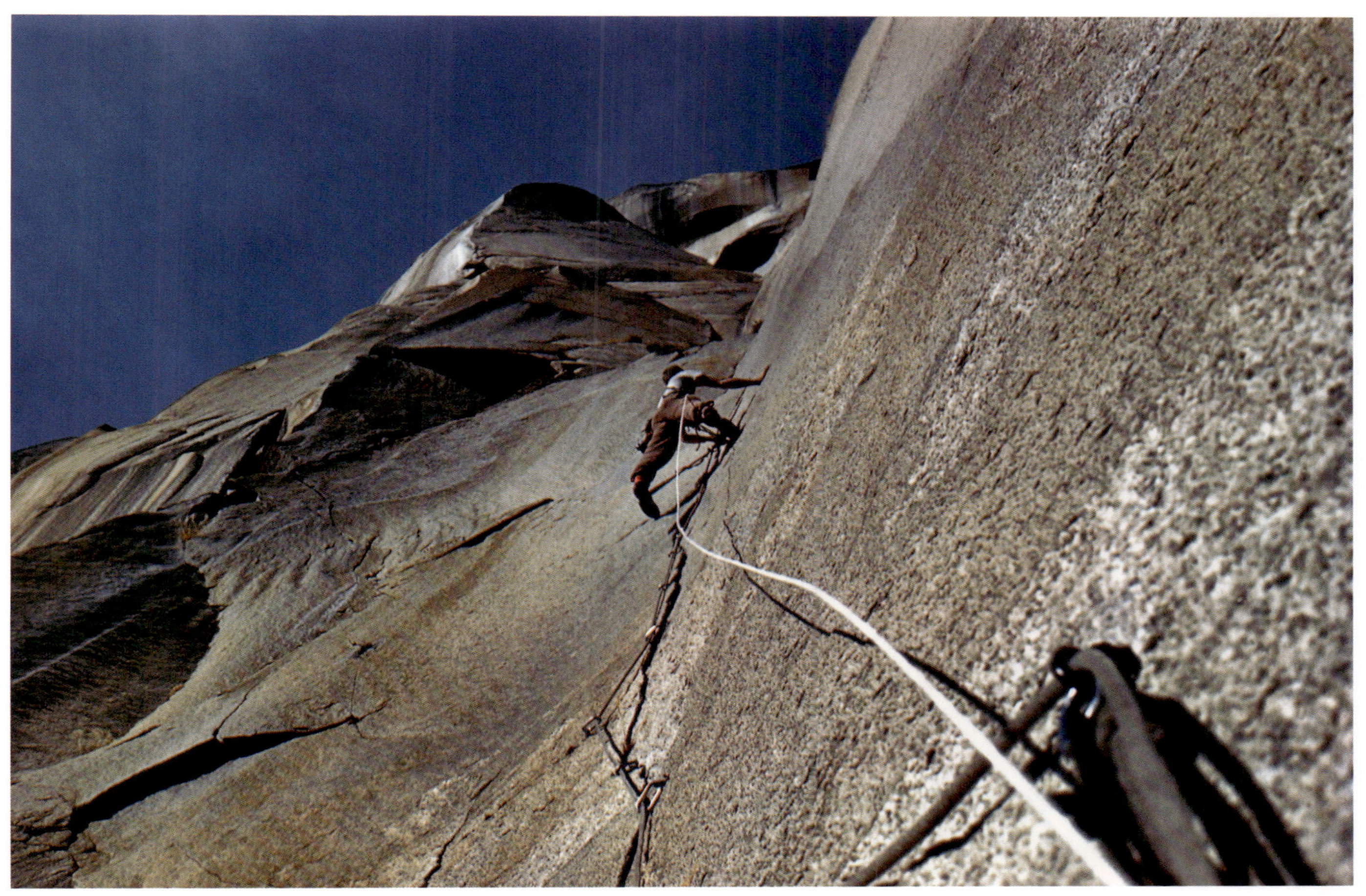

Wayne Merry leads the Pancake Flake Pitch on the first ascent of the Nose Route on El Capitan, 1958. Photo: Warren Harding

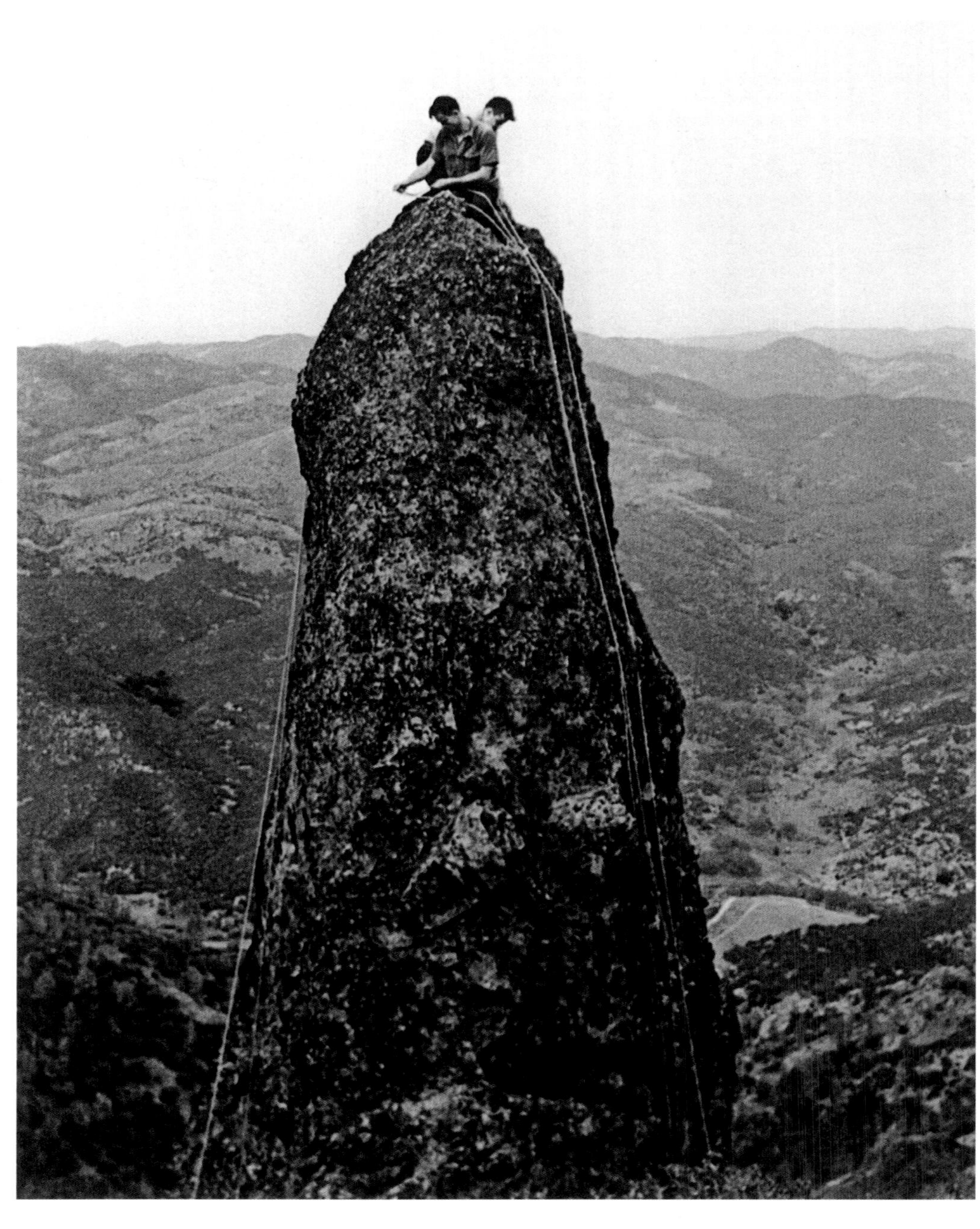

Climbers hunker atop Photographers' Delight, Pinnacles National Monument, California, 1955.
Photo © Richard Irwin, courtesy Stanford University Libraries

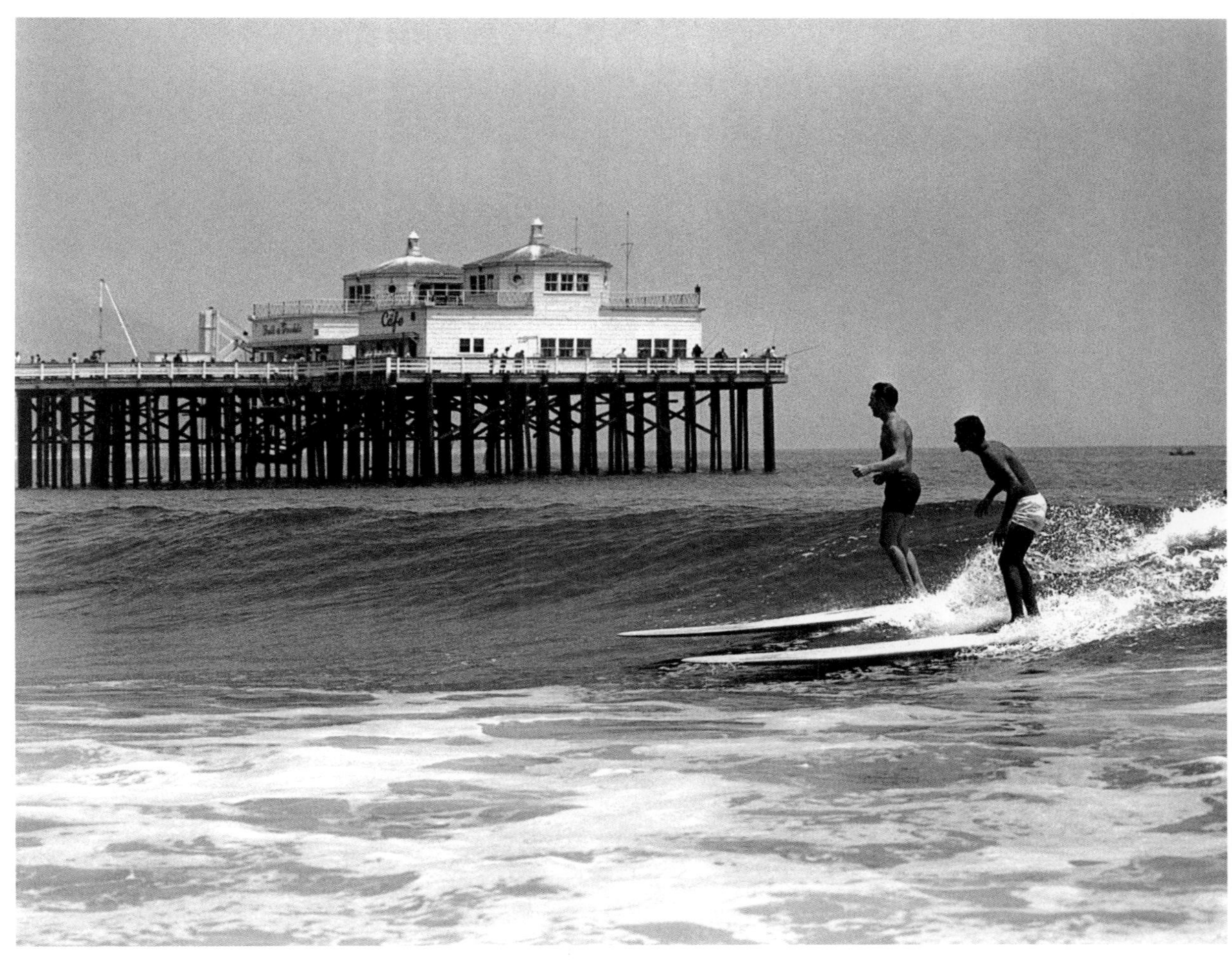

Dave Sykes and Corny Cole trimming Simmon's "concaves" at 1st Point Malibu. Simmons introduced aircraft wing and marine hull design principals to surfboards via his "foiled" shapes, his wide planing-tails tended to spin-out in larger waves. Photo: Joe Quigg

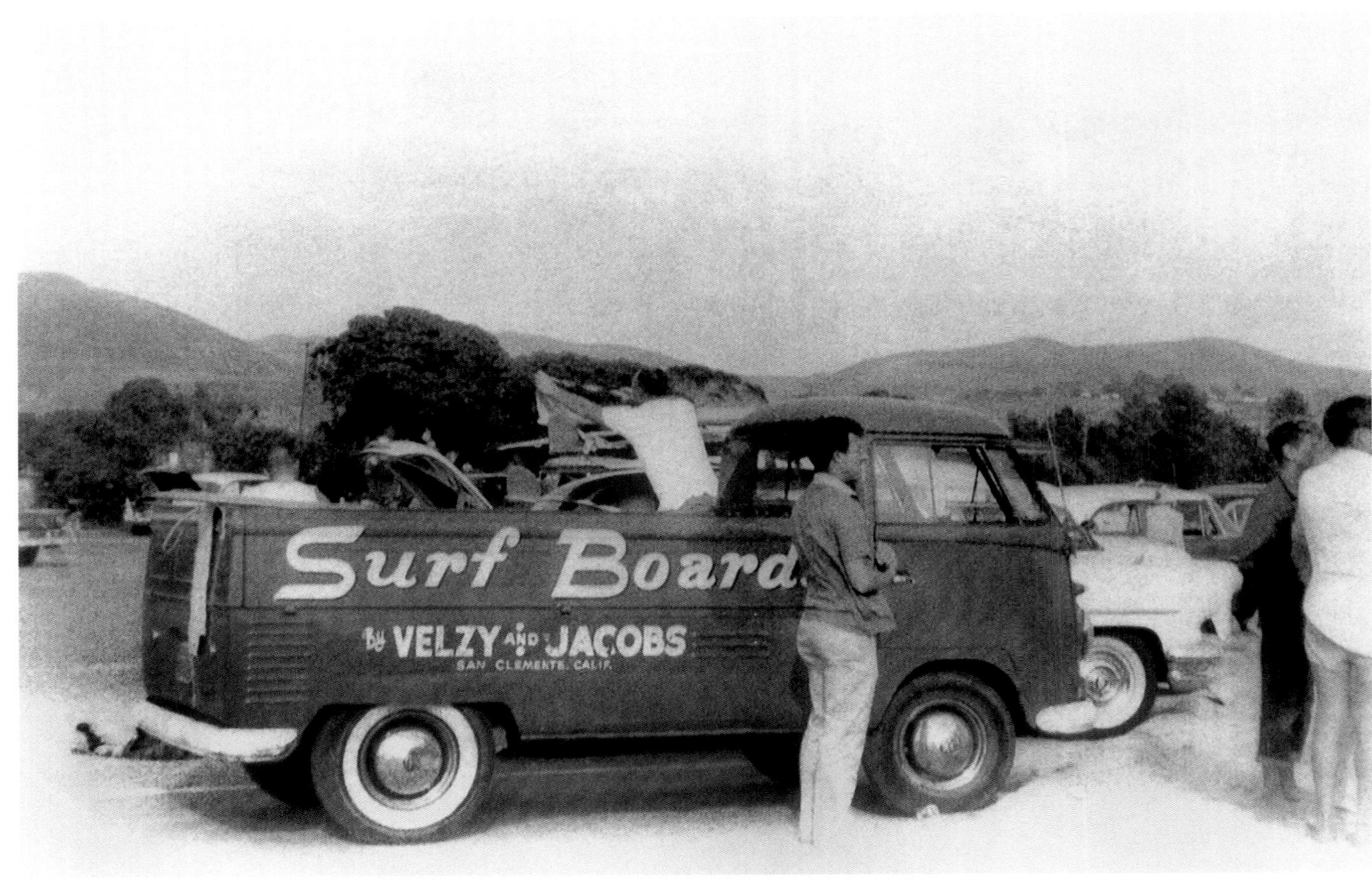

The Velzy & Jacobs' surf mobile at Doheny Beach, 1959. The logos of the few dozen surfboard makers along the coast became clan symbols that kick-started the popularity of screen-printed T-shirts. Photo: courtesy SHACC

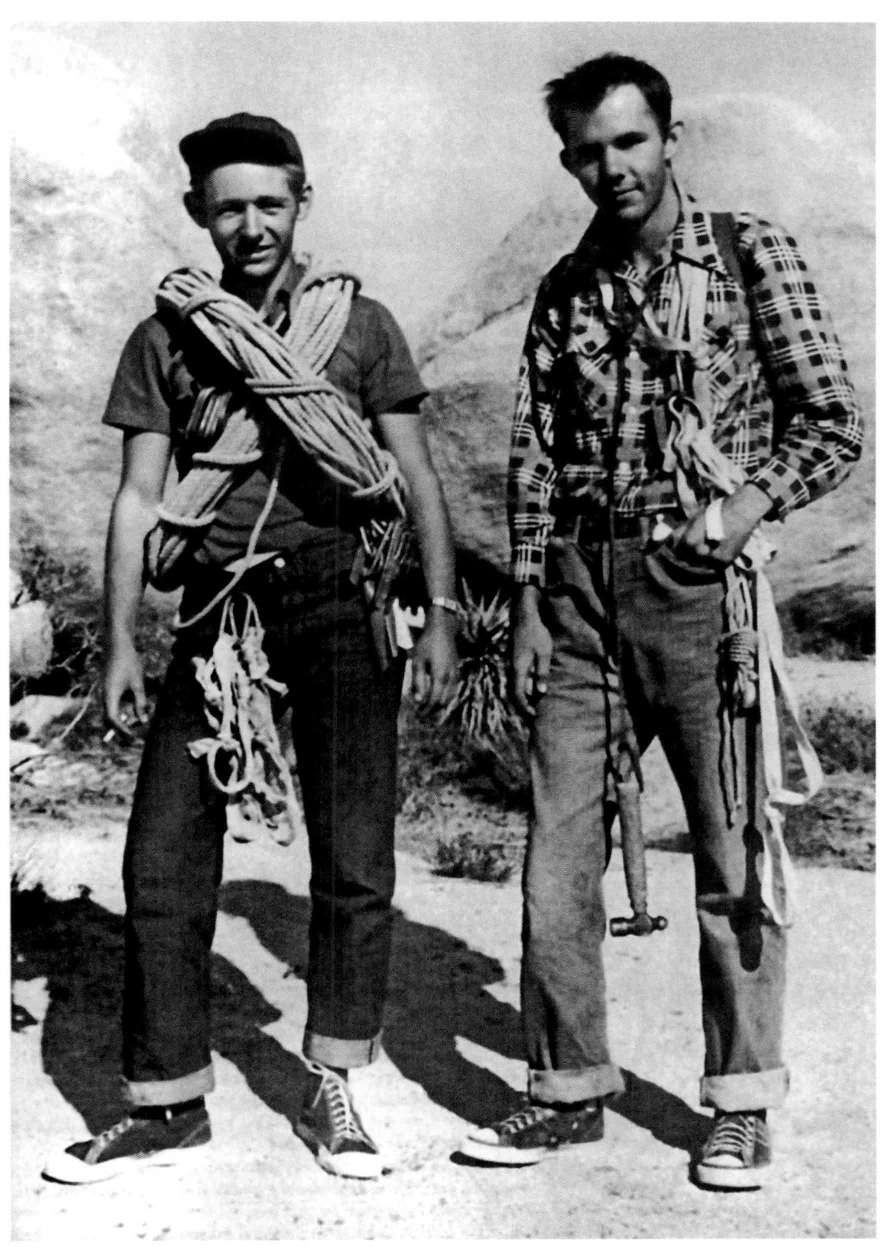

Don Wilson and Frank Hoover decked out in early '50s gear. Photo: Niles Werner, courtesy Frank Hoover collection

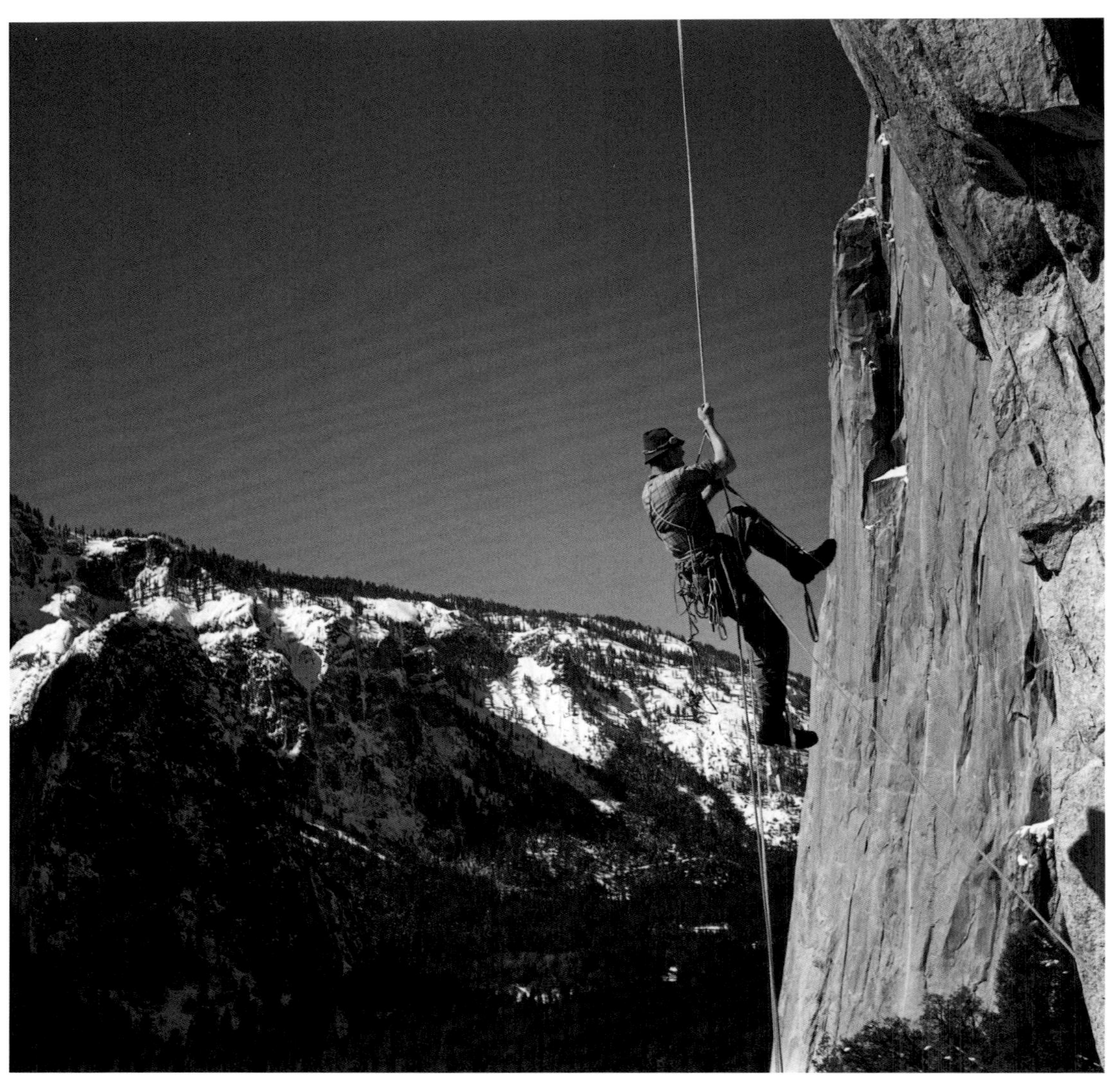

Bob Swift ascends a fixed rope during the first ascent of the route known as El Cap Tree. Photo: Allen Steck (taken with Swift's Zeiss)

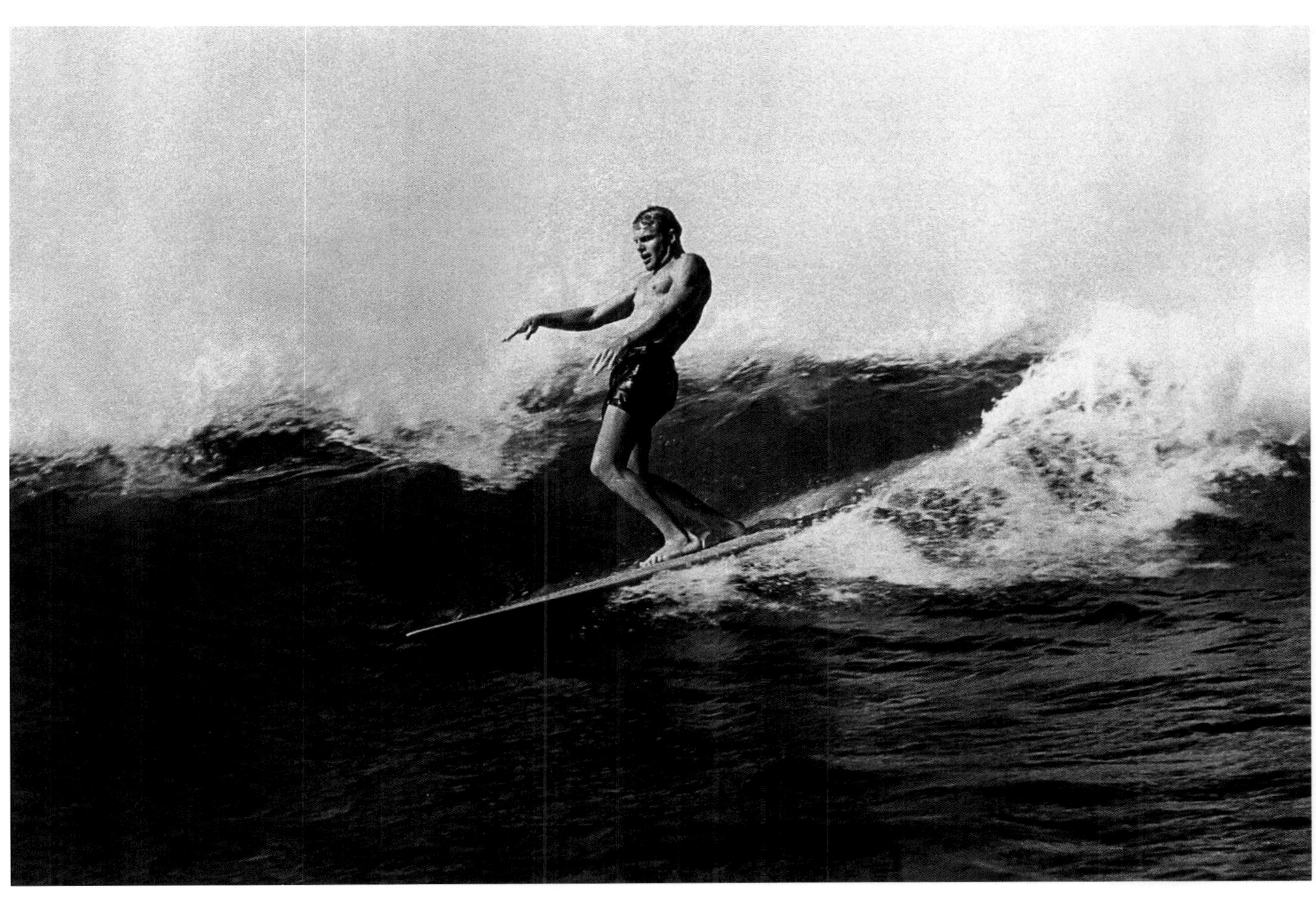

Santa Monica lifeguard/Malibu surfer Tom Zahn, 1955. Zahn served as a catalyst in the advancement of board design by putting up the money to try new things. Quigg, Kivlin, and Zahn would team up to do the work. Photo: Clarence Maki / SHACC

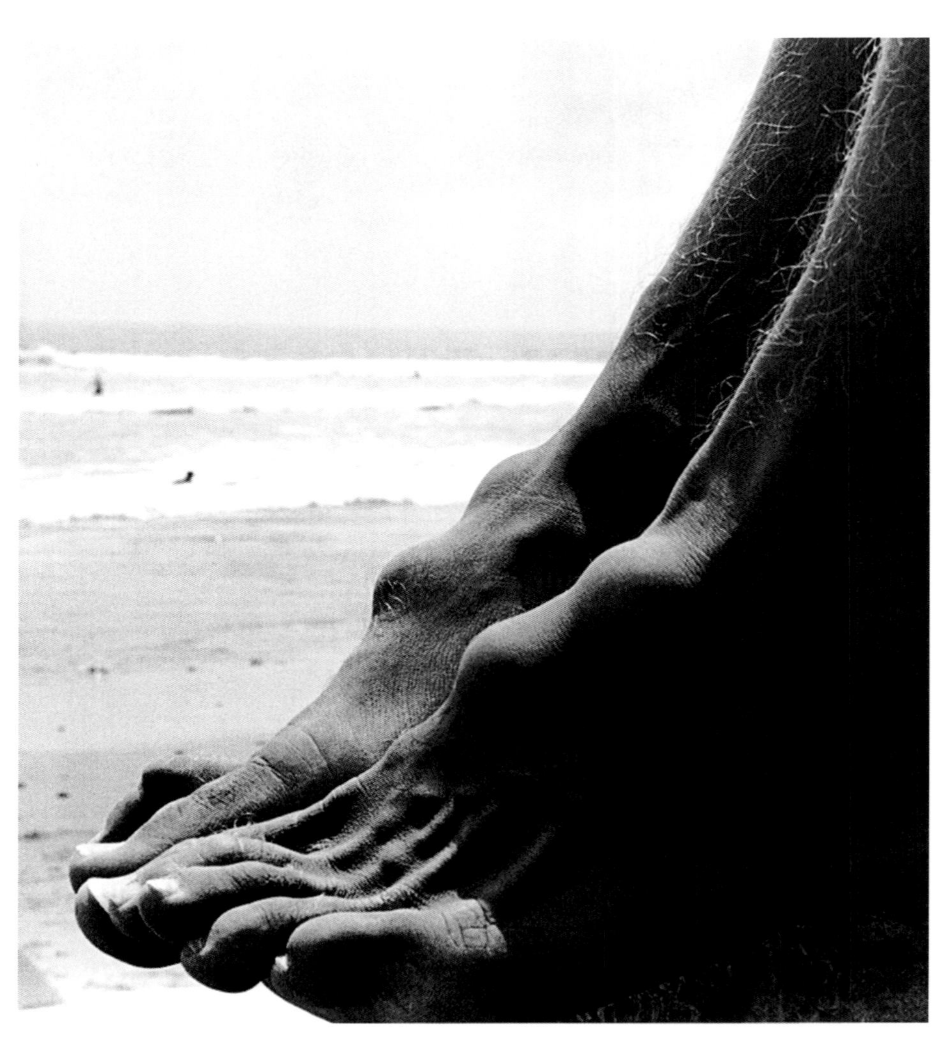

Calcium deposits from knee paddling, "surf knots" became status symbols. Large, oozing ones called "volcano's" could get you classified "1Y" by the draft board. Photo: Ron Stoner, courtesy Jeff Hollenbeck

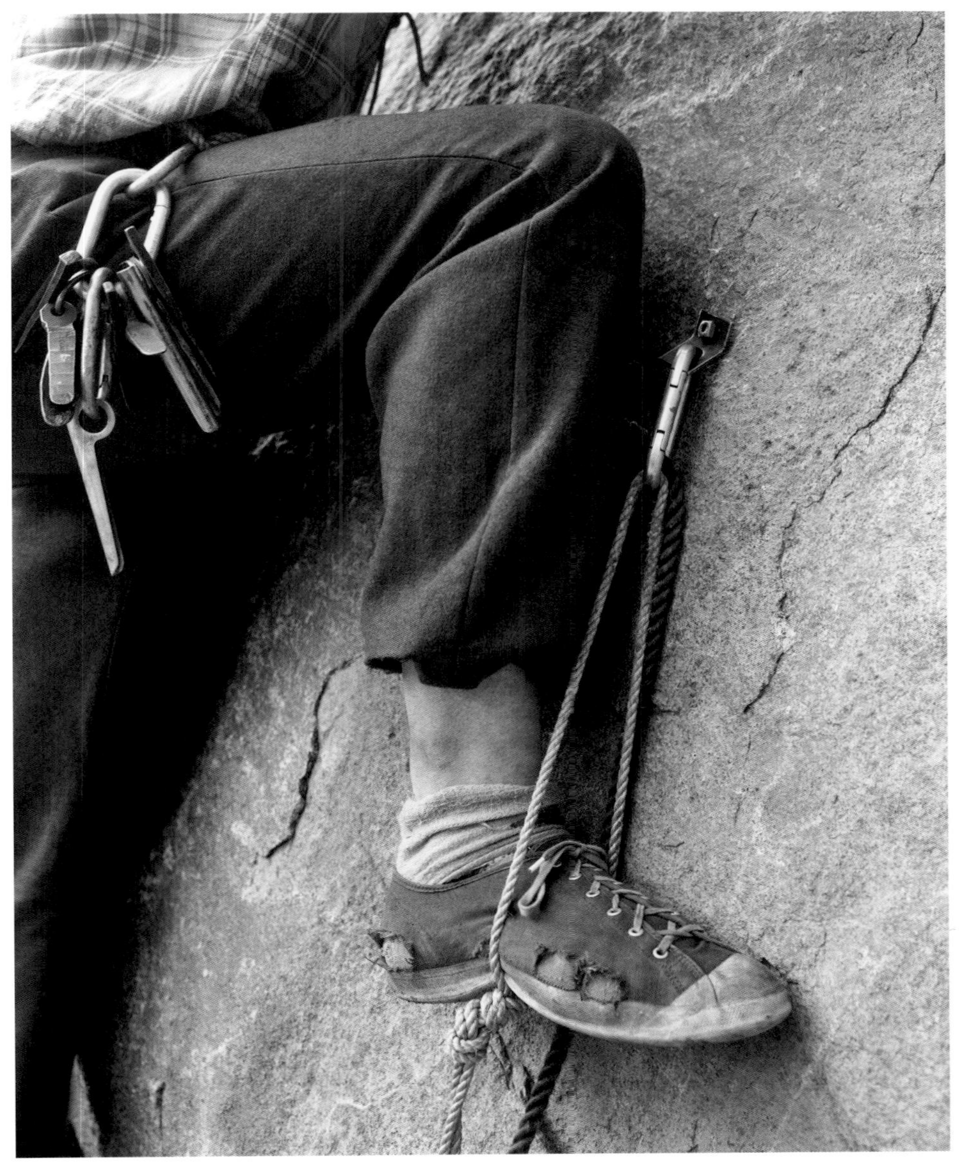

Typical '50s equipment, with tennis shoes, a crude aid sling, and steel pitons.
Photo: Bob and Ira Spring

There were maybe a thousand surfers worldwide, at most. Hawaii was the seedbed from which it all sprang. Surfing was almost invisible, nothing more than an eccentric pasttime picked up by a few who had been to the Islands, or were adventurous, athletically inclined, alternative lifestyle addicts that someone had turned on. They were all individuals, each discernible from a mile away. They all pretty much knew, or had heard of, each other. It was a small tribe operating to the beat of a secret joy, in the midst of a society that didn't have a clue about them, being consumed by the abstract of an atomic age. Surfing waves still seemed unique to certain areas.

Surf craft were balsawood, with deeper fins, which—after decades of trying bolts, nails and glue—at last firmly attached by a fiberglass coating that allowed sudden turning and banking without spinning out. The flight had become suddenly much freer, more exhilarating, and spontaneous. The trappings of Hawaii were brought home and planted like rootstock. Surf trunks, with longer legs to protect from thigh rash and lace-up fronts to keep them from being swept off, indicated you knew where to get such things. This was while Balboas with combs in the rear pocket were being worn at public pools. Island thrift stores were loaded with cheap, comfy, loose-fitting and colorful silky shirts with outlandish prints. Rubber shower slaps were all that was needed. It was all about casual comfort—and it was different.

The small tribe unconsciously adopted that style. Grass shacks were erected at Onfre' and Windansea. Ukes and slack key strumming wafted in the breeze. These few weirdos had thrown off their parents' depression-era security paranoia and had become beach bums; even the employed acted like they weren't. Night jobs allowed free days to chase waves. They waited tables, tended bar, hustled. The point was to stay free to ride. The ride was the magic thing; being moved by a wave of cycling molecules that resulted from wind caused by the sun's heat waves warming our atmosphere. It was a cosmic attachment that, though it went unspoken, was shared by those who had felt it firsthand. It was a secret thrill. The world was lame. We were not. They'd white-knuckle grasped onto a truth that was different than the one we'd discovered. Both theirs and ours were merely theoretical constructs about how to live life; that much we did know.

That little world was just beginning to crack open. Joe Quigg was shaping formative balsa chips in the early fifties along with Matt Kivlin, and both worked with Bob Simmons in a Venice garage building remarkable Styrofoam/plywood sandwich boards, all glued together in a curved jig, then adding shaped balsa rails. Then came Quigg and Velzy's lighter, more fun, easy riders that would entice the first wave of teenaged kids to surf. A surfer/diver named Bev Morgan was building a urethane surf vest, the first ever surf wetsuit, for Buzzy Trent, using a piece of experimental material a Scripps scientist had given him.

Down south, Lorrin Harrison was also in his prime in the fifties. By then he was an experienced, expert all-around waterman, who fished lobster and abalone from a skiff out of Dana Cove. Post WWII, he was the first to commercially dive Abalone Cove in Laguna Beach. Those delicious shellfish had multiplied untouched for a hundred years, having had no natural enemy since the sea otter had been hunted out of existence. That first day, he told me, they took seven hundred dozen! They didn't know better then. He rode Corona Del Mar before the jetty, surfed San O the first day ever, shaped redwood balsa planks with Pete Petersen at Pacific System Homes, brought an outrigger canoe back from Waikiki to plant that sport here, and built his own boards in his barn. One day I asked him if he'd rather have been born a little later, when the equipment had gotten better and we knew more about all the waves around the world. He shook his head and told me, "Naw, I liked my slice." — Steve Pezman

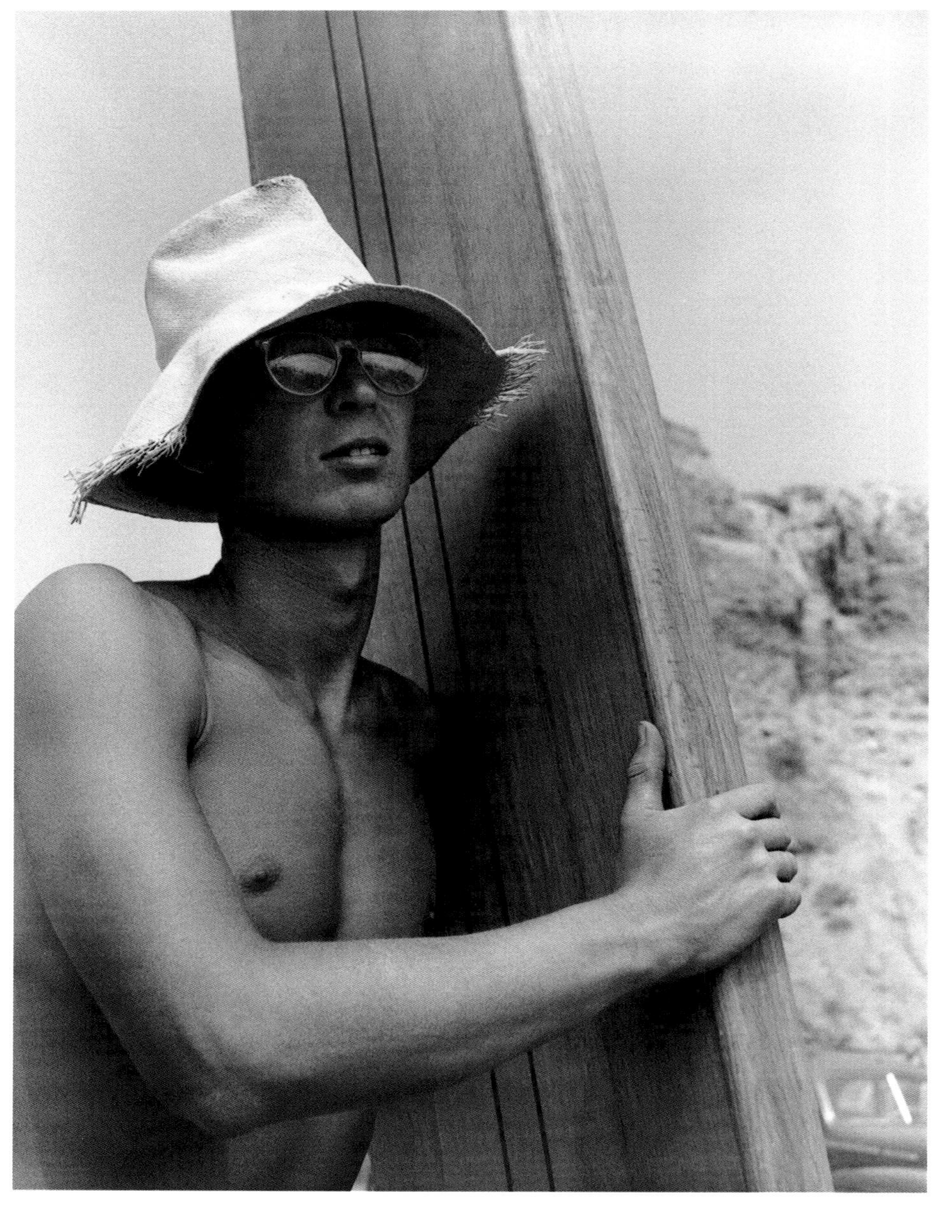

"Huckleberry" sporting 'Nofre garb and an obsolete but serviceable varnished redwood-railed balsa, circa-1950.
Some considered San Onofre a backwater of surfboard evolution, more about beach fun than riding waves. Photo: Joe Quigg

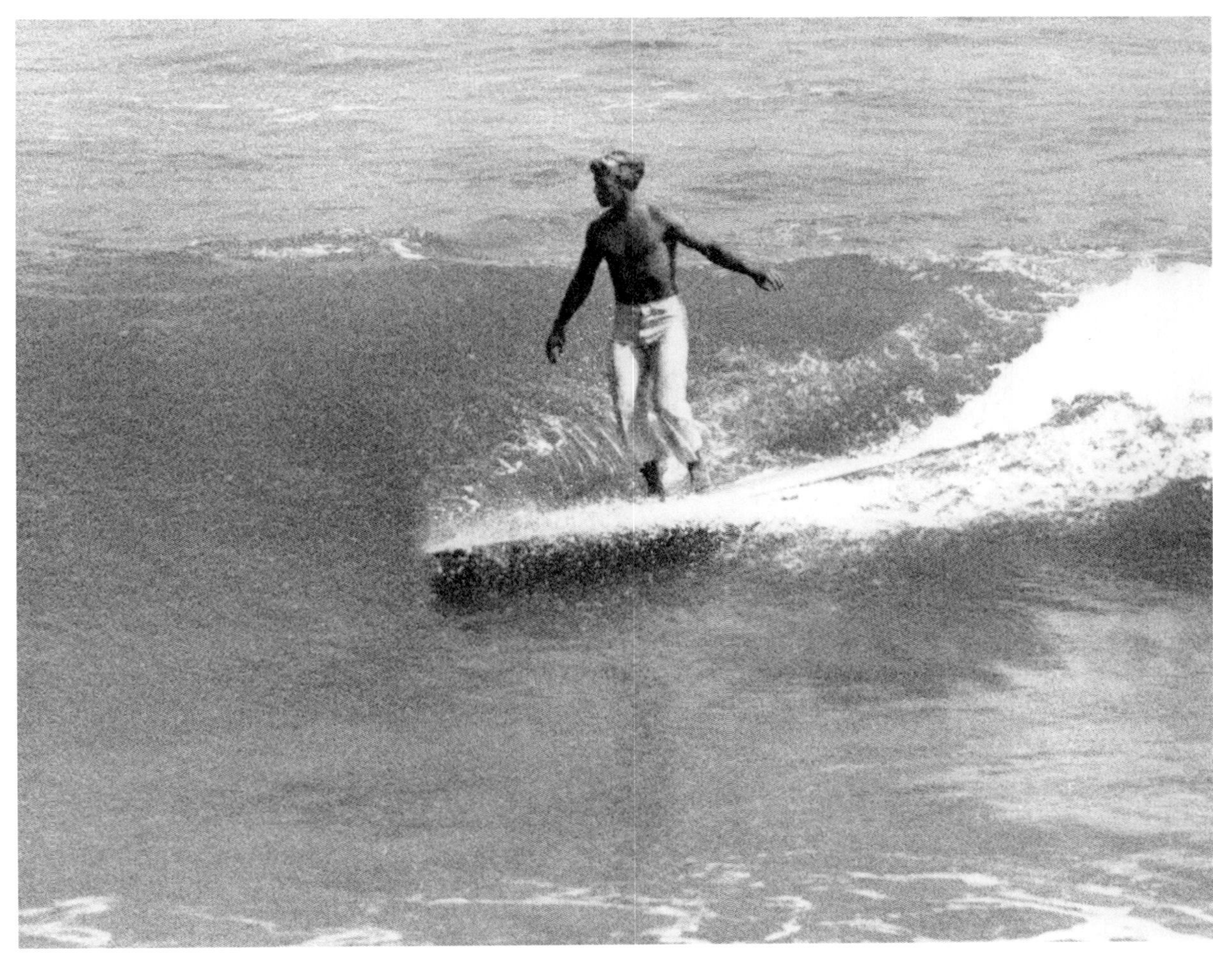

Bev Morgan slotted on an ultra-short eight-footer named "Sylvester the Cat" that Quigg had built for himself, then was bought by Velzy for young Greg Noll, and went from there to Bev, who passed it on to a kid named Phil Edwards. Malibu, 1951. Photo: Joe Quigg

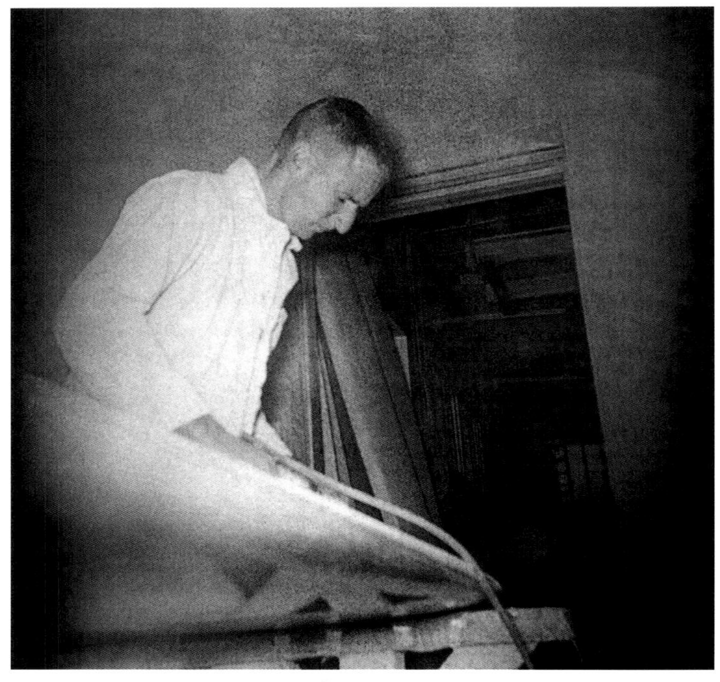
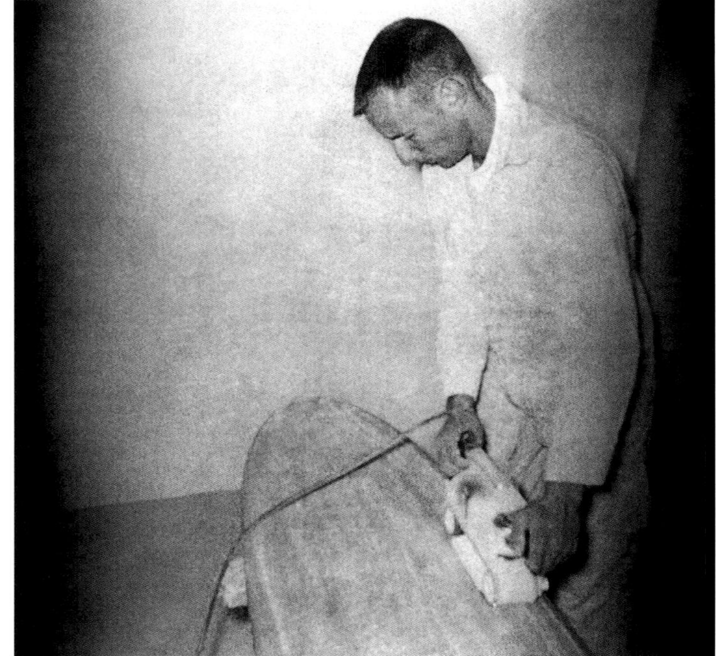

Rennie Yater mowing balsa on sawhorses at Hobie surfboards, circa-1954/'55. The shaping process would become more refined but remained essentially the same: envision the desired shape within a mass of material and deftly remove the excess. Photo: John Thurston / SHACC

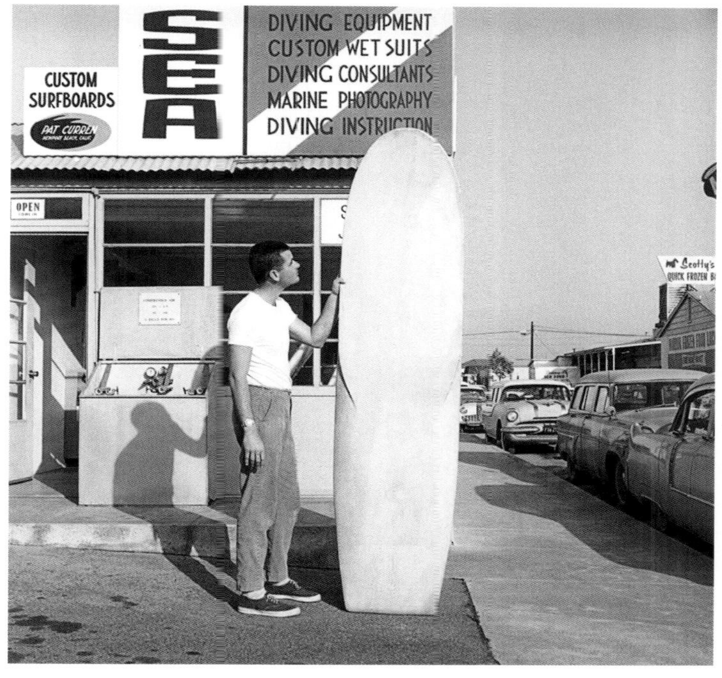

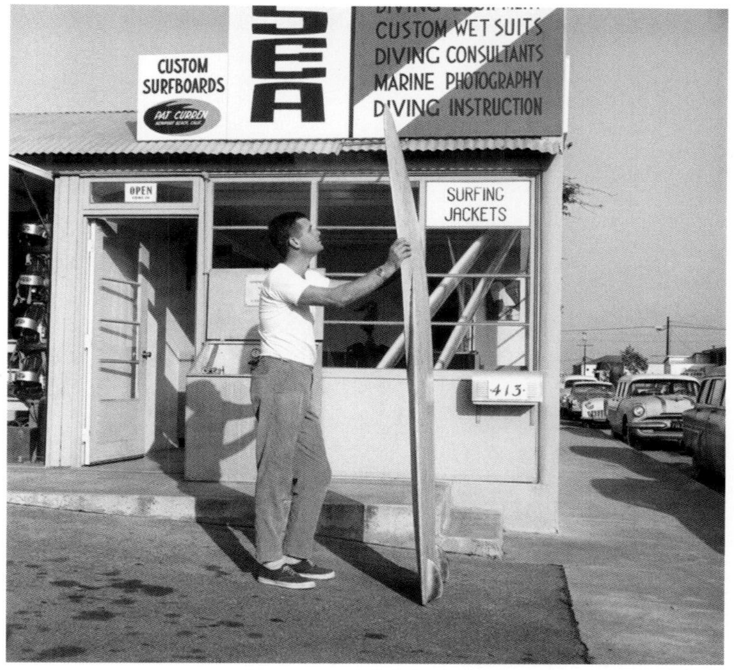

Ramsey Parks showing off an early '50s "Slot" board at his and Bev's wetsuit/dive shop on the Newport Beach Peninsula. Simmons intended the Slot to let the laminar water flow shortcut the path from entry to tail. Photo: Bev Morgan / SHACC

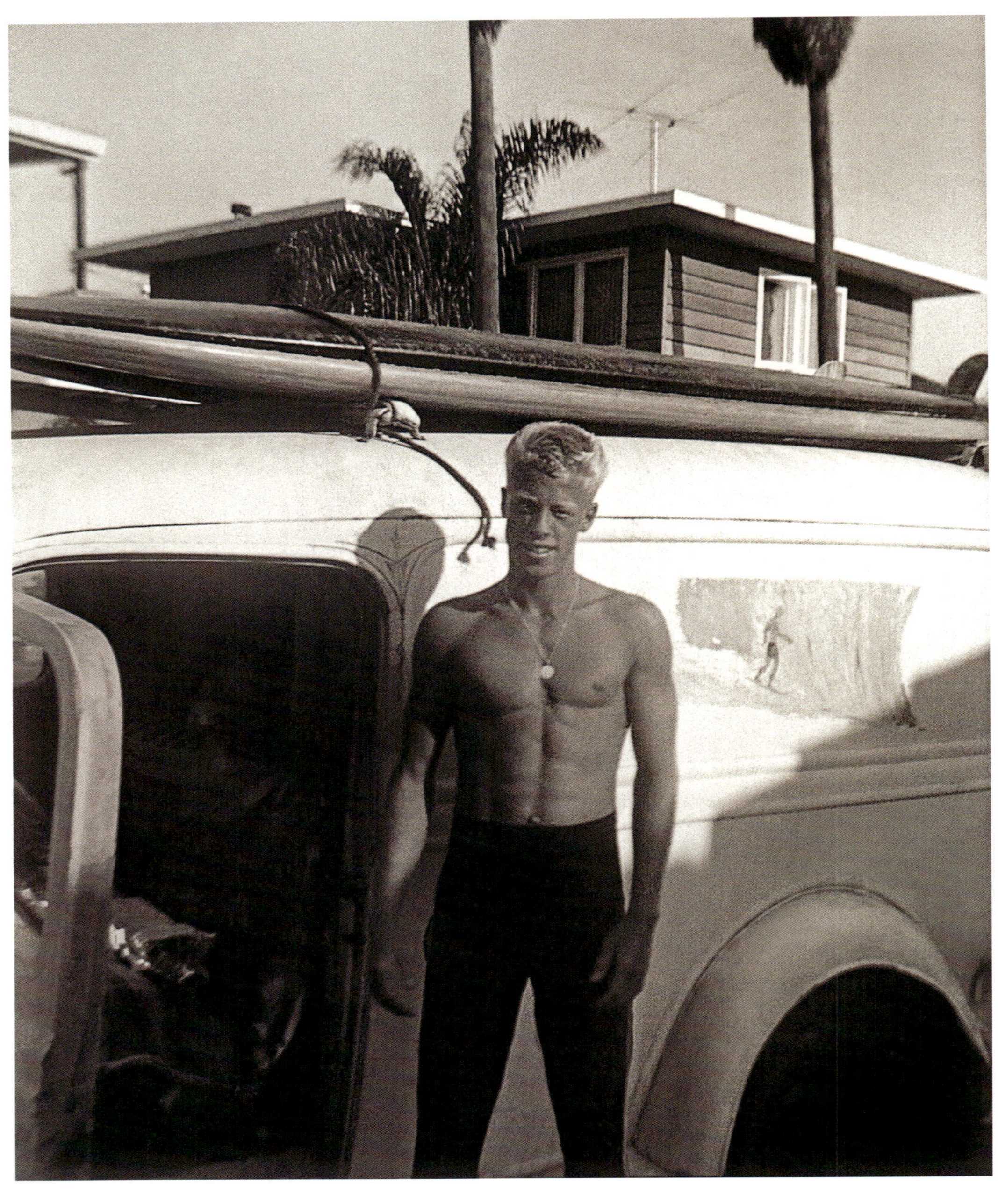

Long Beach Wilson High Schooler Bruce Brown, twelve years prior to making his seminal surf film, "The Endless Summer," at his family's bay front home on Treasure Island, Alamitos Bay, 1954. Photo: Bruce Brown collection

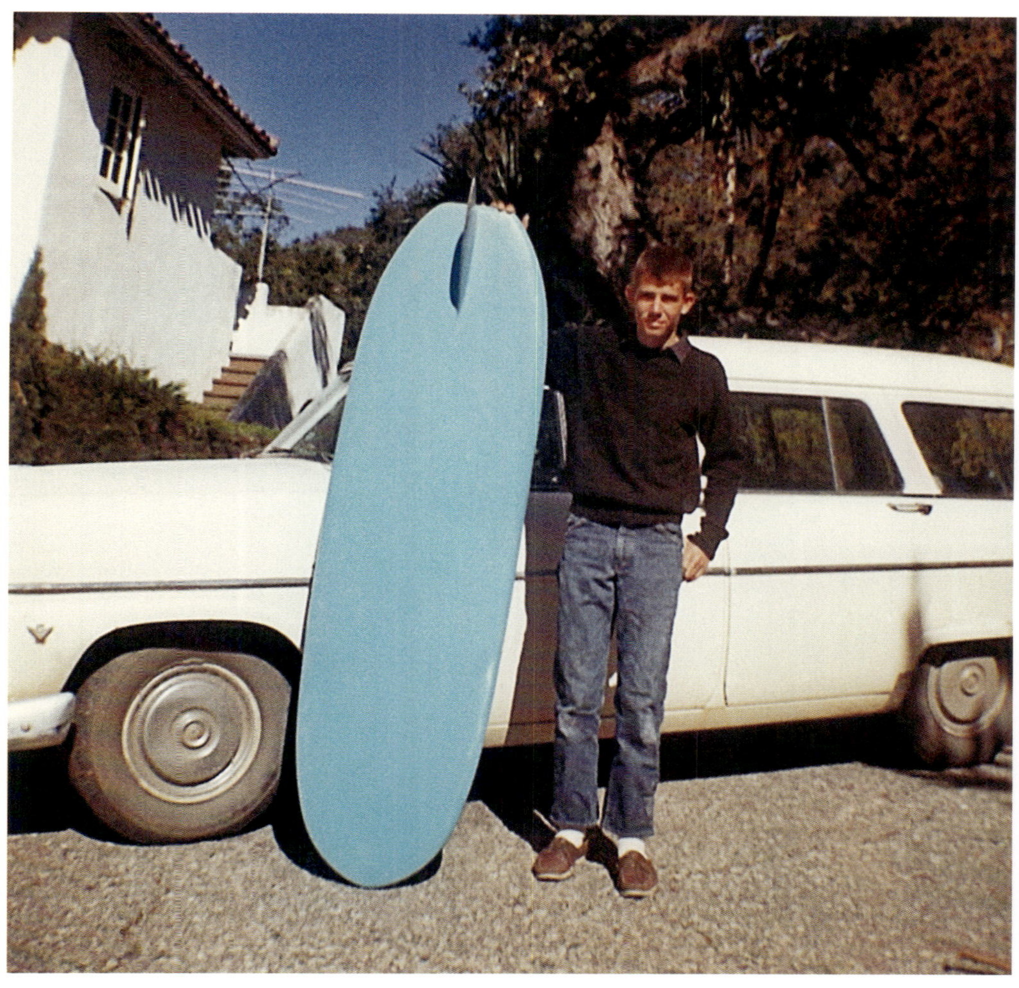

Santa Barbara High Schooler George Greenough, with self-made board at the family home in Montecito, 1958. His progression to deep carving kneeboards in the '60s inspired a profound sport-wide "short board" movement. Photo: George Greenough collection

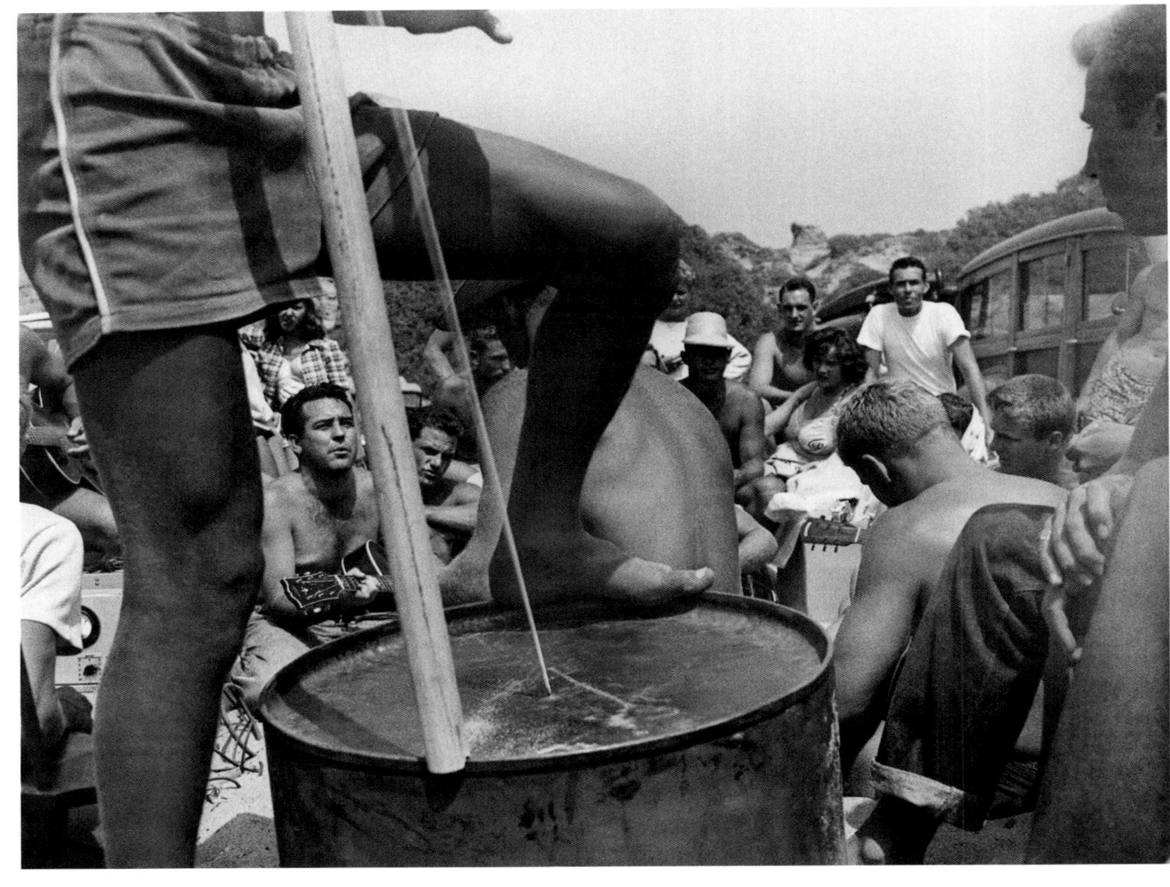

Afternoon jam at 'Nofre with "Viking" on the oil-drum-bass. Hawaiian Beachboys, most all skilled entertainers, inspired visiting surfers to return home with slack-key guitars and uke's along with outriggers and a passion for grass shacks. Photo: Joe Quigg

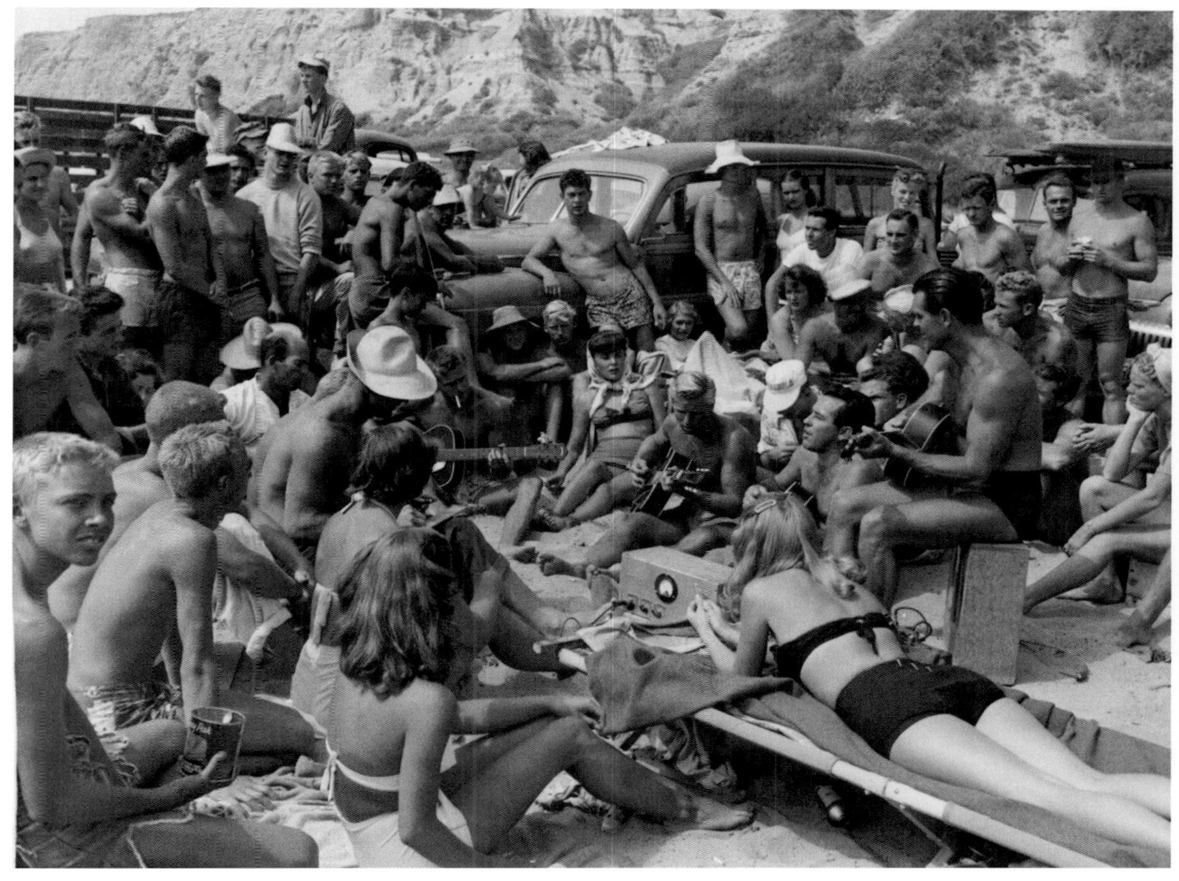

San Clemente dentist Barney Wilkes perched on his electric amp across from Pete Petersen in the white hat at a July 4th shin-dig. Regulars with particular skills gradually improved the rather remote beach with amenities. Photo: Joe Quigg

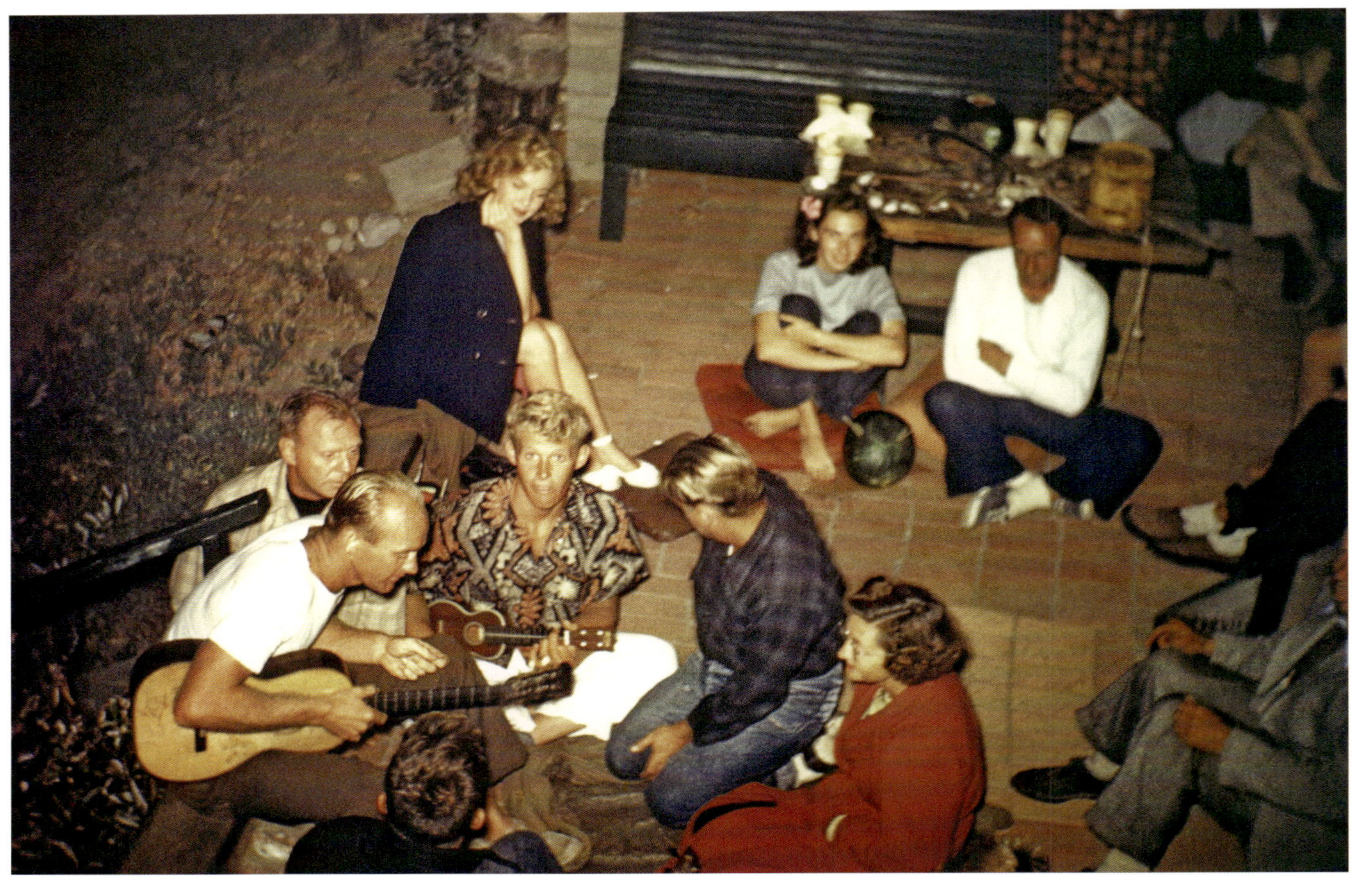

Pete Peterson playing guitar with Whitey Harrison on uke, entertaining friends at an impromptu sing-a-long near Malibu Colony. Zahn's date, Norma Jean Mortenson (Marilyn Monroe) with Navy Pea coat over her shoulders, listens in. Photo: Tom Zahn collection / SHACC

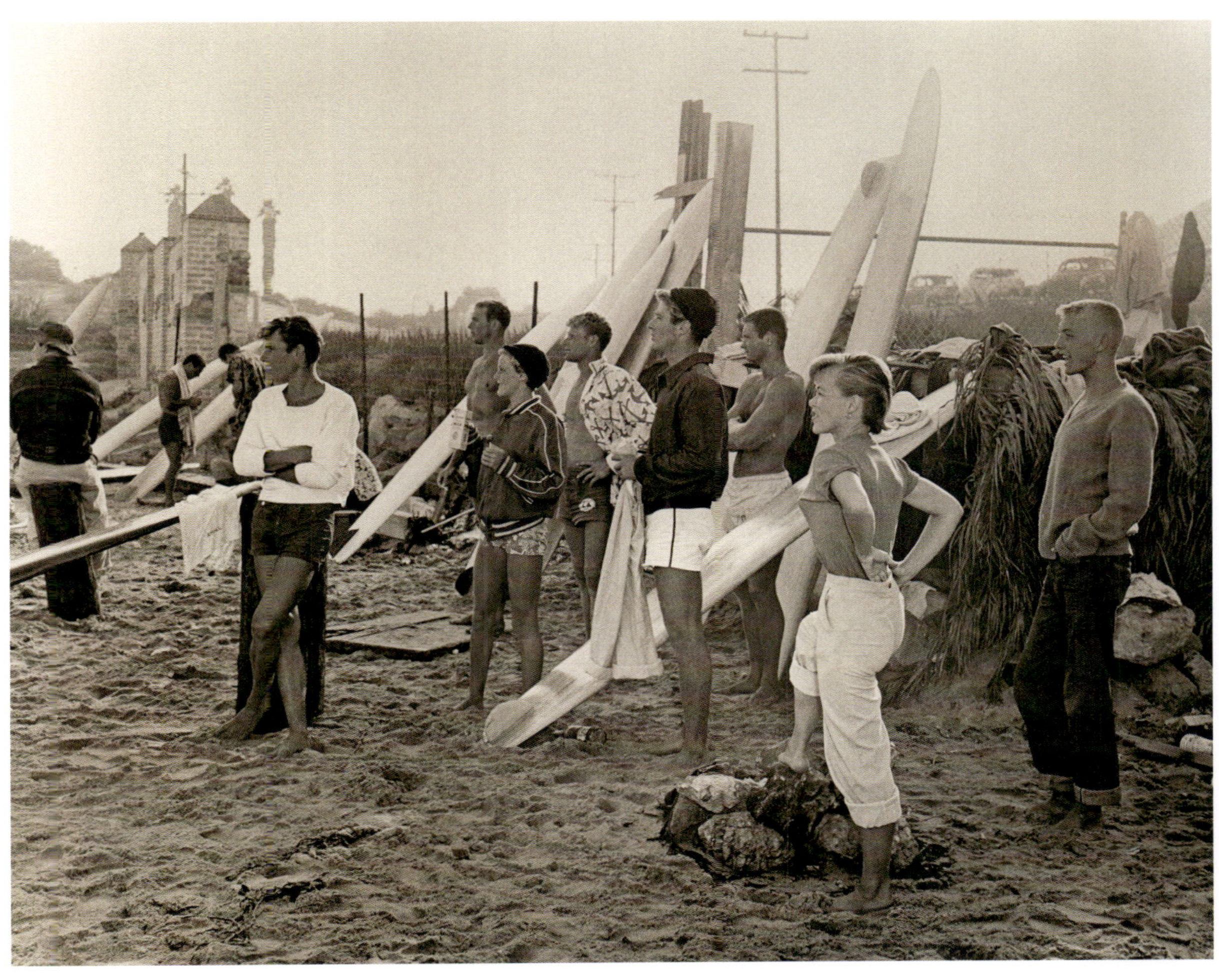

Malibu, 1950. (L to R) Don Drazen, Bill Stevens, Robin Grigg, Dave Rochlen, Peter Lawford, Tom Carpenter, Molly Dunn and Tim Lyons, all captivated by a set forming on the point. Photo: Joe Quigg

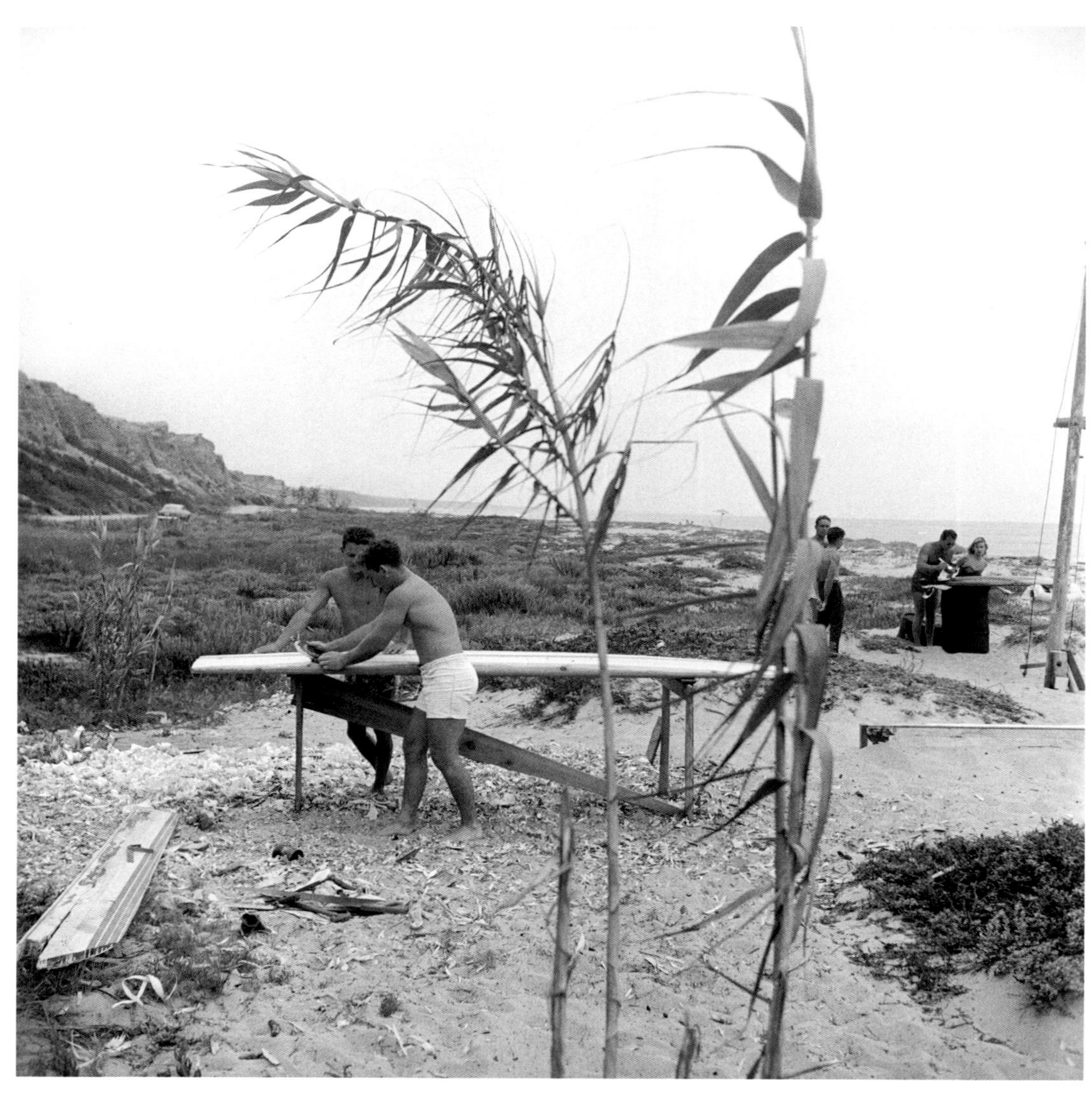

On site board building: roughing out a balsa blank with hand tools at San 'O, 1950.
Better than the garage; no cleanup required. Photo: Loomis Dean

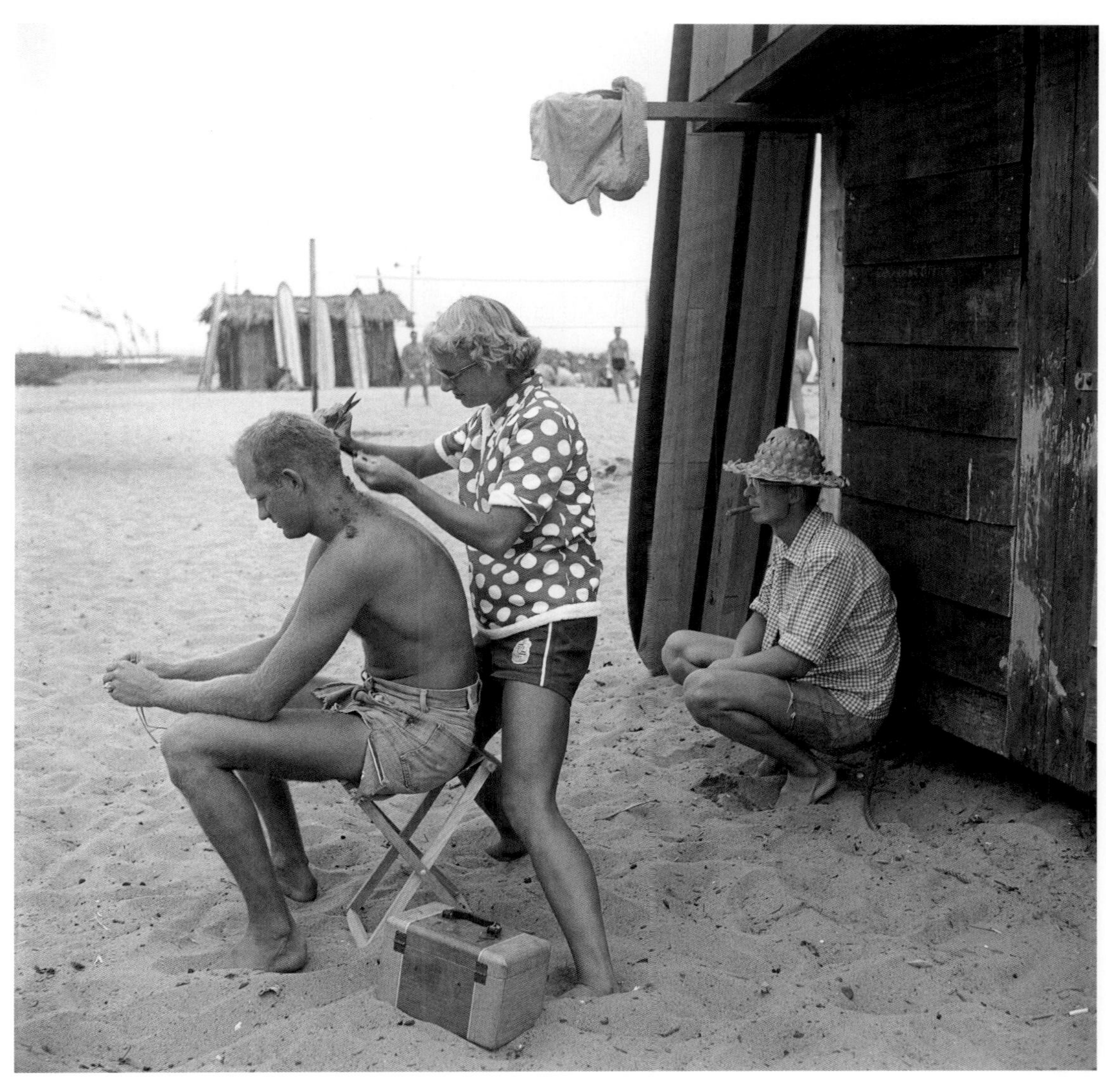

Ski film pioneer Warren Miller getting a hair cut from Myra Roche, July, 1950. At San 'O you could drive in and park right on the sand, which meant you could bring along all kinds of neat stuff. Photo: Loomis Dean

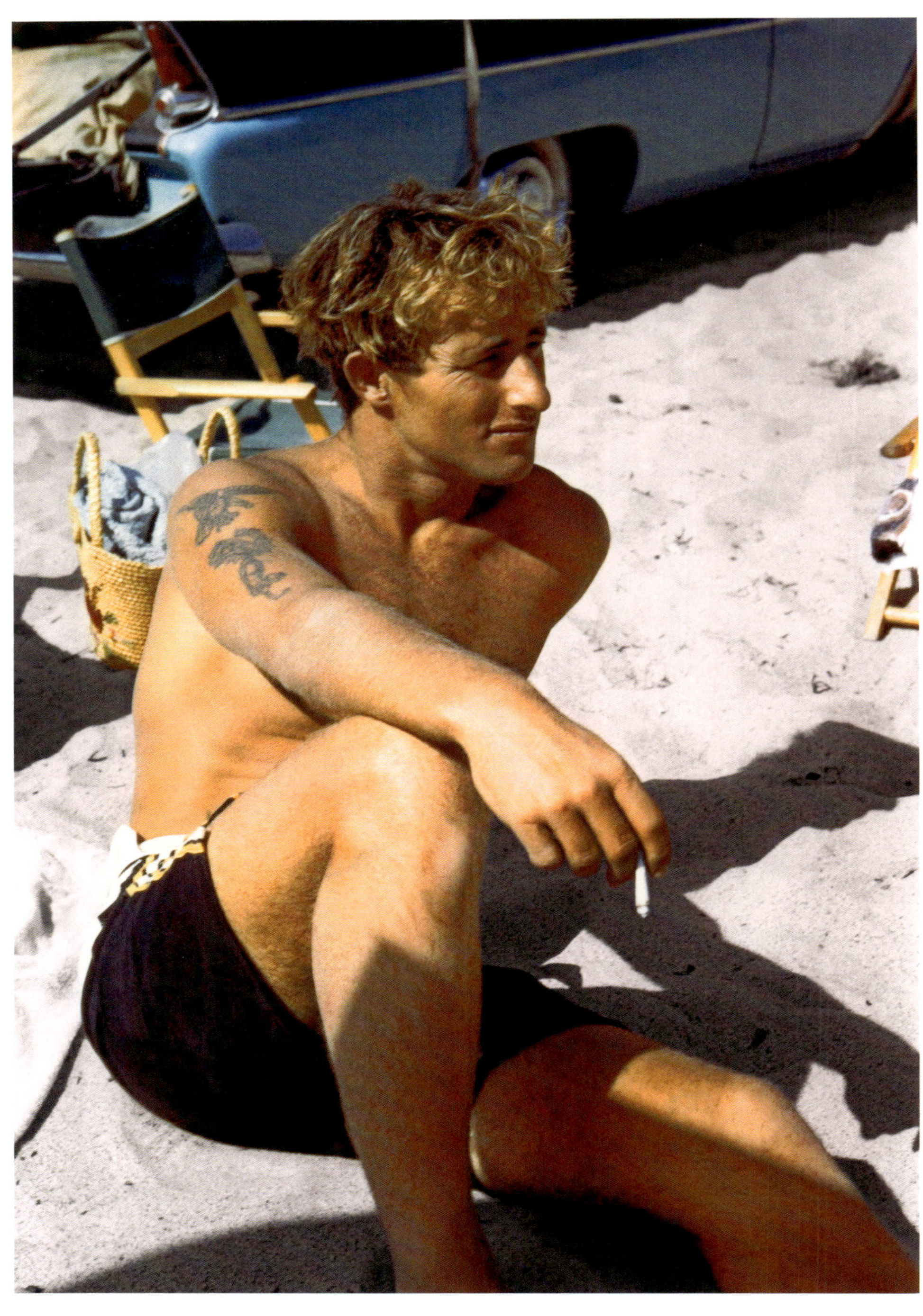

Dale Velzy relaxing at 'Nofre, mid-50s (judged by the tail light). He wasn't a tough guy but he had attitude, even for the beach crowd, and could back it up. Photo: Steve Barlotti collection / SHACC

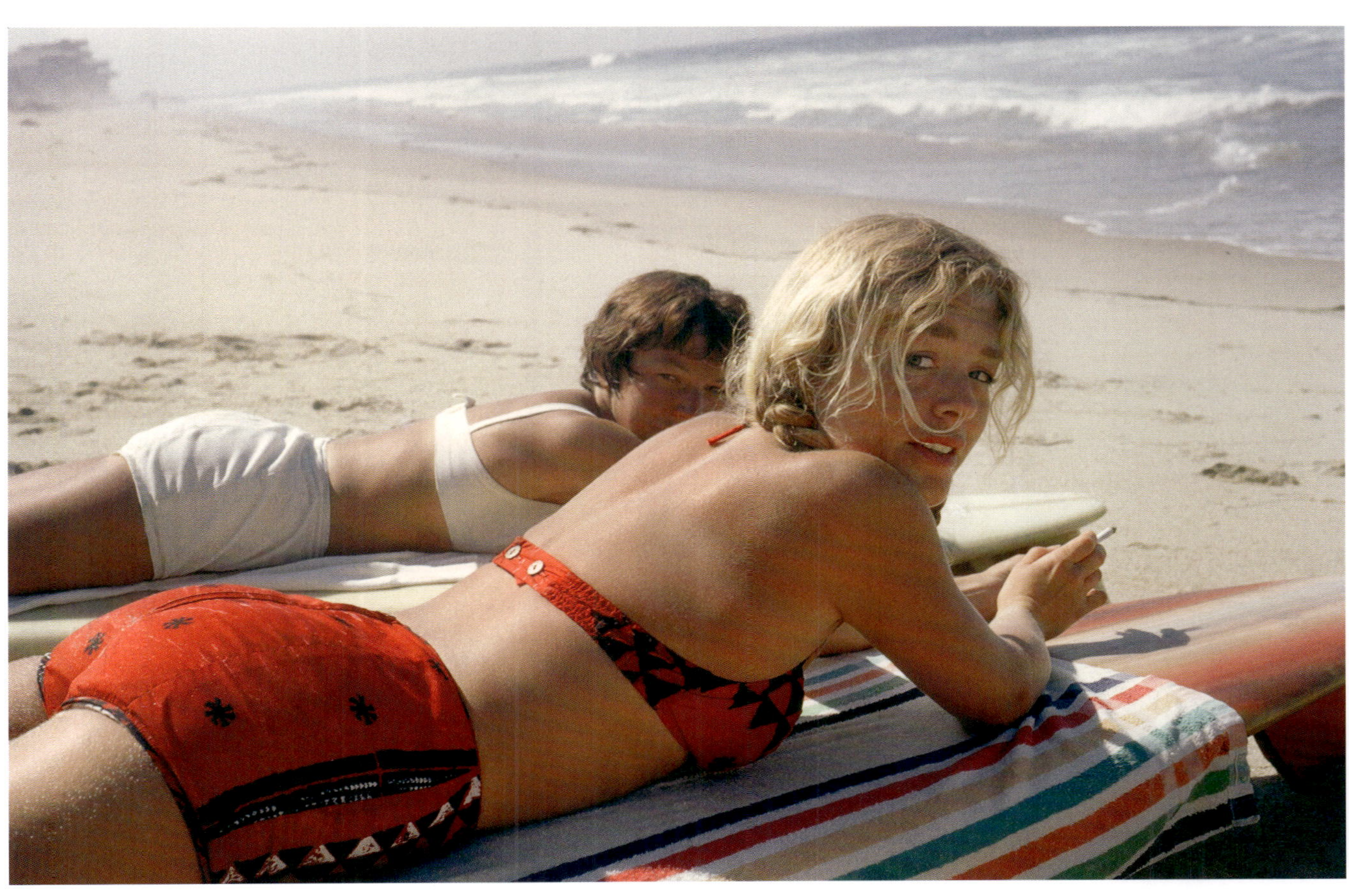

Oak Street, Laguna Beach, late '50s, photo taken by Dick Metz. The two gals were certainly invited to a party at his place later that evening. Photo: Dick Metz collection / SHACC

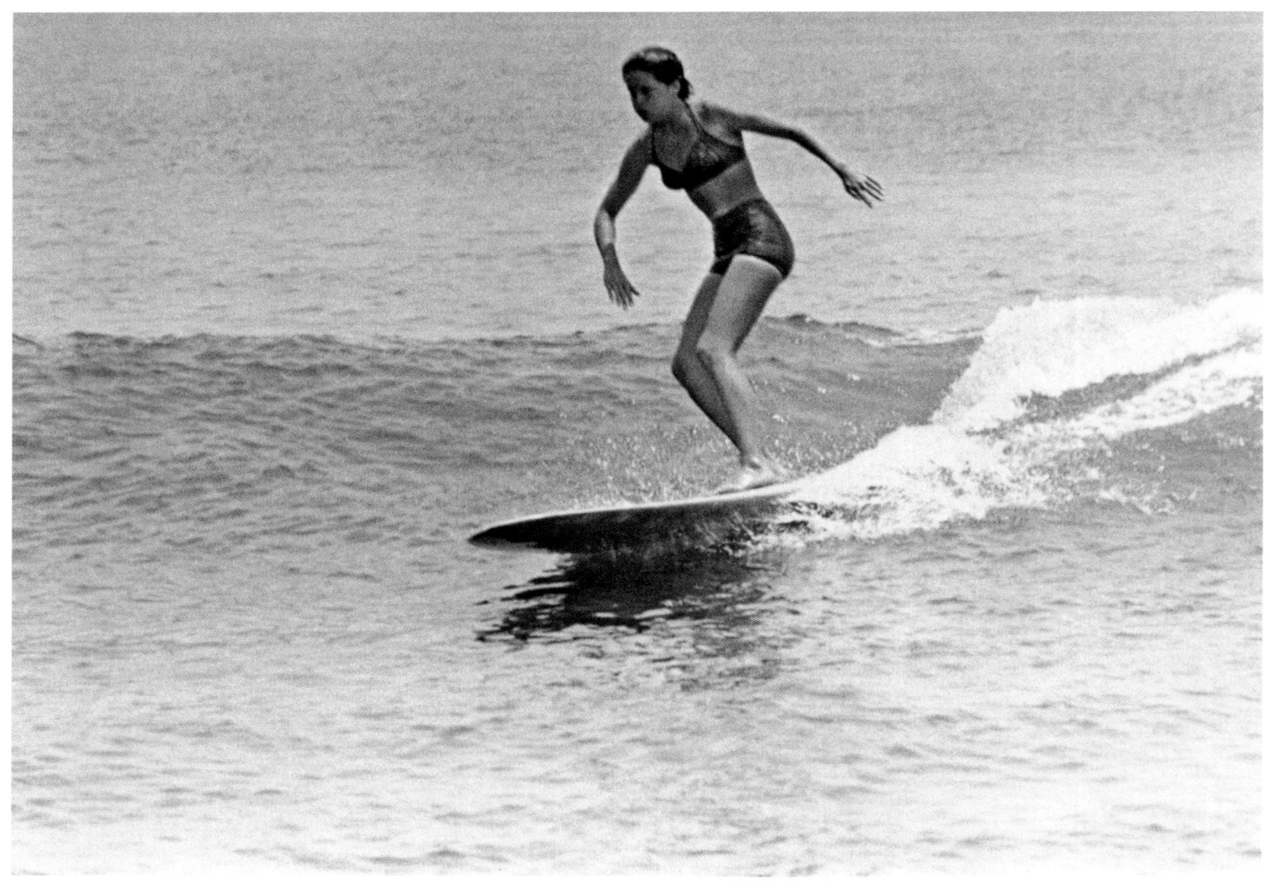

Aggie Bane, the future Mrs. Quigg, riding her 16th birthday present from Joe. When guys tried the shorter, lighter "girlfriend" boards with Quigg's innovative rail rocker, the "hot-dog" fuse was lit. Photo: Joe Quigg

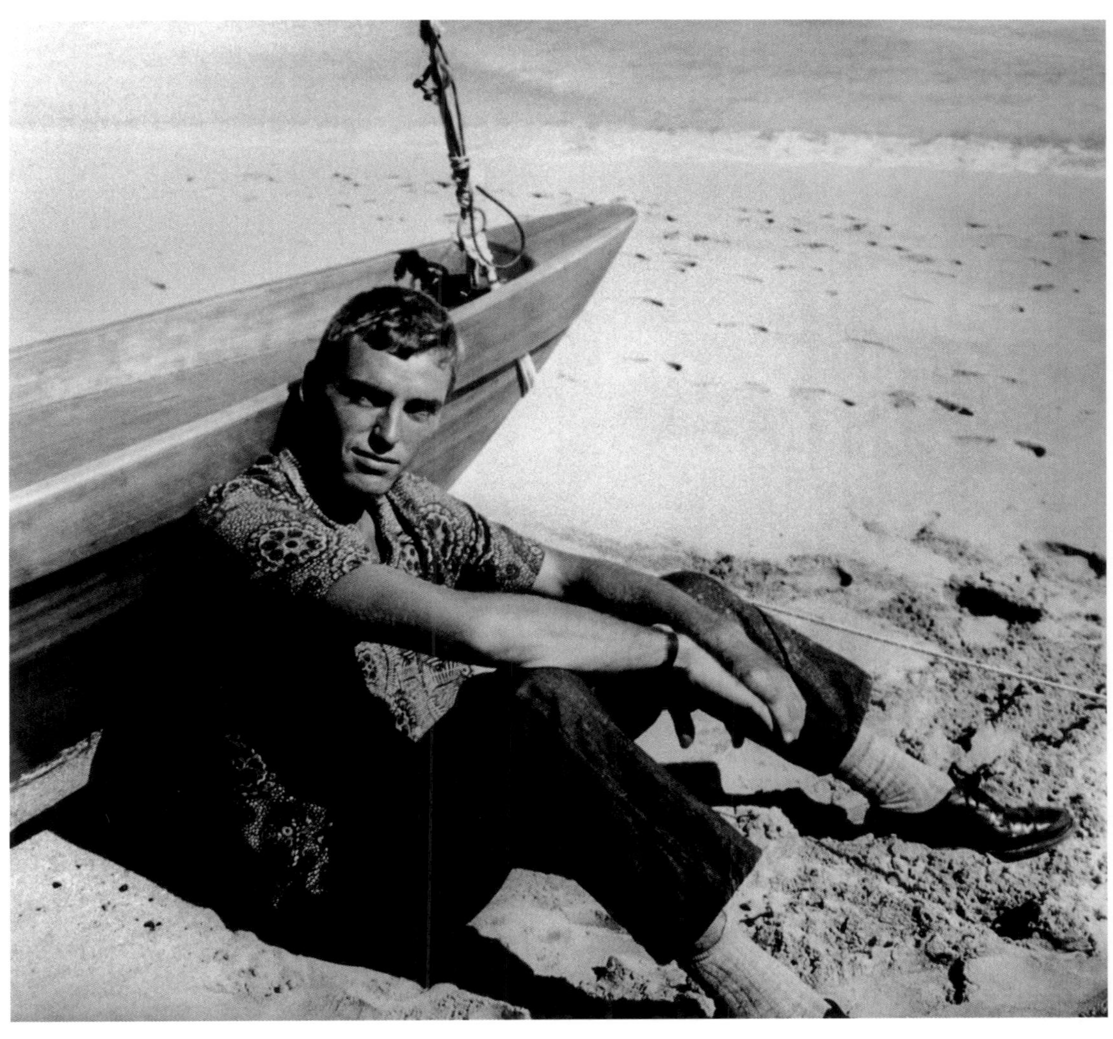

Joe Quigg, over from California, relaxing against the side of his first multi-hull, a trimaran, in front of Waikiki Surf Club.
Photo: Joe Quigg collection

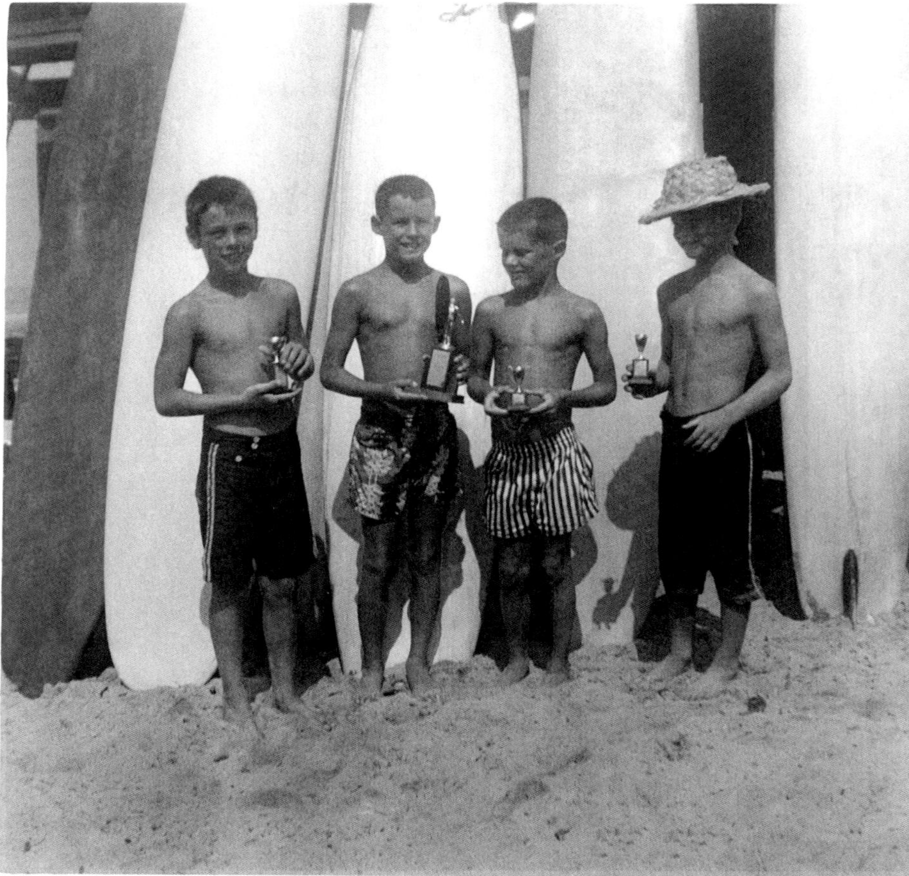

Stoked "Gremmies" with mini-balsa "chips", winners of the boy's 9-11 division at the annual San Onofre Club contest.
Photo: Jim Galloon / SHACC

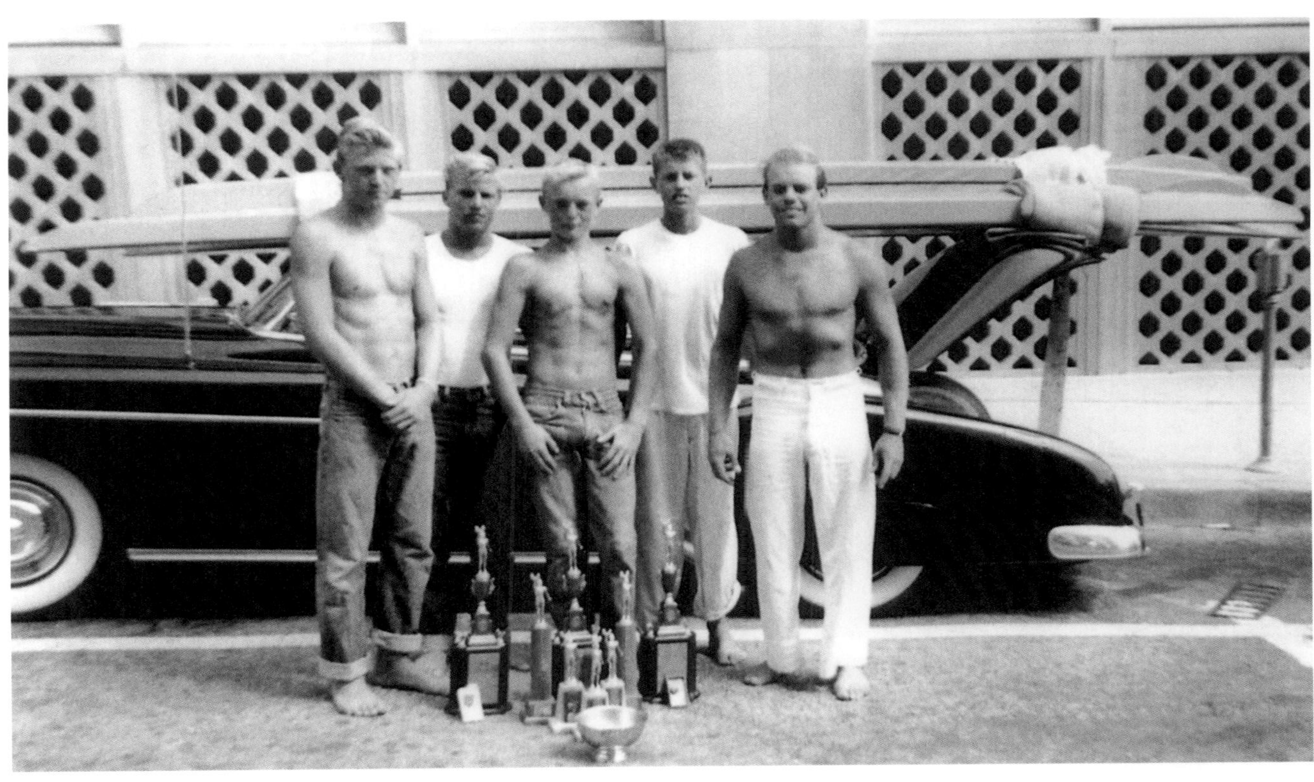

Bing Copeland, Bev Morgan, Greg Noll, Dick Medvie and Bob Hogan in front of Bev's Chevy, 1951, at a Santa Monica paddleboard race. Back then, somewhat of a teenage tough, Noll would become an entrepreneurial surf filmmaker, noted board builder, and historic big wave rider. Photo: Bing Copeland collection / SHACC

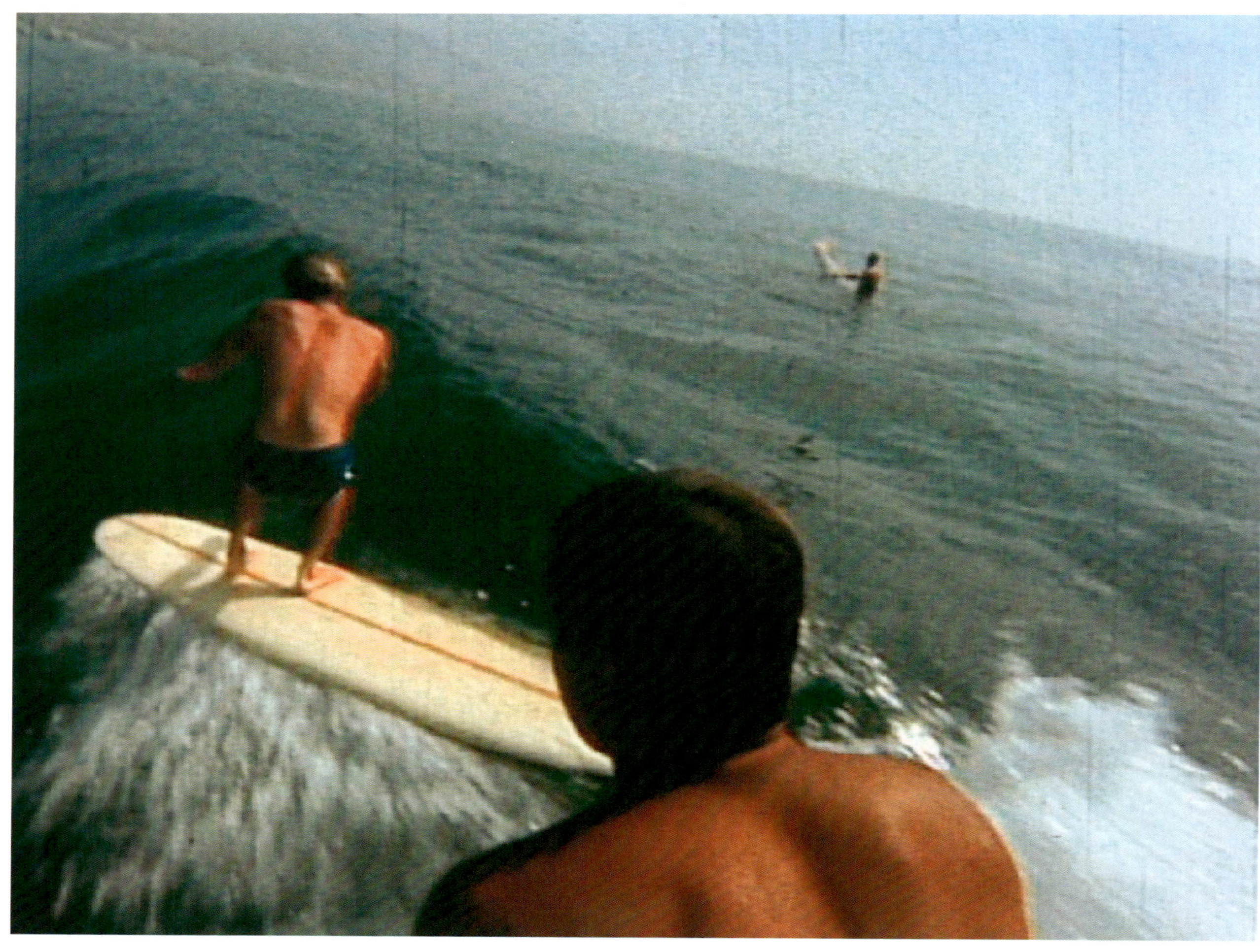

Miki Dora haunting Johnny Fain at Arroyo Secos near the L.A. County Line;
(an innovative aft-mounted camera perspective captured by Grant Rohloff in 1959). Photo: Grant Rohloff, courtesy Chris Rohloff

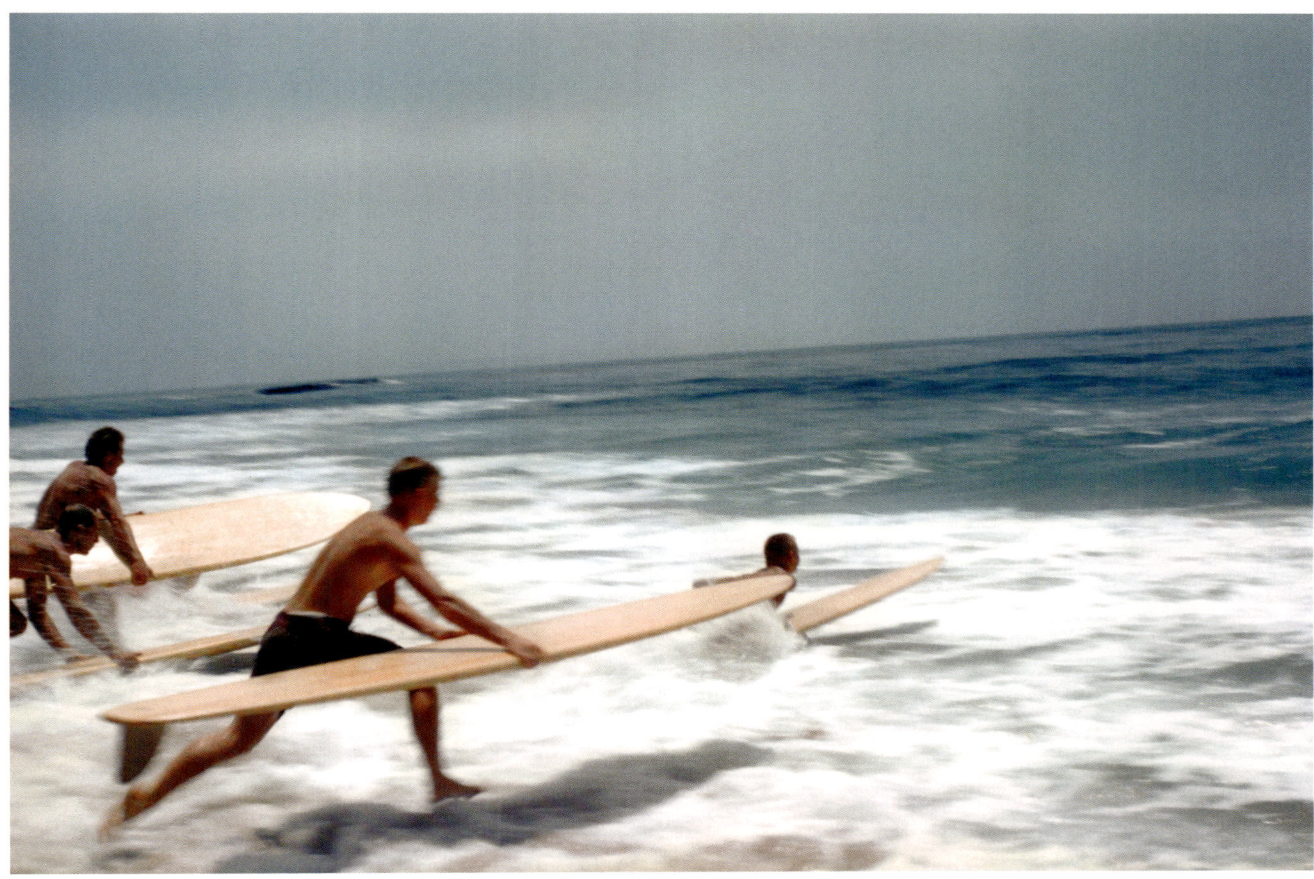

Start of the paddle race at the Brooks Street Surf Contest. Begun in 1954, the strictly local event run by the Laguna Beach Rec. Department is the oldest continuously run surf competition in the world. Photo: Dick Metz collection / SHACC

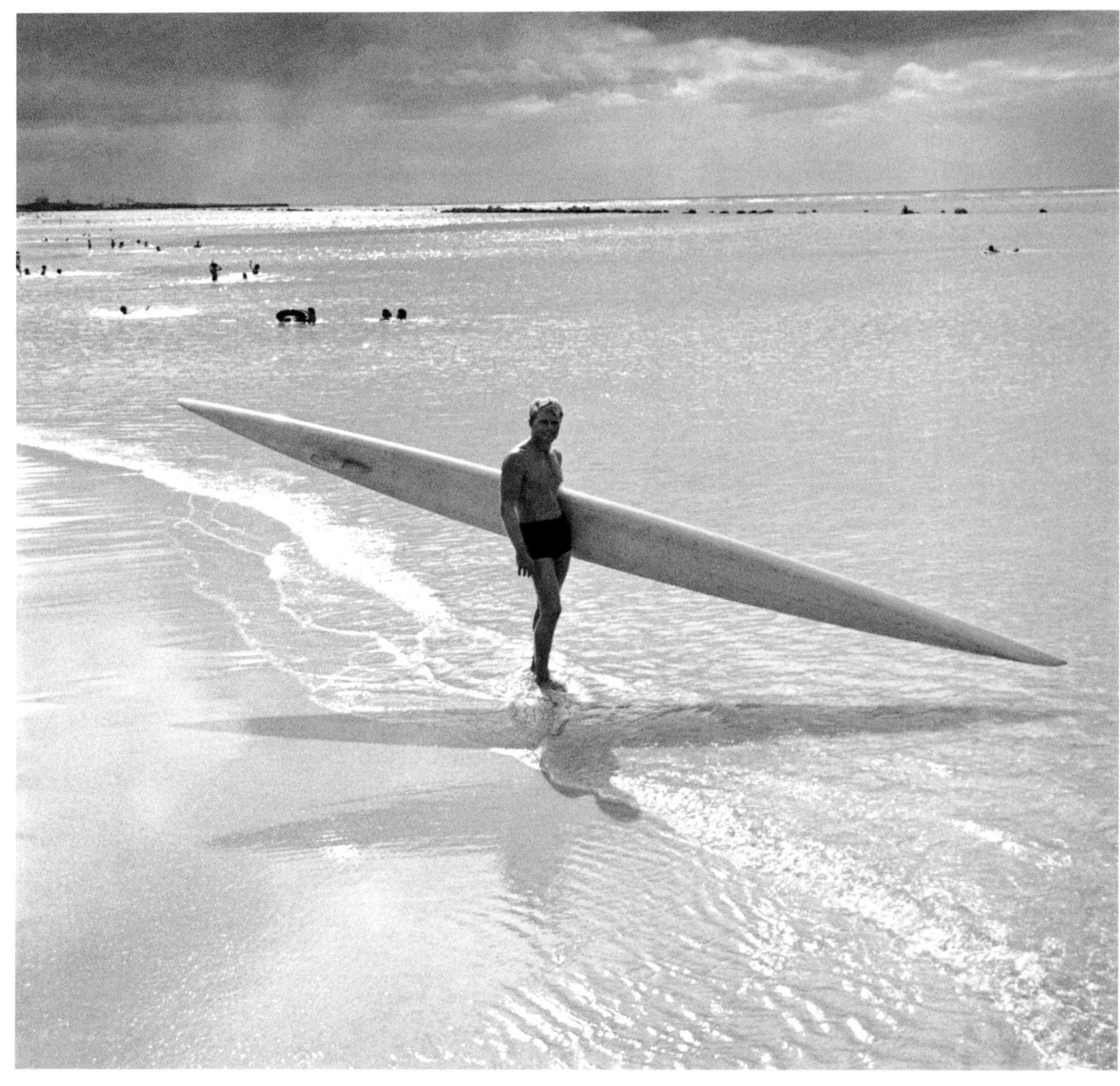

Tom Zahn with the "Stradivarius" paddleboard, a balsa skin over a ½″ balsa bulkhead, 19′L x 16″W, 20LBS., that Quigg originally built for himself. Zahn won several Catalina to Mainland races with this board. Photo: Joe Quigg

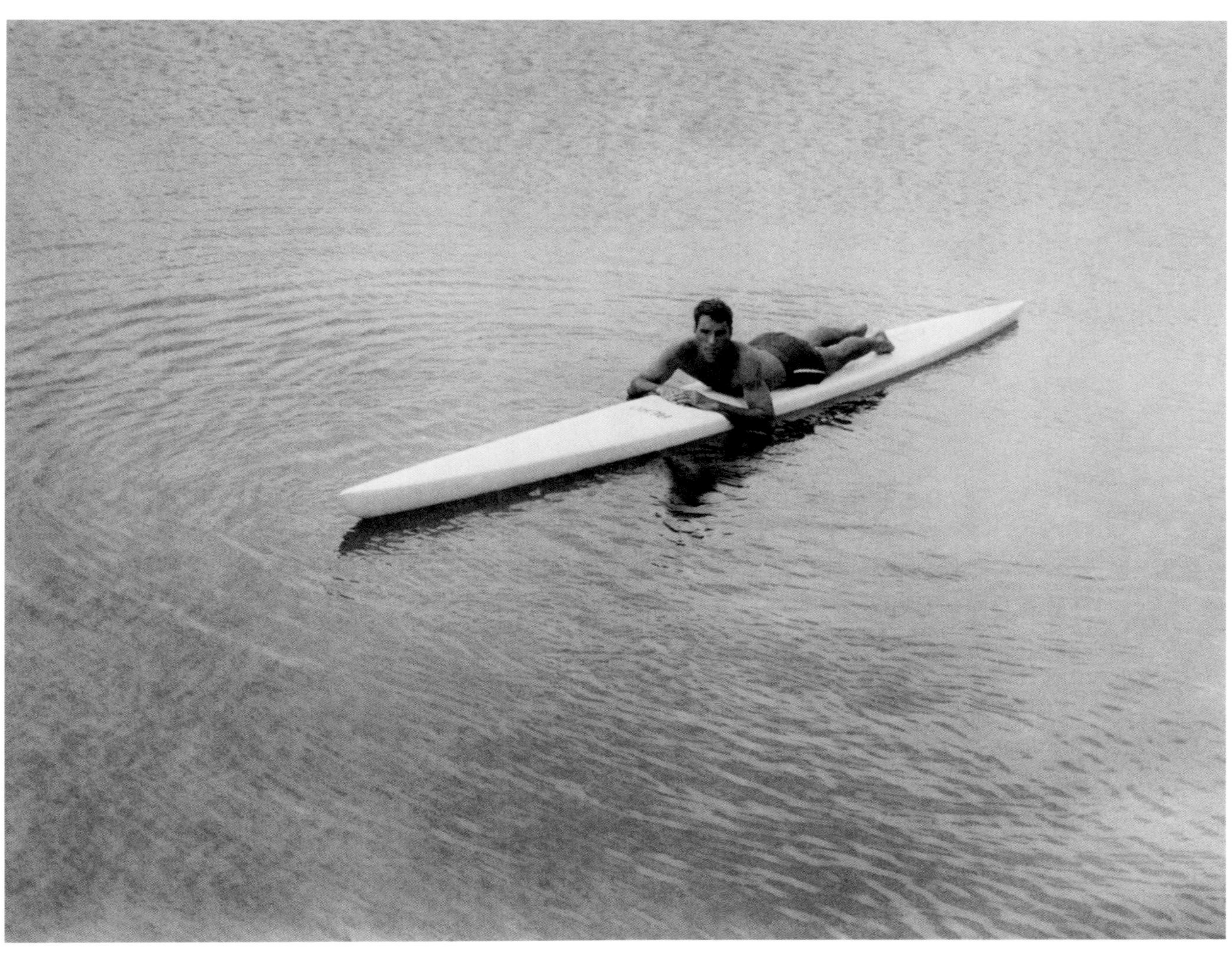

Built prior to the "Stradivarius", Joe Quigg finished second place in the Diamond Head race paddling this 20′ board he crafted.
Photo: Aggie Quigg

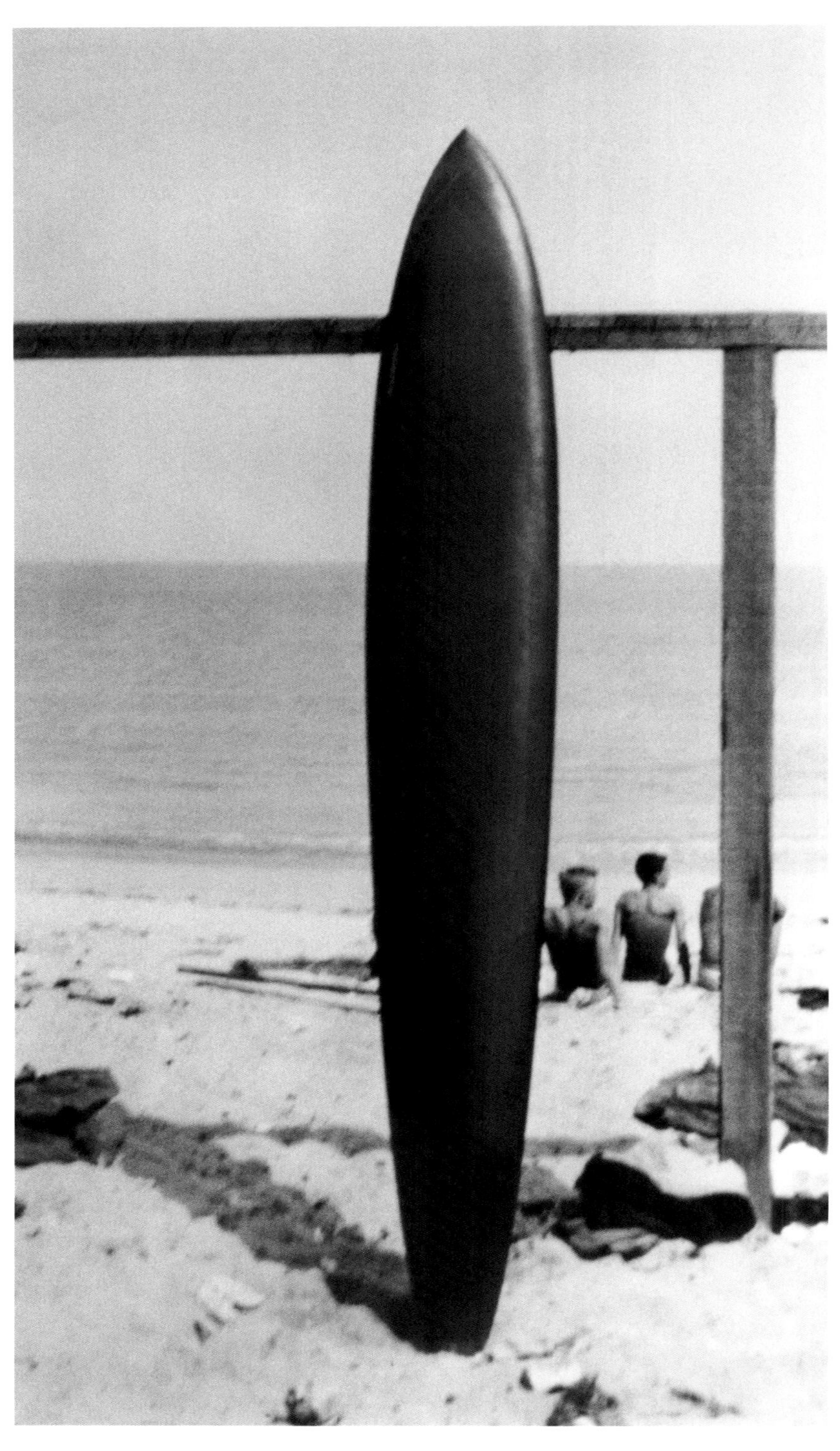

Wally Froiseth brought his Hawaiian hot-curl "Super Castle" (standing against the remnants of the old Malibu fence) on an early trip to California. The Pit crew had slowly dismantled the fence for firewood. Photo: Joe Quigg

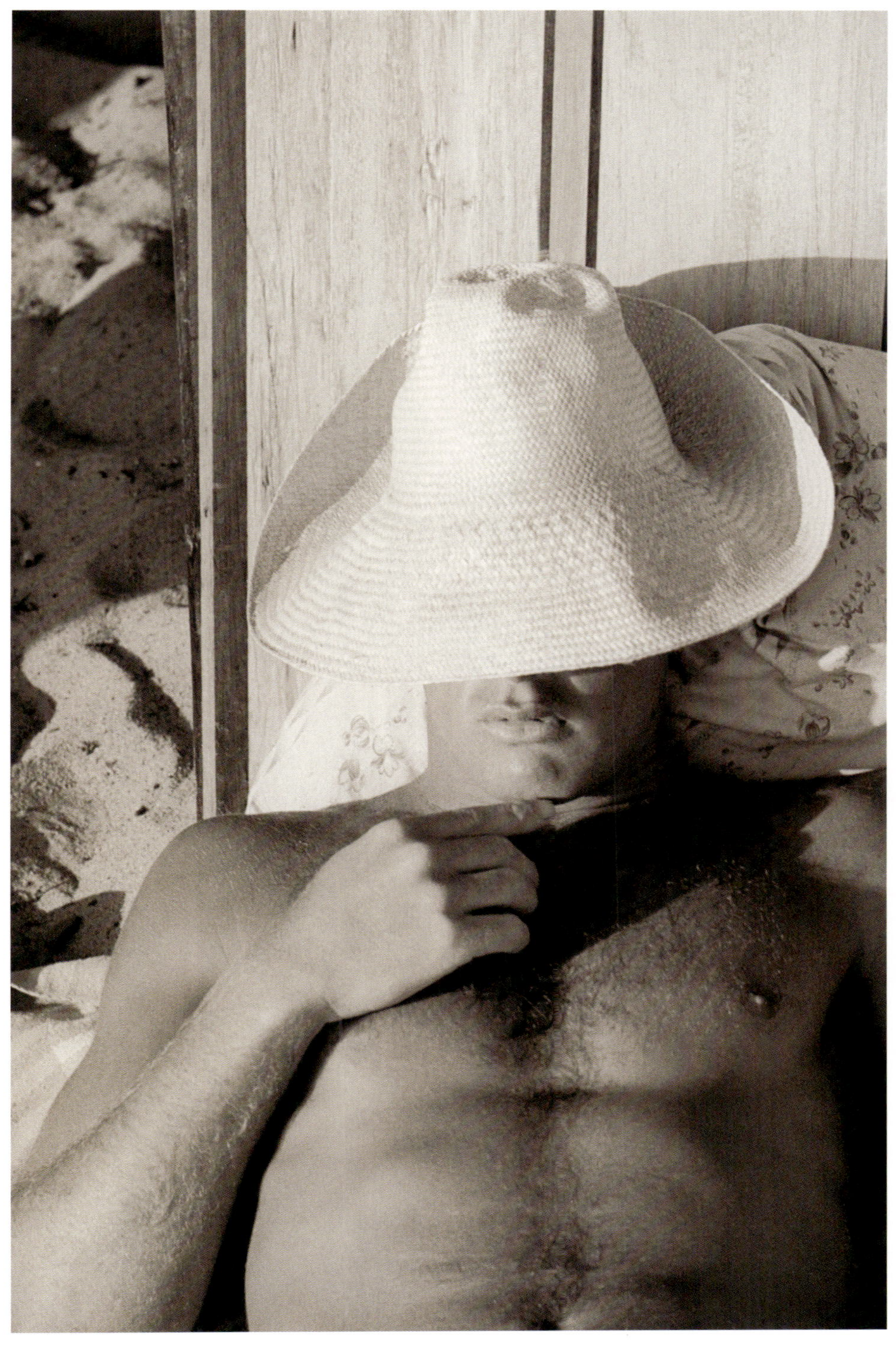

A 1950 image by Loomis Dean for a Life magazine article on San Onofre;
such media attention was a sign that the sport was beginning to take on a romantic "aura." Photo: Loomis Dean

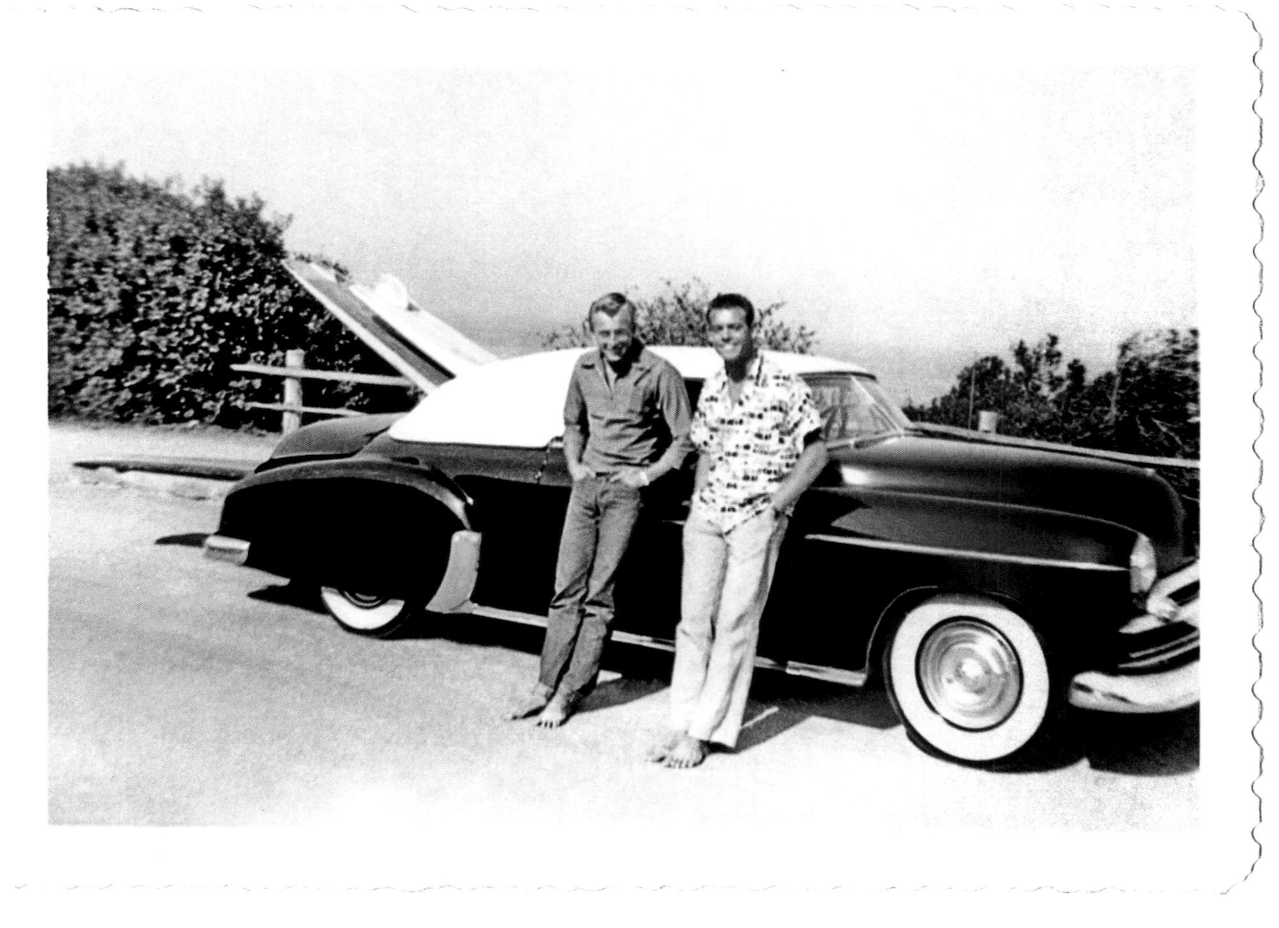

Barney "Google" Briggs and Bob Hogan with Bev's '49 Chevy, chopped with Carson top and McGurk modified engine, loaded with balsas. The two cultures often intermixed. Photo: Bev Morgan collection / SHACC

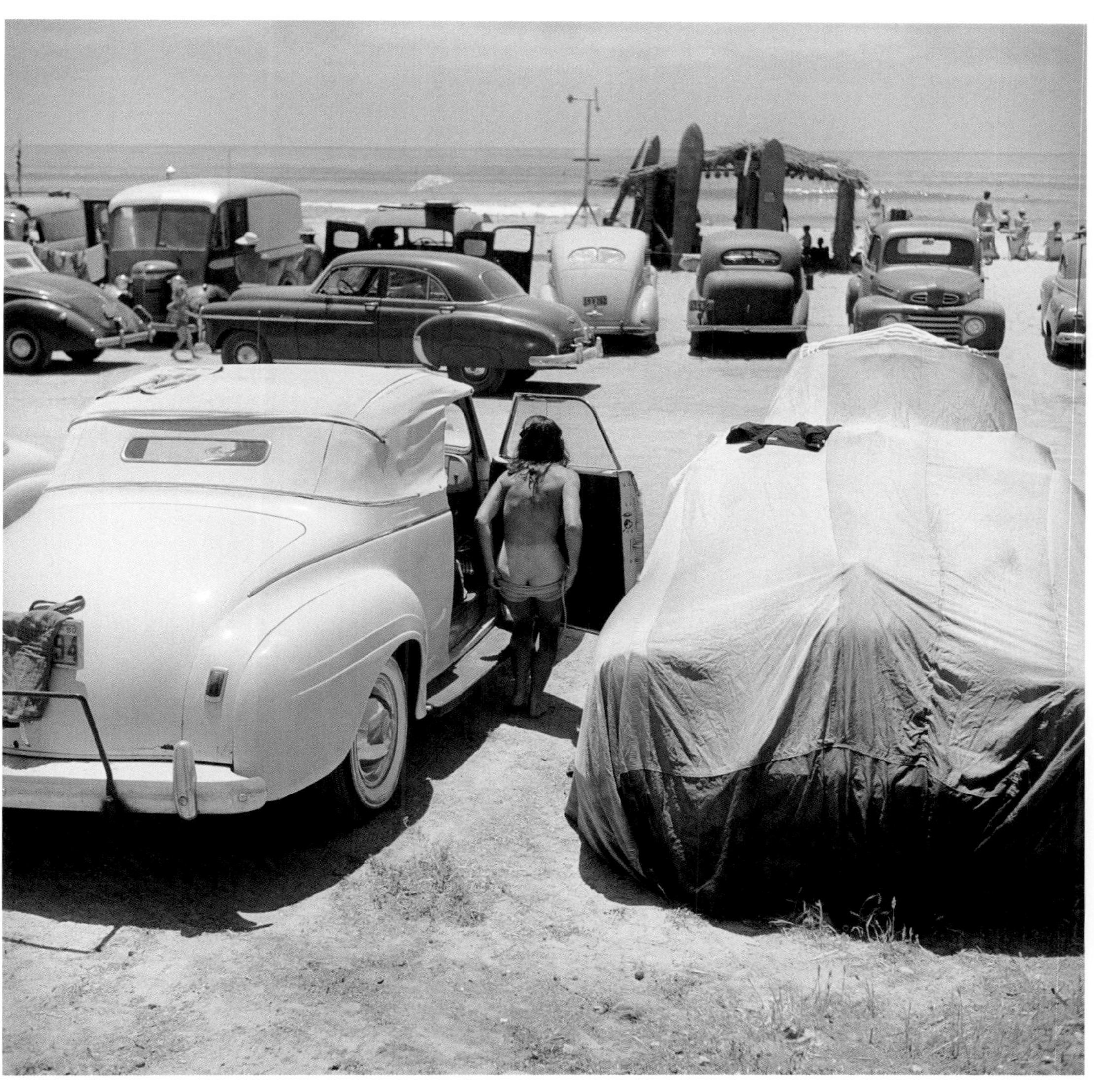

Quick changing at San Onofre on a July weekend, 1950.
If the law caught you doing that at Malibu you'd be arrested for indecent exposure. Photo: Loomis Dean

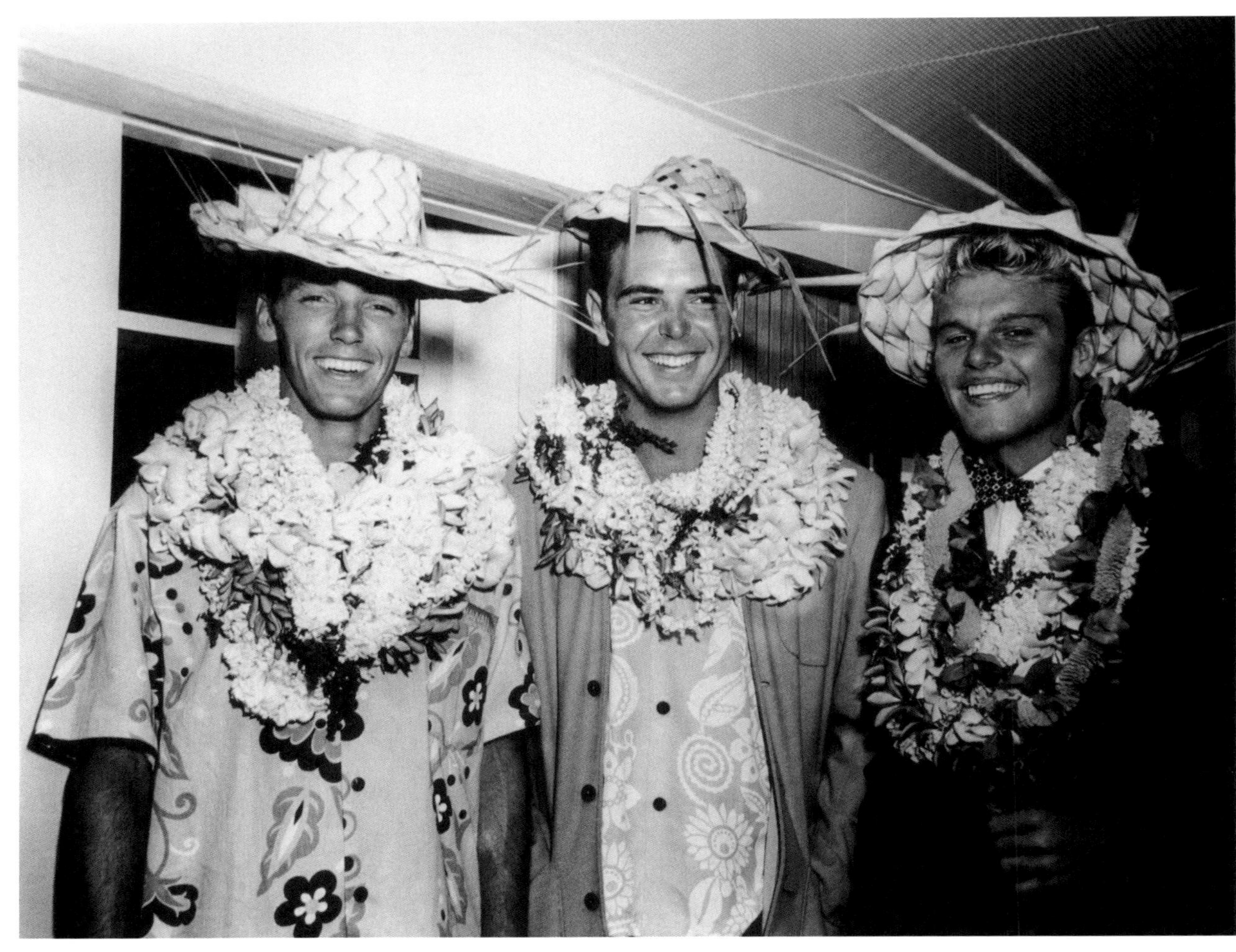

Joe Quigg, Matt Kivlin, and Tom Zahn on their first trip to Hawaii in the late '40s. Once there, they were profoundly influenced by the style and techiniques of the Hawaiian surfers. Upon their return to California, they shared that experience. Photo: Joe Quigg collection

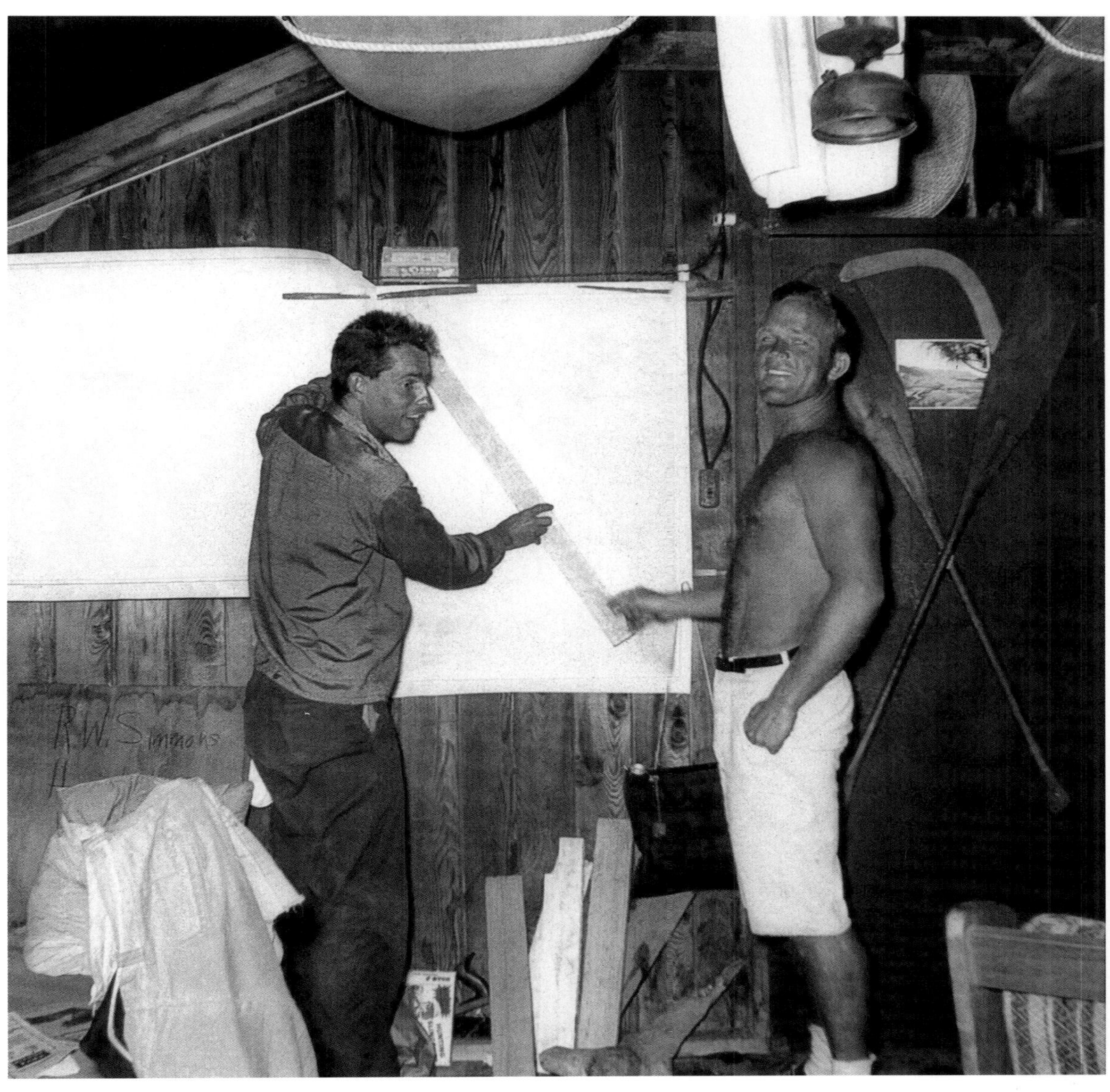

Bob Simmons diagraming Makaha's swell angle, peak shift, and bottom structure
for fellow Californian Buzzy Trent in their Waianae Quonset hut. Photo: Walter Hoffman

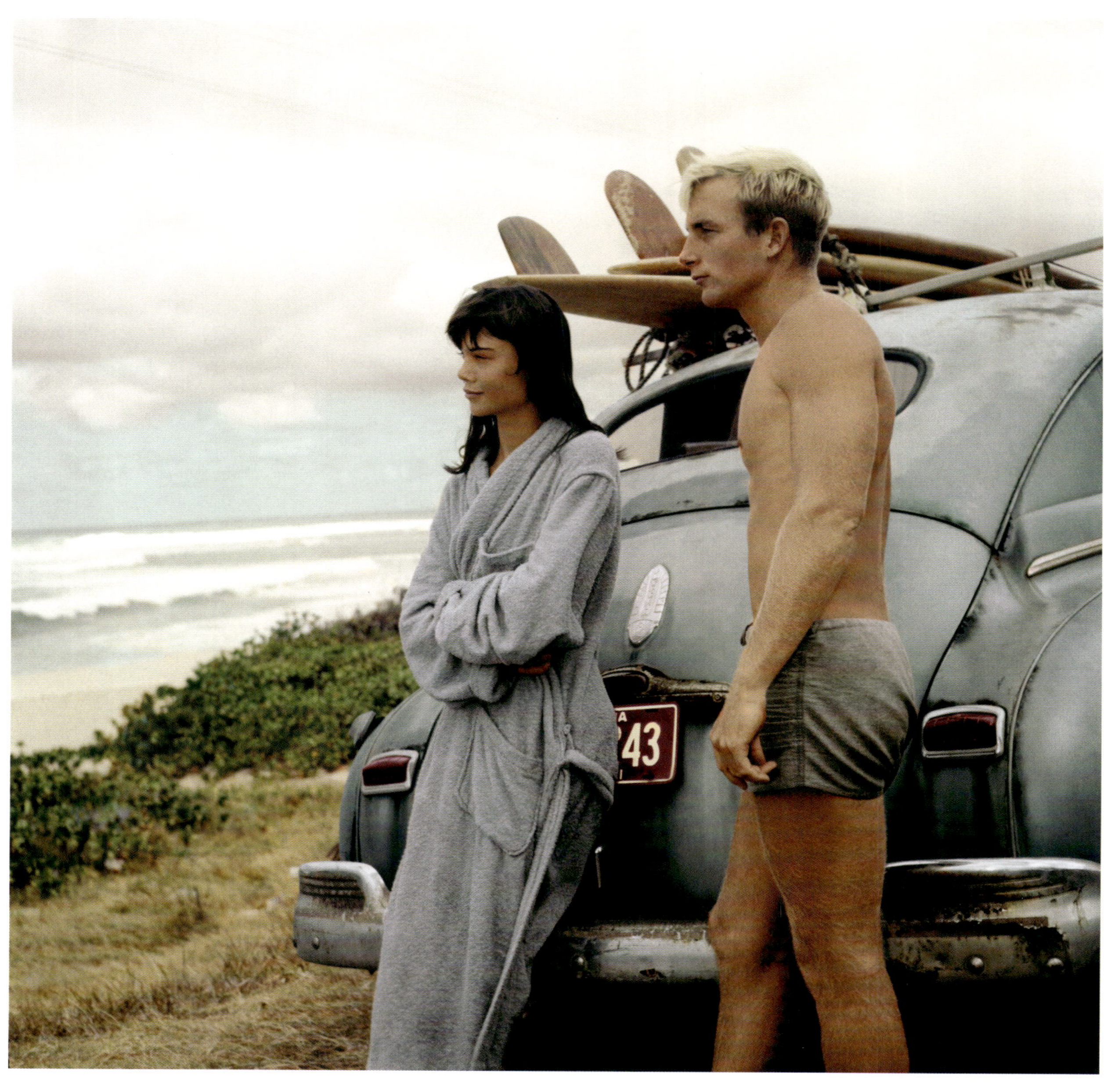

Californians Wendy Wagner and Tom Carlin on a drive around Kaena Point.
A shortcut to the North Shore from the West side, the track along the jagged rocks got hairy in spots. Photo: Bev Morgan / SHACC

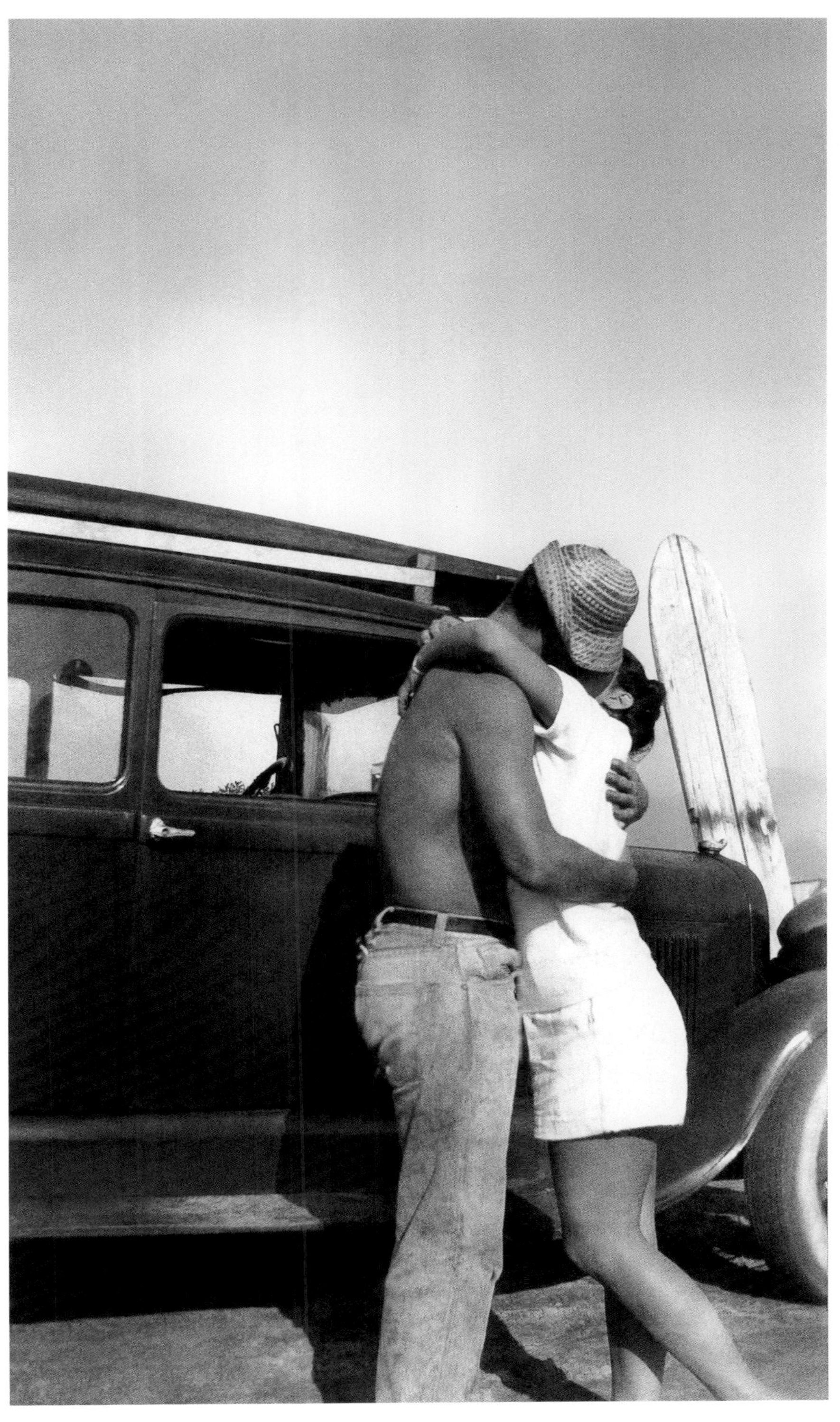

San Onofre's comfortable sand beach and array of soft-waves made for a perfect surf date, a family surf destination, and a place where the accoutrements of beaching approached high art. Photo: SHACC collection

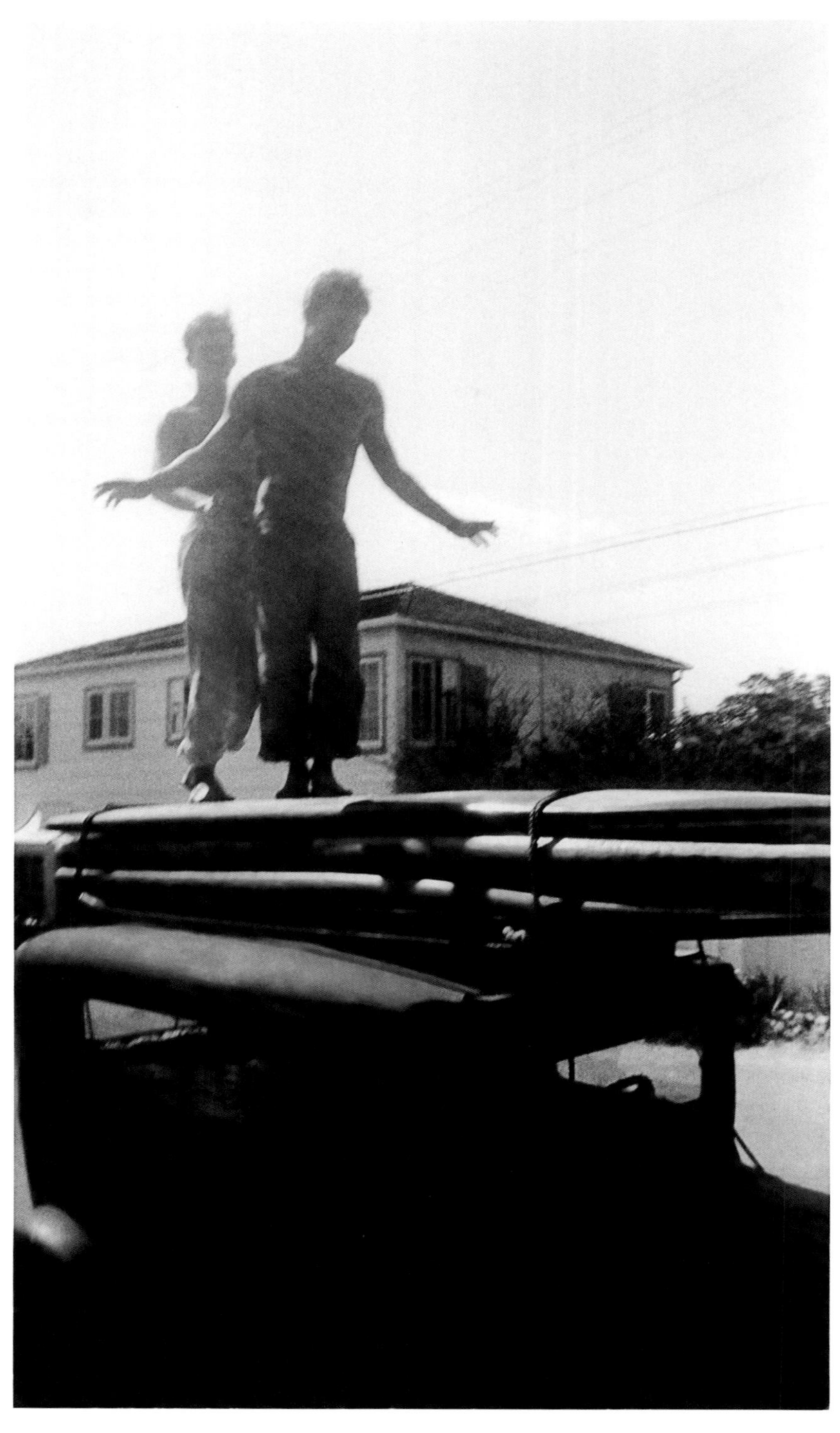

Young "surf rats" goofing around before driving to the South Bay from some mid-city Los Angeles neighborhood. Just ten miles apart, the two worlds existed in different universes. Photo: Bev Morgan collection / SHACC

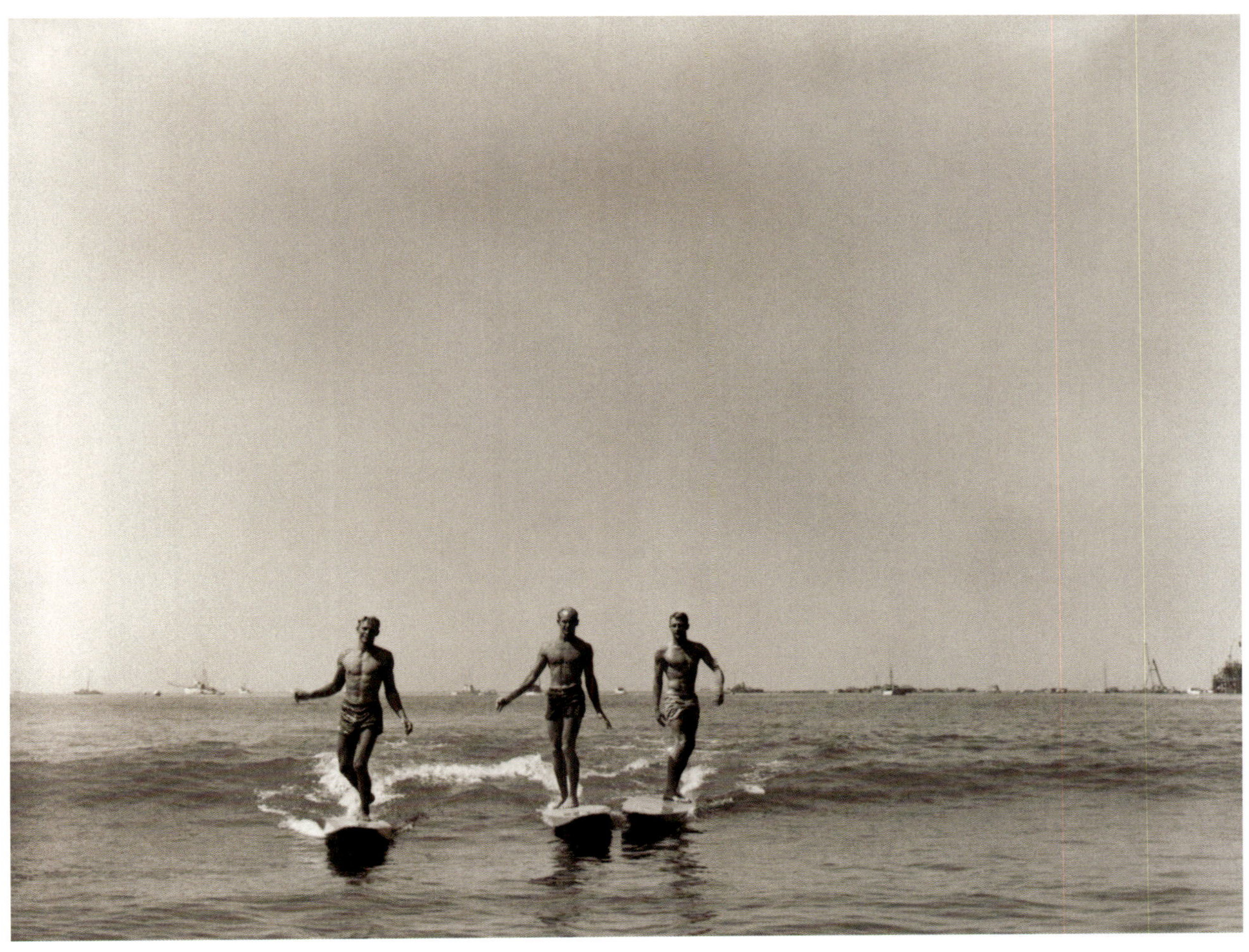

Dave Rochlen, recently back from the war, Pete Peterson, considered the greatest waterman of the 20th century, and Tom Volk sharing a nondescript beach break at the finish of the Santa Monica Lifeguard paddle race. Photo: Joe Quigg

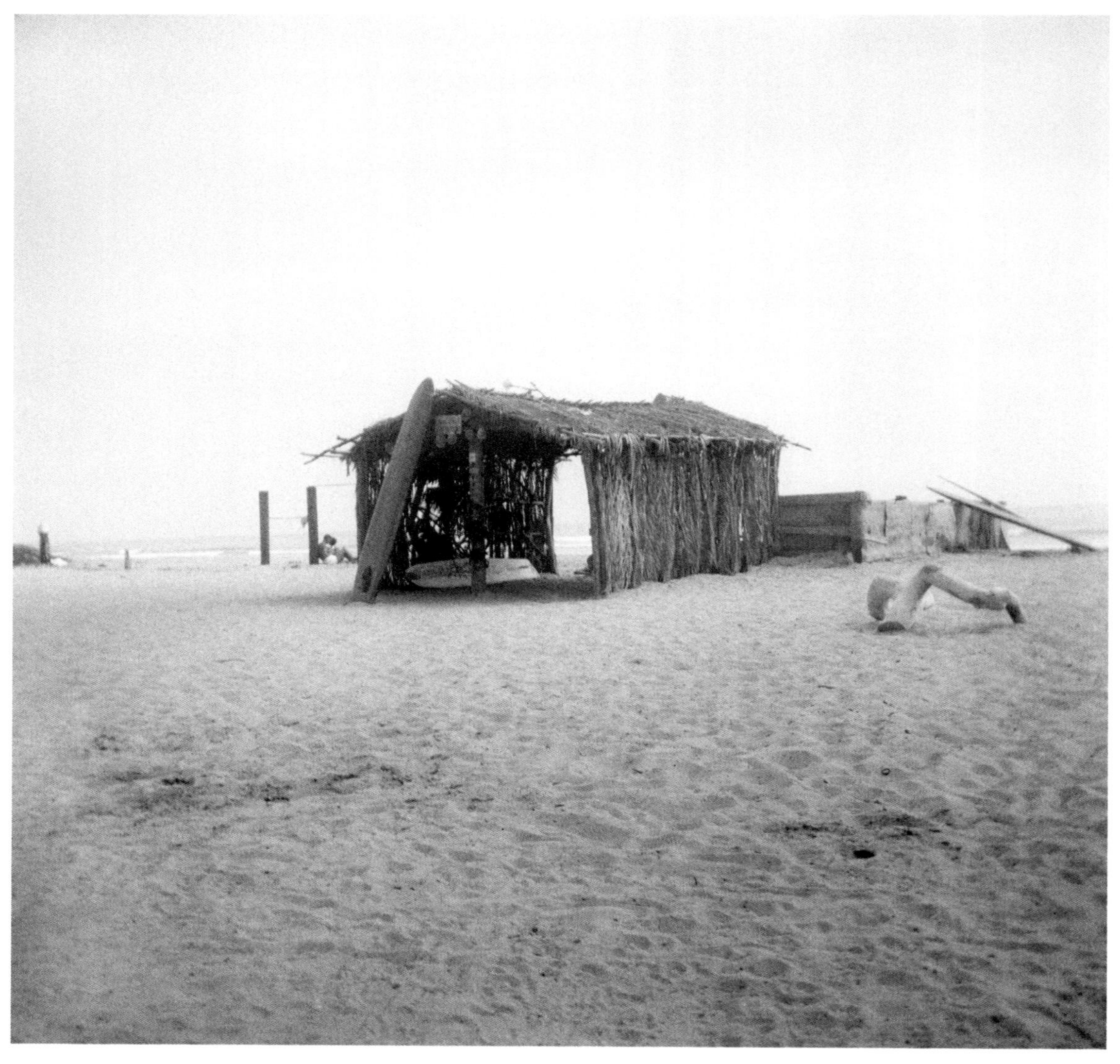

One in a series of beach habitats erected at 'Nofre over the years by surfers to provide shelter from the elements and who knows what else? It can get windy there in the afternoon. Photo: Dick Metz collection / SHACC

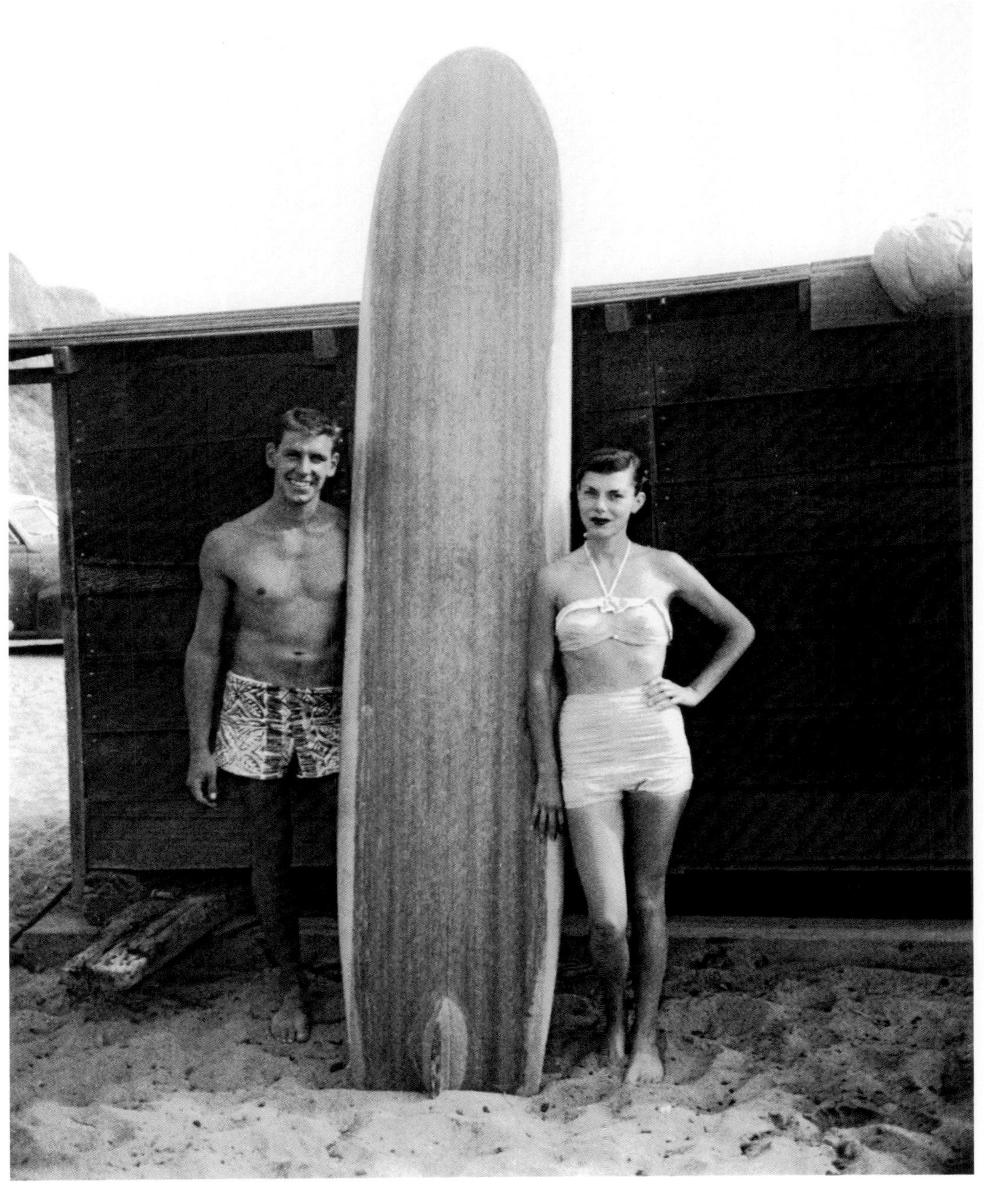

Jim Galloon and friend with a Simmons "sandwich". Roughly 200 were built by Bob circa-1950 with Kivlin and Quigg's help, using Styrofoam cores decked with thin veneer, edged with hand-shaped balsa rails, all bonded together in a rocker'd jig. Photo: Jim Galloon / SHACC

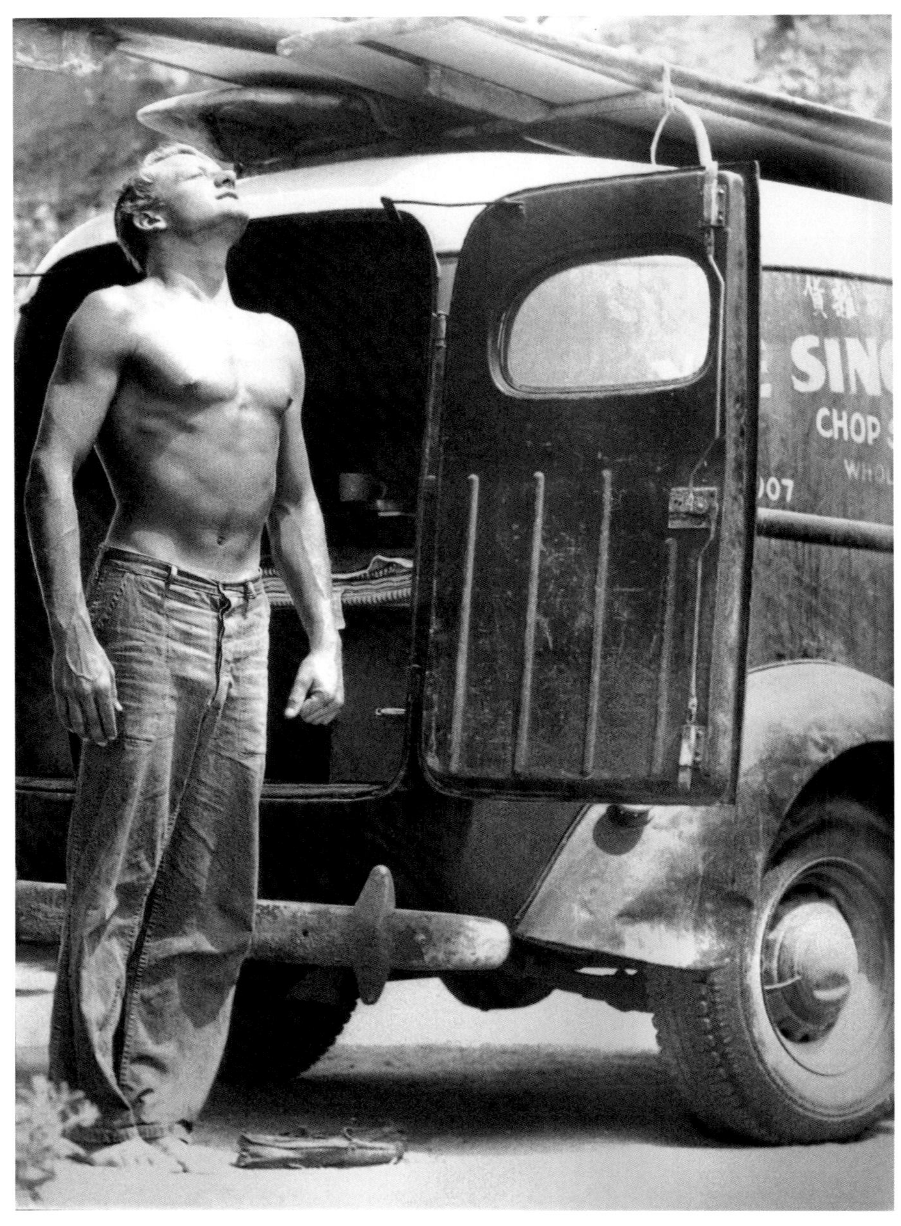

"Jungle" Joe Sokolich taking sun at the rear of a typical period surf vehicle adaptation, once a Chop Suey delivery van, now top-loaded with shallow-finned planks. Photo: Paul W. Luton

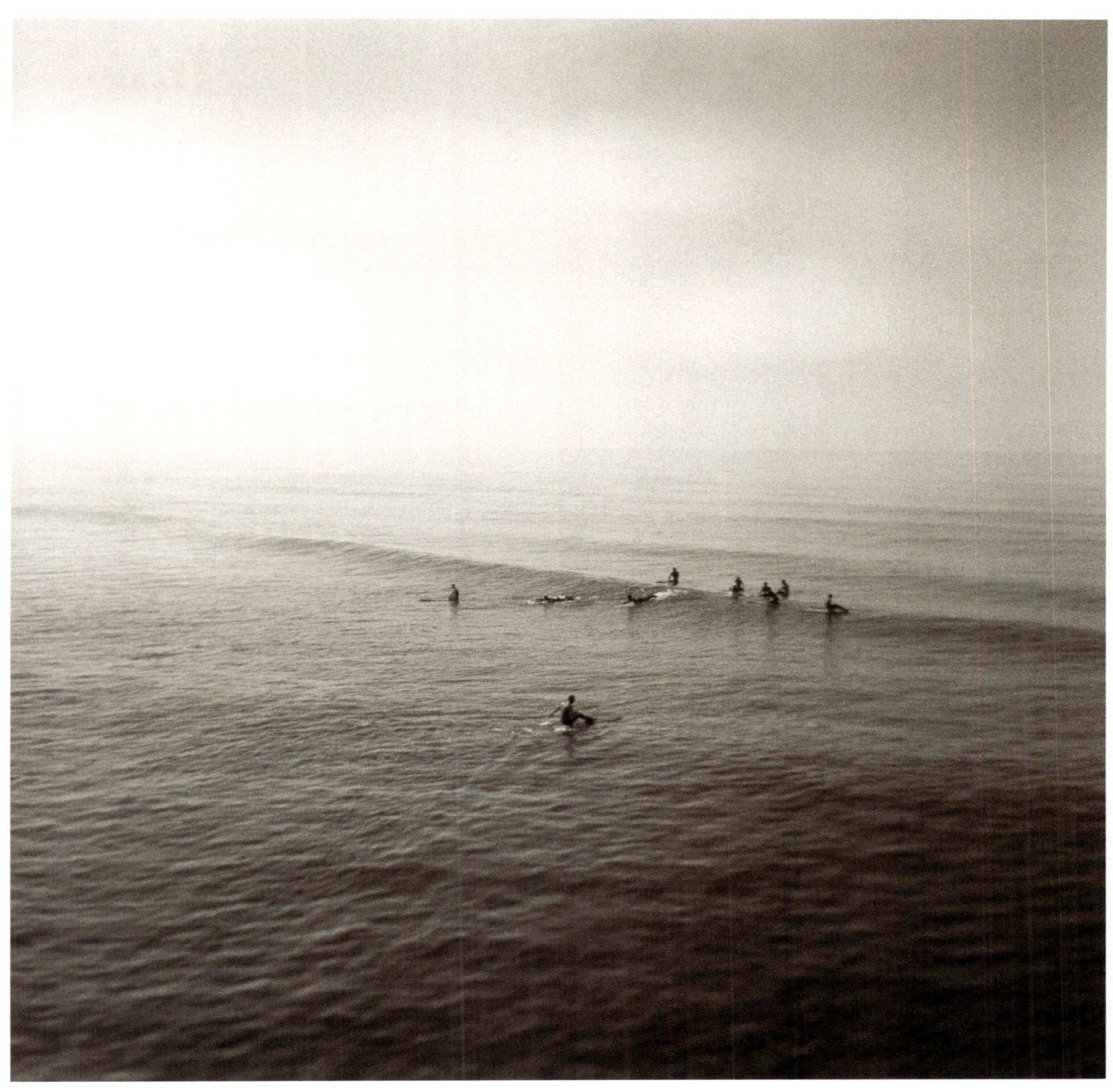

Morning glass on the south side of Manhattan Beach Pier, circa-early '50s. Recalled Bev Morgan, "We'd be sitting out there and Velzy'd ask us, 'See all those cars heading to their 9-5's? Whose got it wrong? Them or us?'" Photo: Alayne Raistin / Bev Morgan collection / SHACC

At long last the Second World War ended. Not surprisingly, most of the innovative Yosemite climbers of the 1930s had, by 1946, become working men with families, and with little ambition to once again tackle the somber granite walls of the Incomparable Valley. Wars disrupt, and it was time for new upstarts to make their mark, which they did, gradually at first. The decade of the 1950s in Yosemite climbing history is a classic example of a sea change in style, equipment, and attitudes toward "impossible" walls, the ones the Thirties pioneers had shunned.

To be sure, the "decade" of the 1950s was really from late 1948 to late 1958. But that's quibbling. The beginning of the Golden Age of Valley Climbing was the first ascent of the Lost Arrow Chimney, and the end of the initial phase of this era was the first ascent of El Capitan's Nose. Later climbers, naturally, put up routes of startling difficulty, and the decade of the 1960s, the subject of many climbing books (including this publisher's *Yosemite in the Sixties* and my *Camp 4: Recollections of a Yosemite Rockclimber*) was indeed equally groundbreaking. But this is a book about those hard men of sixty years ago, as climbers and surfers alike explored new ways of pondering the "great outdoors" in a freer and more committed way than had their forebears.

Yosemite's walls had hardly been touched in the early 1930s. Richard Leonard, one of the leading climbers of that long-ago generation, had once gazed upon the Lost Arrow with friends and quivered. "It was unanimously agreed," he wrote in 1935, "that we would never attempt it." The Arrow was a smooth, slender needle detached from Yosemite's rim, and it would be a problem even from that rim, let alone from its base, where a long, crack system called the Lost Arow Chimney led up to the notch behind the pinnacle. By 1948, however, a few brave men (no brave female climbers back then—that would come many years later) invented specialized equipment and regarded the new nylon ropes manufactured during the war as lifesavers because of their strength and stretch. The axiom that the "leader must not fall," because of suspect hemp ropes, was replaced with the idea that short falls might be survivable.

Enter the first of the postwar legends, John Salathé. A Swiss blacksmith who emigrated to the States around 1930, he took to climbing in the San Francisco area at age 45. Developing hard steel pitons ideal for the convoluted cracks of Yosemite, he managed, with Anton Nelson in 1948, the first ascent of the Lost Arrow from its base, a five-day effort, surely the world's most demanding rock climb. During the 1950s it would be repeated only seven times.

Another pivotal figure of the early days was Allen Steck who, in 1950, accompanied the 50-year-old Salathé on the first ascent of the north face of Sentinel Rock, yet another five-day ordeal. Salathé soon dropped out of climbing, but Steck did some excellent Valley routes for a few more years. In the same week that Everest was first climbed and that Elizabeth was crowned, Steck and his friends topped out on the first El Capitan route, an eastern outrider of the main face. Steck still climbs to this day at age 87!

These formative days in the Valley were largely the province of Northern Californian climbers, but that was soon to change. By the mid-1950s Mark Powell, weaned on cliffs in the Southland, was perhaps the finest free climber in the nation. Bold and fast, he put up fifteen Yosemite first ascents in a sixteen-month period. He wrote eloquently about his feats, and one of my favorite Valley sentences is his: "Higher, the necessity of clinging with both hands caused a 70-foot overhanging face to a gnarled tree to be led bereft of pitons."

Royal Robbins had accomplished some remarkable feats in the Valley and at Tahquitz in the early 1950s, but he achieved stardom with his pathbreaking 1957 climb up the sheer face of Half Dome, a wall thought impossible by the old-timers. This five-day ascent, done with Jerry Gallwas and Mike Sherrick, was simply a prelude to Robbins' later dominance in the 1960s, when he became the world's most accomplished rock climber.

Yet another titan, Warren Harding, had lurked in the shadows during the mid-1950s, putting up several short, demanding routes. This was to change in 1958—and Yosemite climbing finally became front-page news. Harding spent forty-five days over eighteen months working on the Nose of El Capitan, a seemingly impossible project because of logistics. Various partners came and went, but in November he, Wayne Merry, and George Whitmore topped out after "Iron-Man" Harding spent a frigid night drilling holes for twenty-six bolts on the summit pitch.

Valley climbing routes exploded during the 1950s. The exceptional rise of these accomplishments can be explained not just by equipment advances, but also by changes in society. Climbers had more leisure time, access to the cliffs was easier, and a new breed of adventurers got into superb shape by living in the Valley for weeks at a time.

But it should be clear also that the Fifties climbers had learned lessons from their predecessors. And the Sixties climbers to come built upon the exploits of their predecessors. And so it goes, decade after decade. — Steve Roper

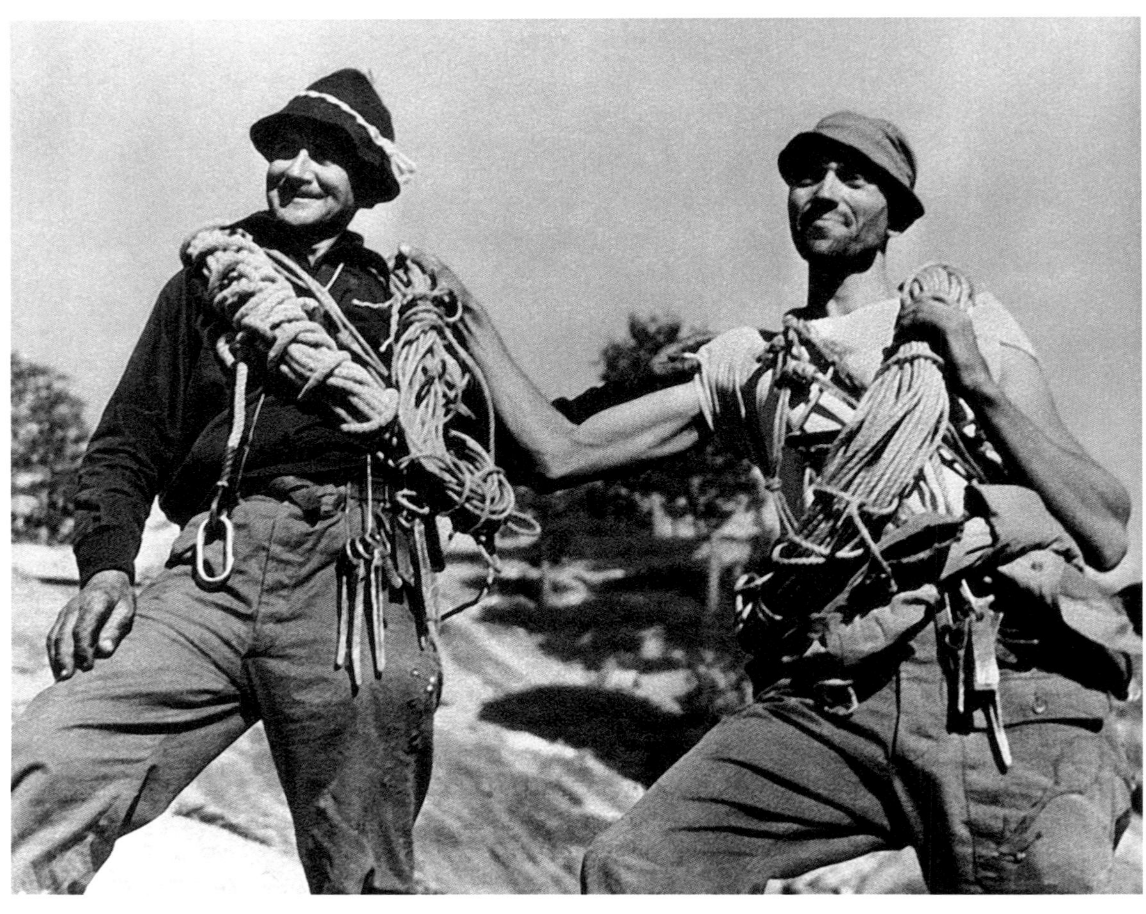

John Salathé and Anton ("Ax") Nelson after their historic five-day climb of the Lost Arrow Chimney,
Yosemite Valley, 1947. Photo: courtesy Glen Denny collection

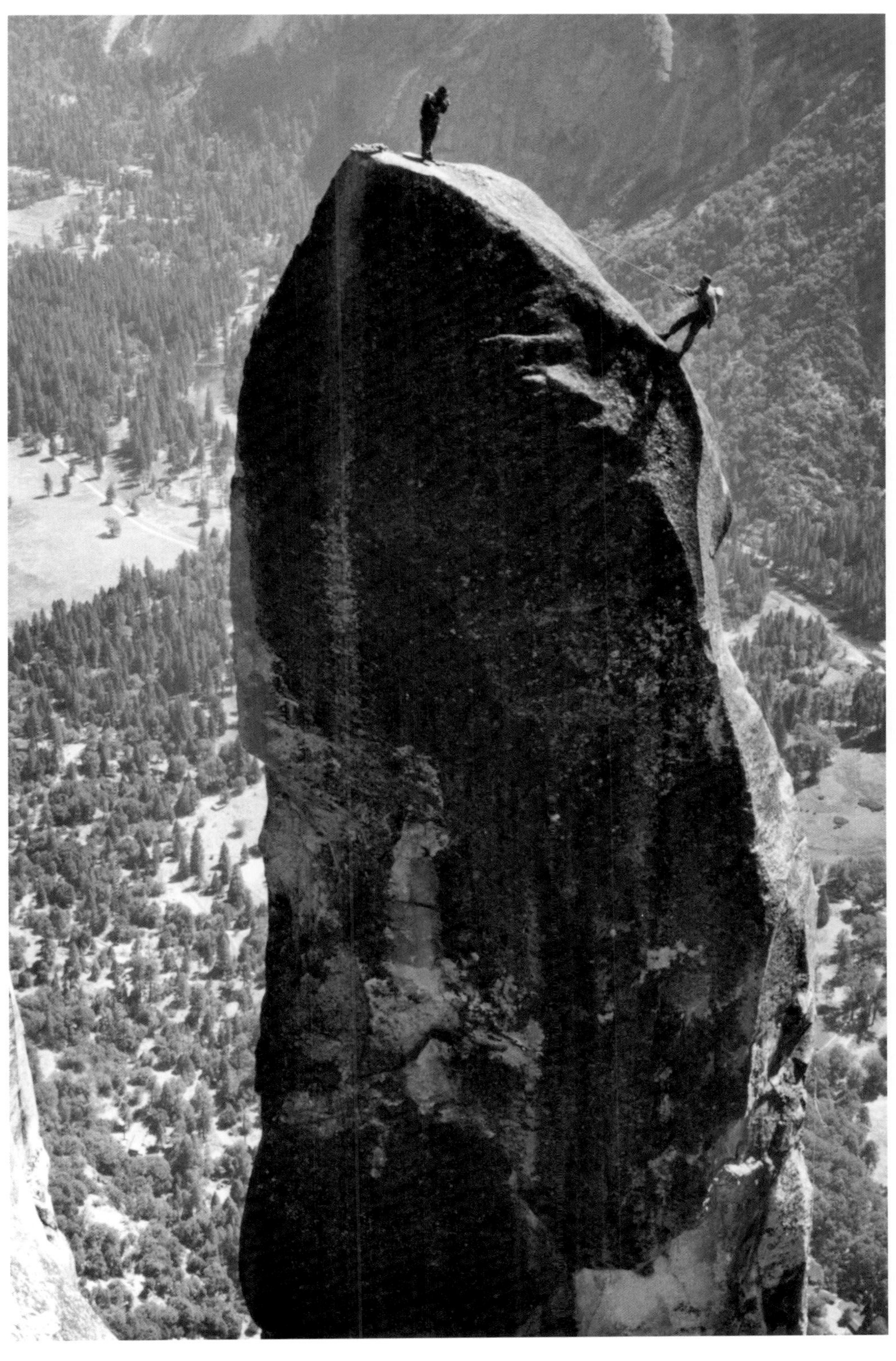

John Salathé and Anton Nelson get ready to leave the summit after their climb of the Lost Arrow Chimney.
Photo: Ansel Adams © 2013 The Ansel Adams Publishing Rights Trust

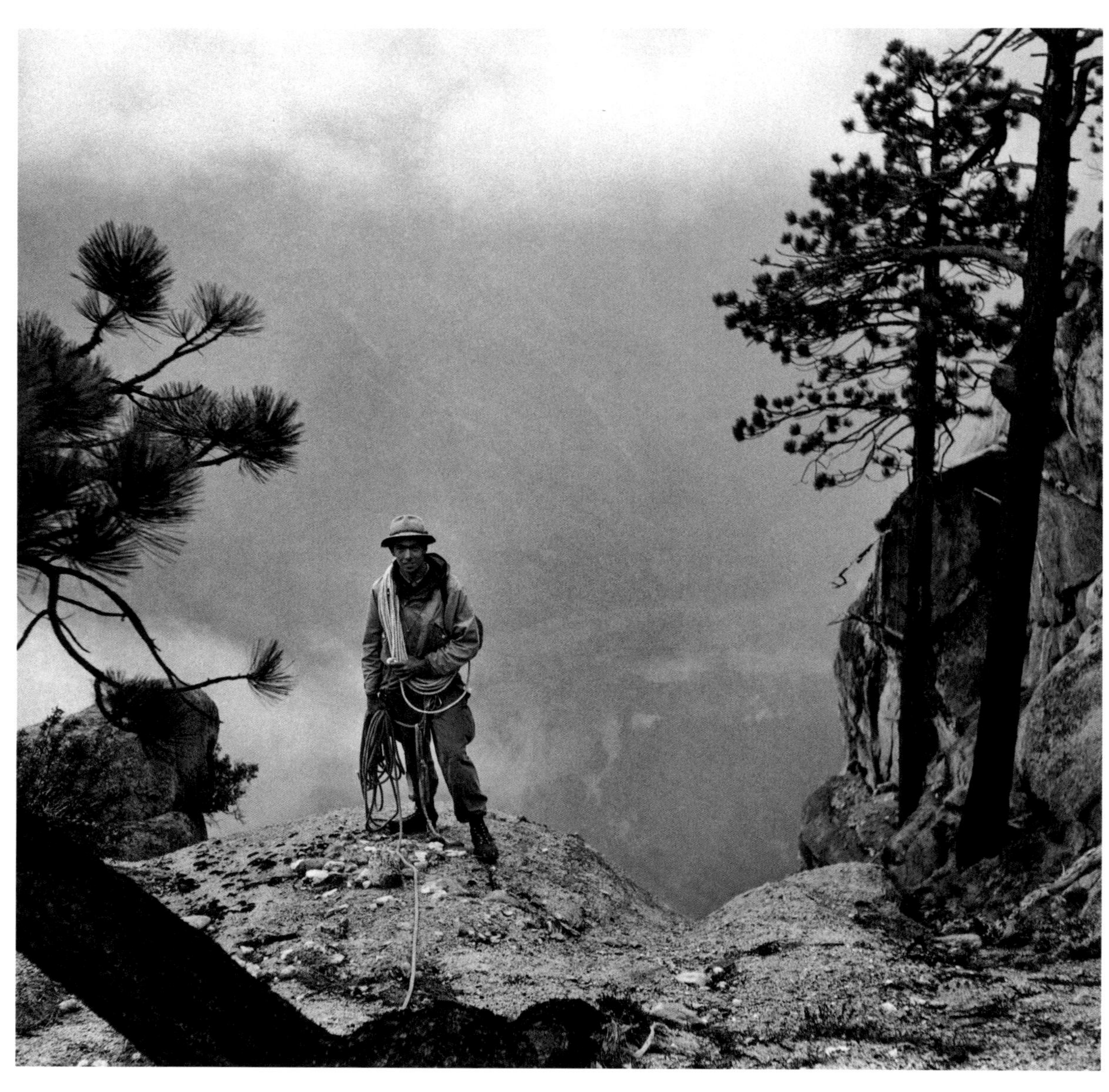

Bob Swift takes a breather atop Yosemite Point Buttress after the first ascent, 1952. Photo: Allen Steck

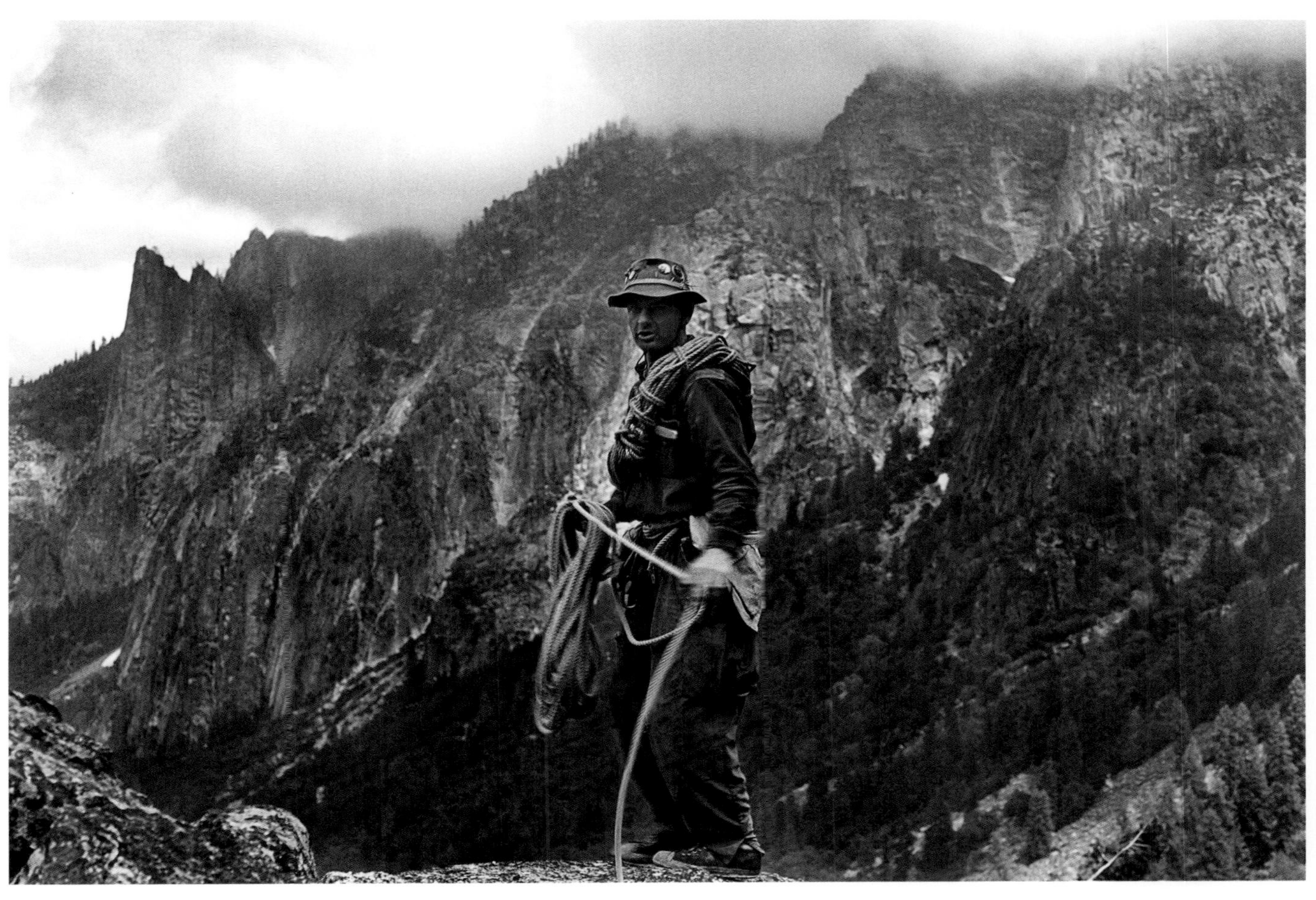

Phil Bettler on the summit of Lower Cathedral Spire, Yosemite Valley. Photo: Bob Swift

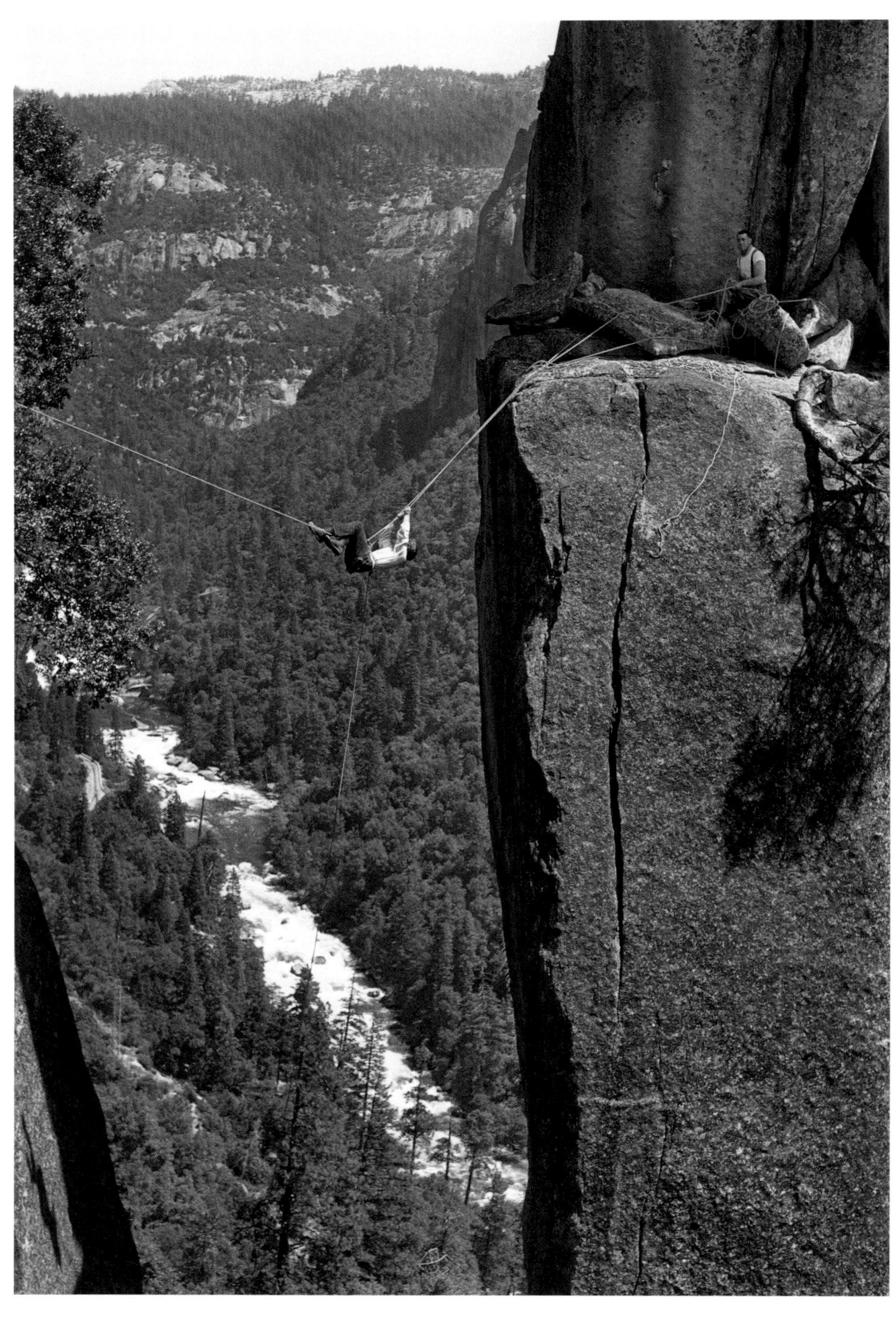

A Tyrolean Traverse, a fun method of leaving a spire to get to solid land. Corky Corthell is heading for the pinnacle with Bob Swift belaying.
Kat Pinnacle, Yosemite National Park. Photo: Frank Tarver, Bob Swift collection

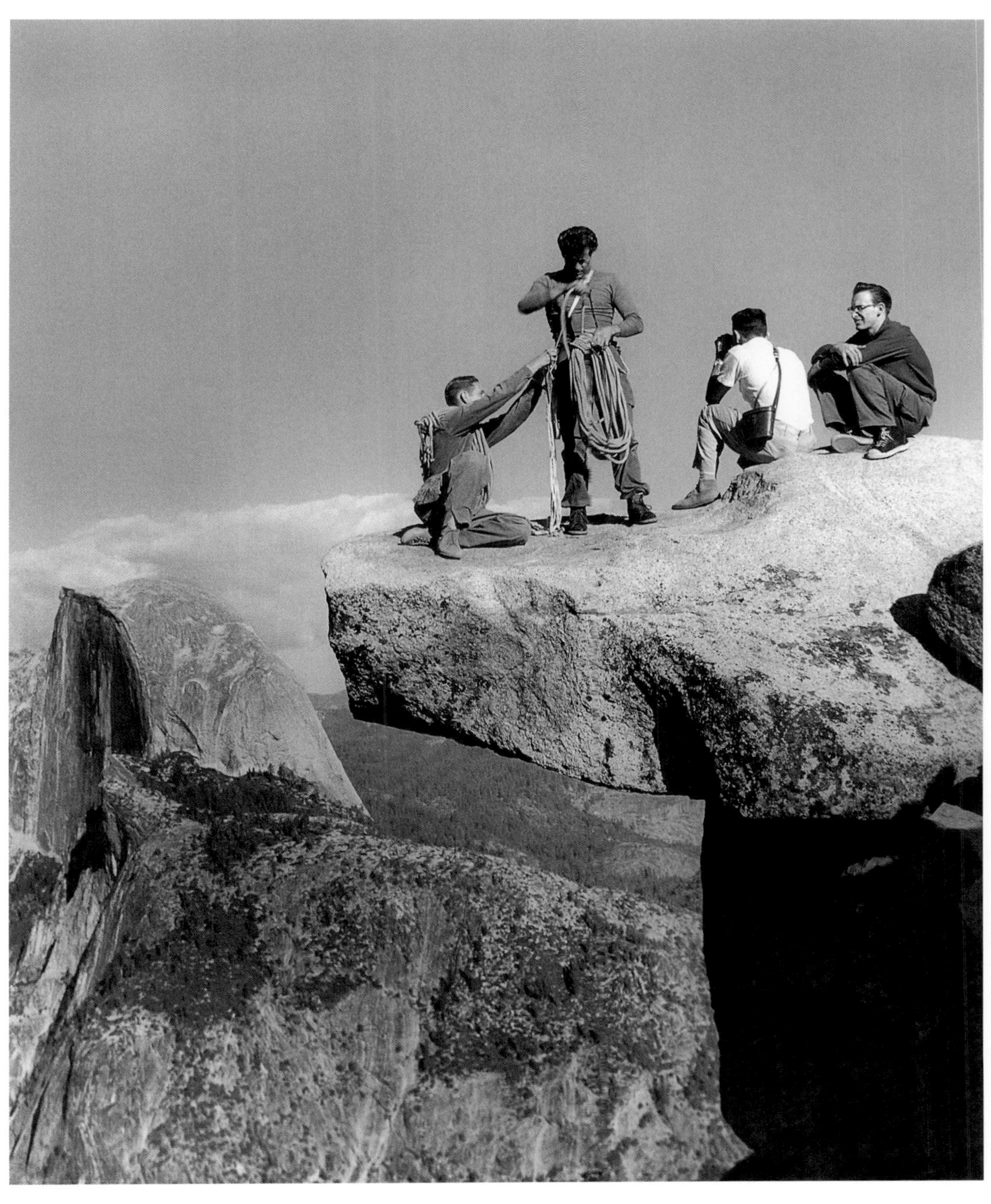

Don Wilson, Warren Harding, Jerry Gallwas, and Royal Robbins ham it up on Glacier Point, Yosemite Valley, 1955.
Photo: courtesy Jerry Gallwas collection

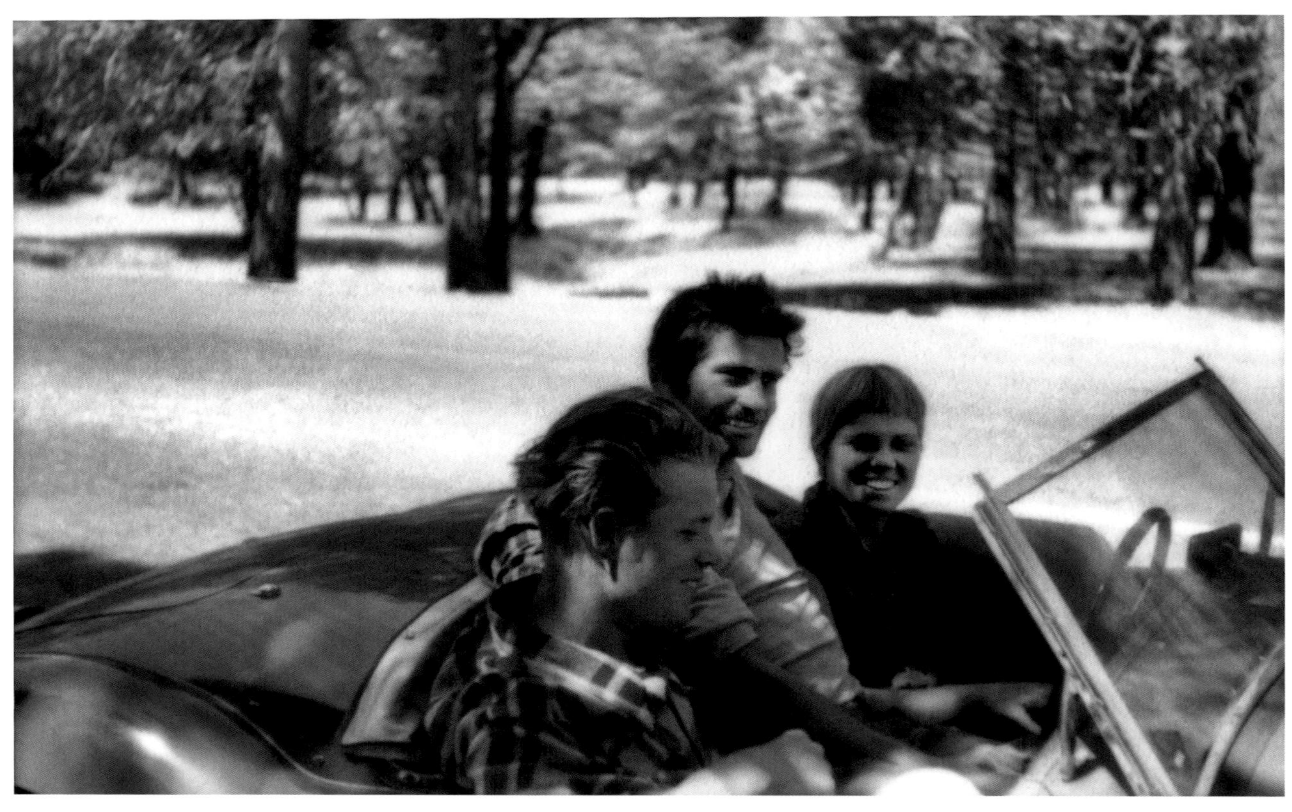

Mark Powell, Warren Harding, and Bea Vogel, Yosemite Valley, 1957. Photo: Frank Hoover

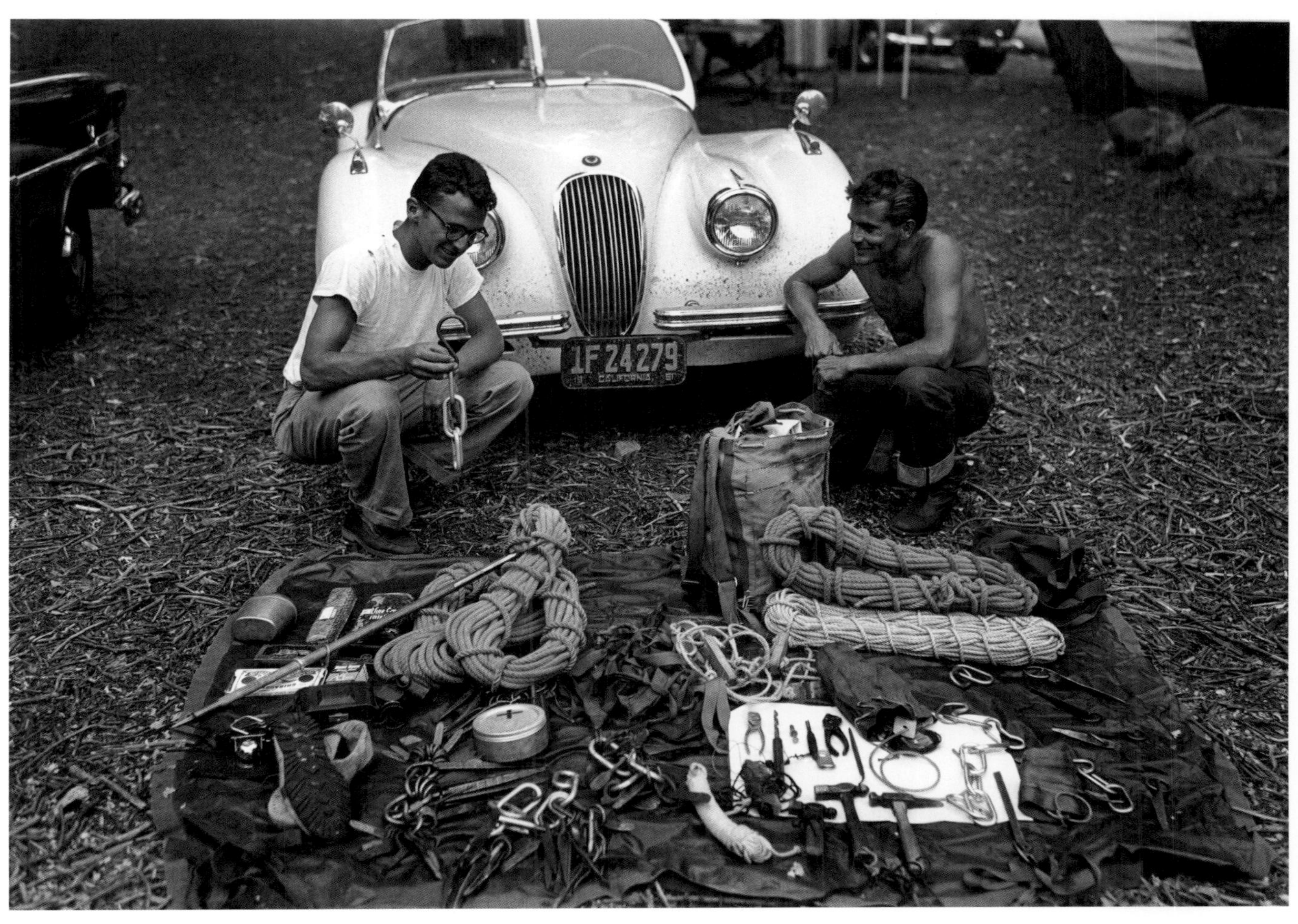

Frank Tarver and Warren Harding sort gear for their climb of the Lost Arrow Chimney, 1954. Photo: Bob Swift

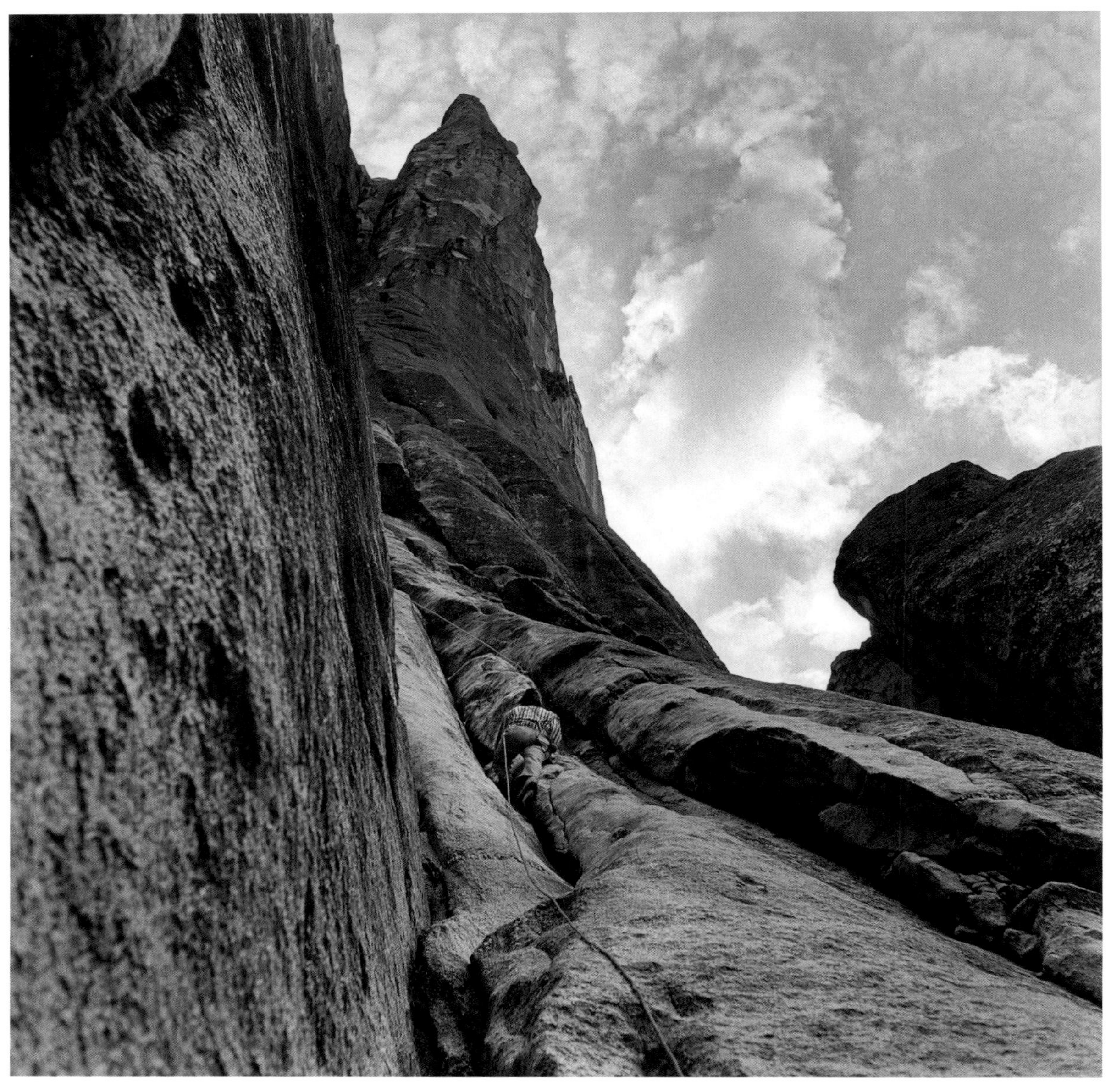

Frank Tarver low on the Lost Arrow Chimney Route during the second ascent, 1954. Photo: Bob Swift

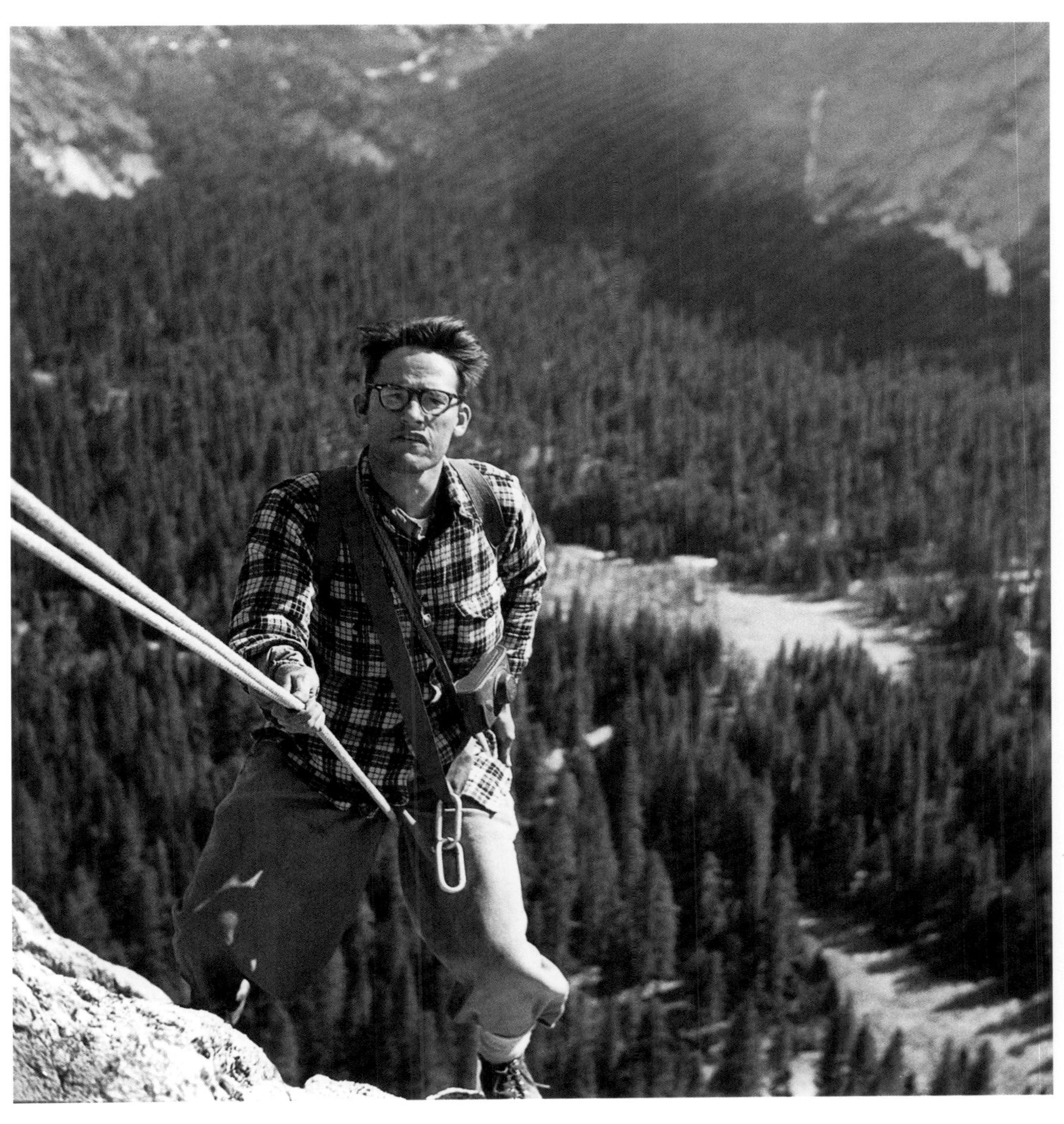

Allen Steck rappeling, late '50s, Yosemite Valley. Photo: Allen Steck Collection

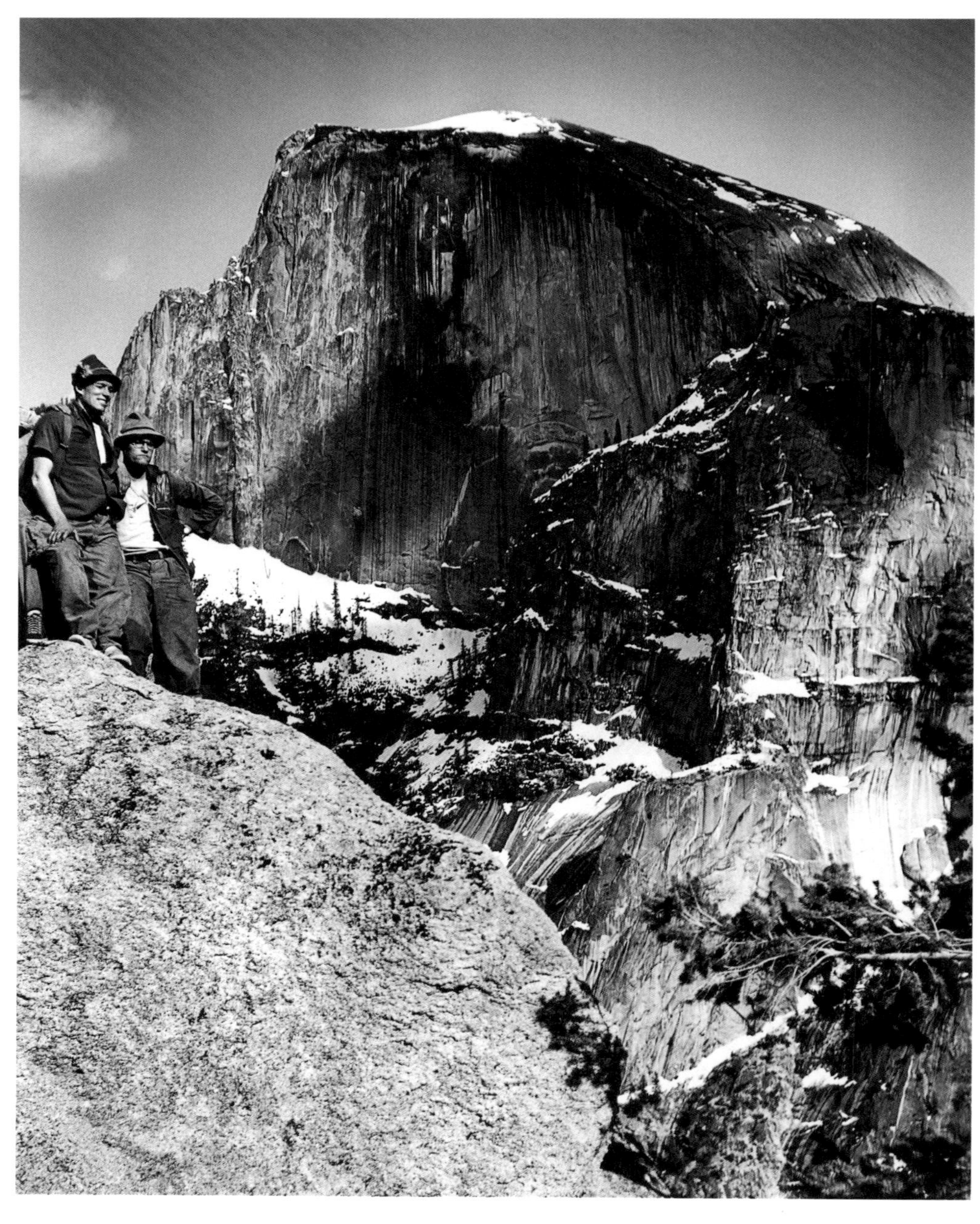

Bill Long and Allen Steck ignore the Northwest face of Half Dome looming in the background. Photo: Bob Swift

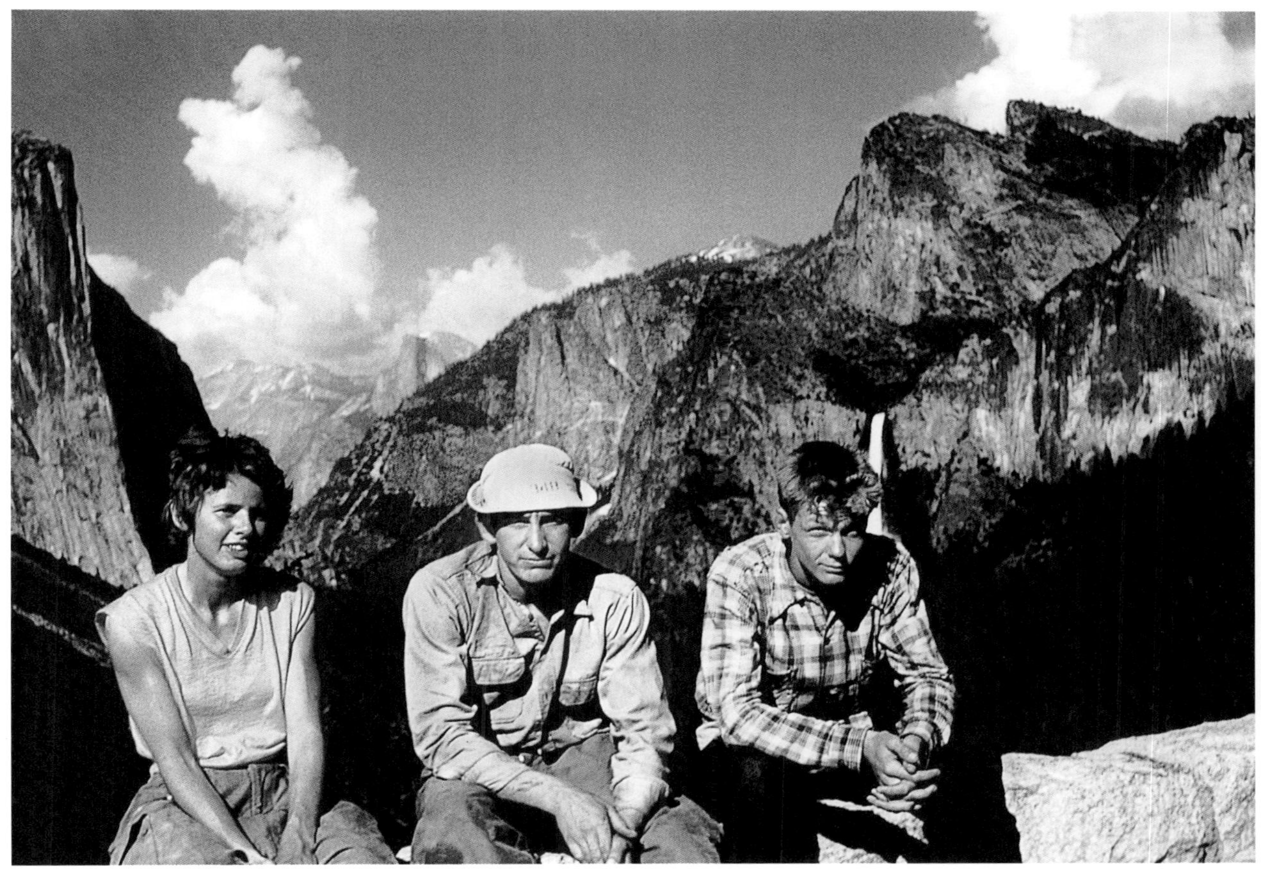

Barbara Lilley, Royal Robbins, and Gary Hemming (said to be the role model for the protagonist in James Salter's *Solo Faces*) at the Wawona Tunnel overlook, with El Capitan on the left and Bridalveil Fall on the right. Photo: courtesy Barbara Lilley collection

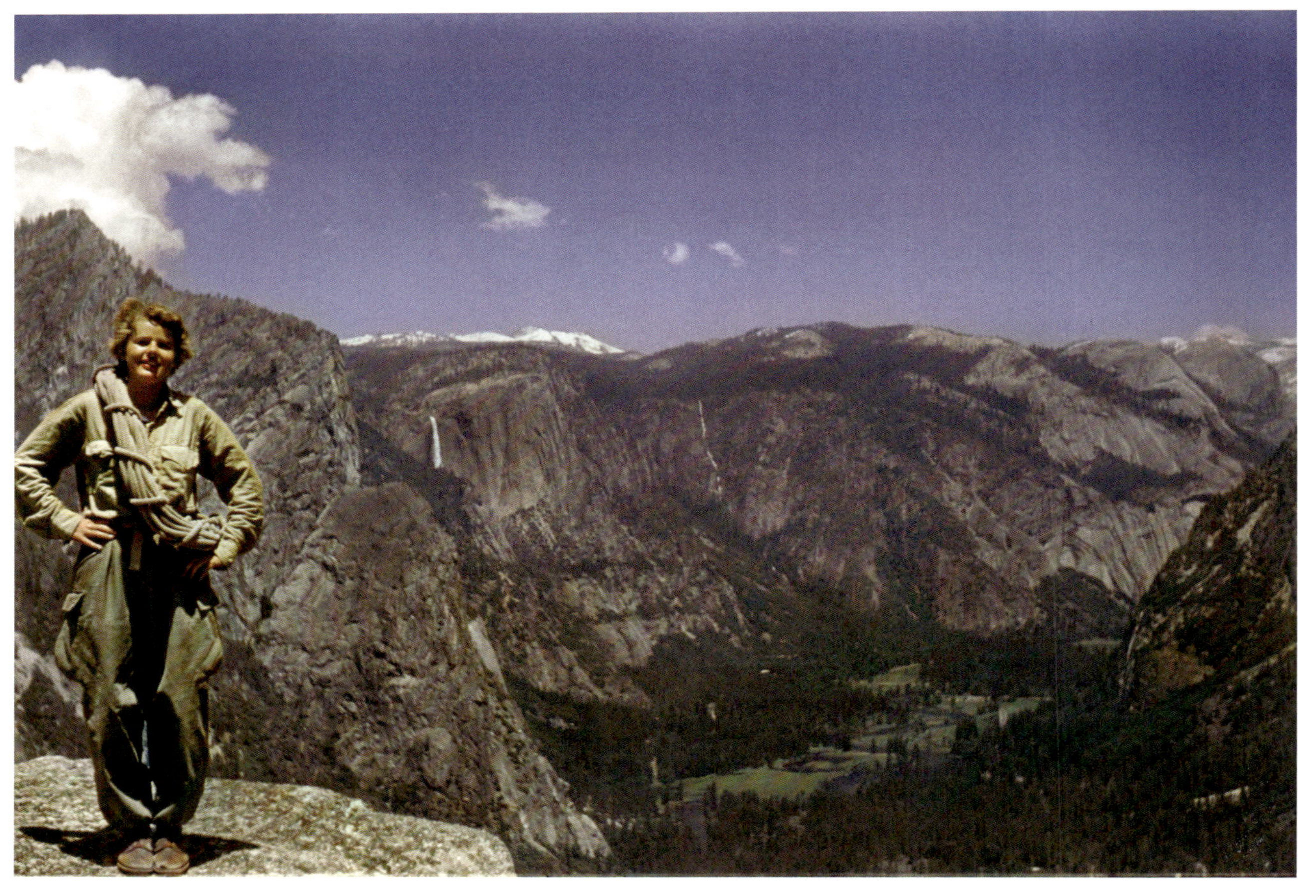

Barbara Lilley on top of the Lower Cathedral Spire, Yosemite Valley. Photo: Don Wilson, Barbara Lilley collection

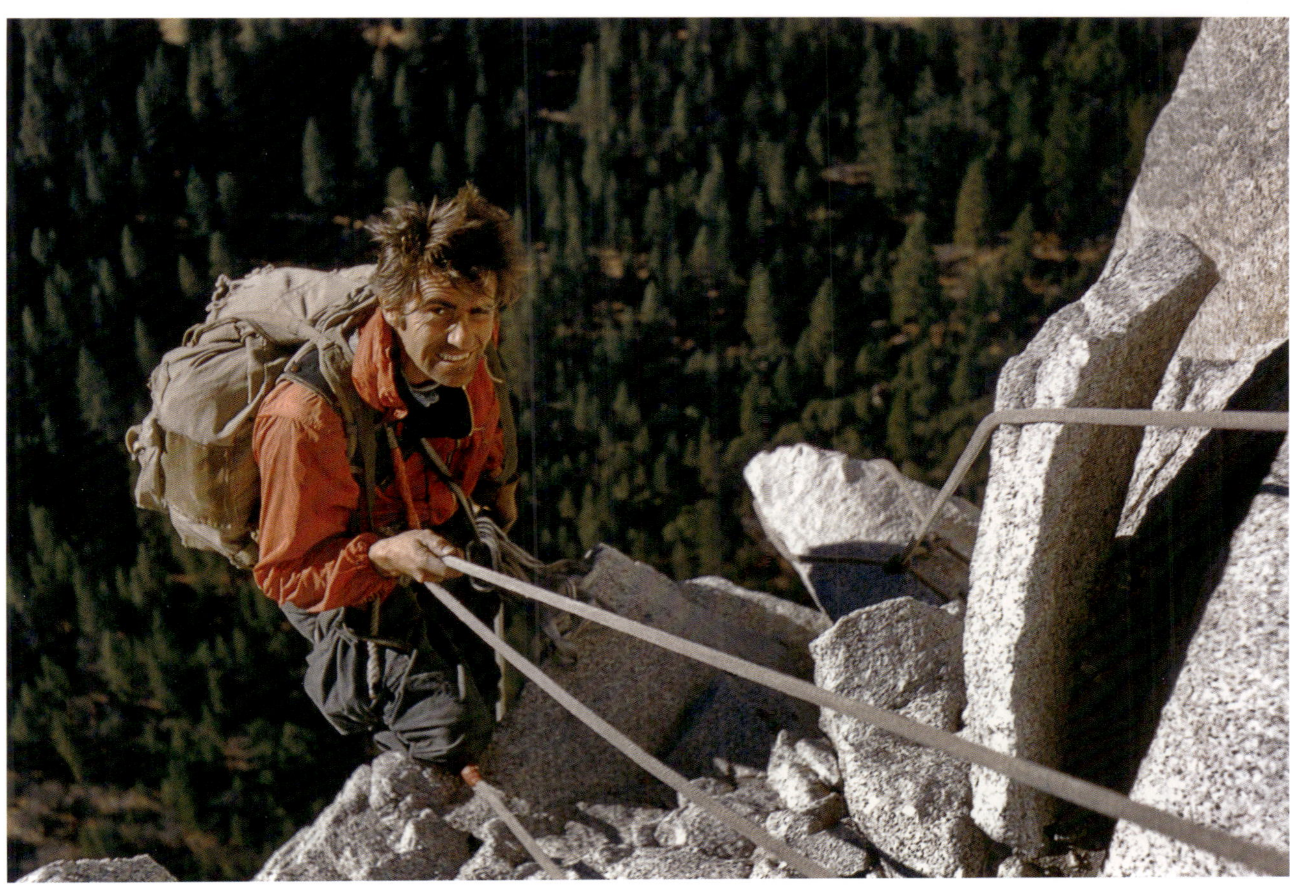

Warren Harding on El Capitan, 1957. Photo: Allen Steck

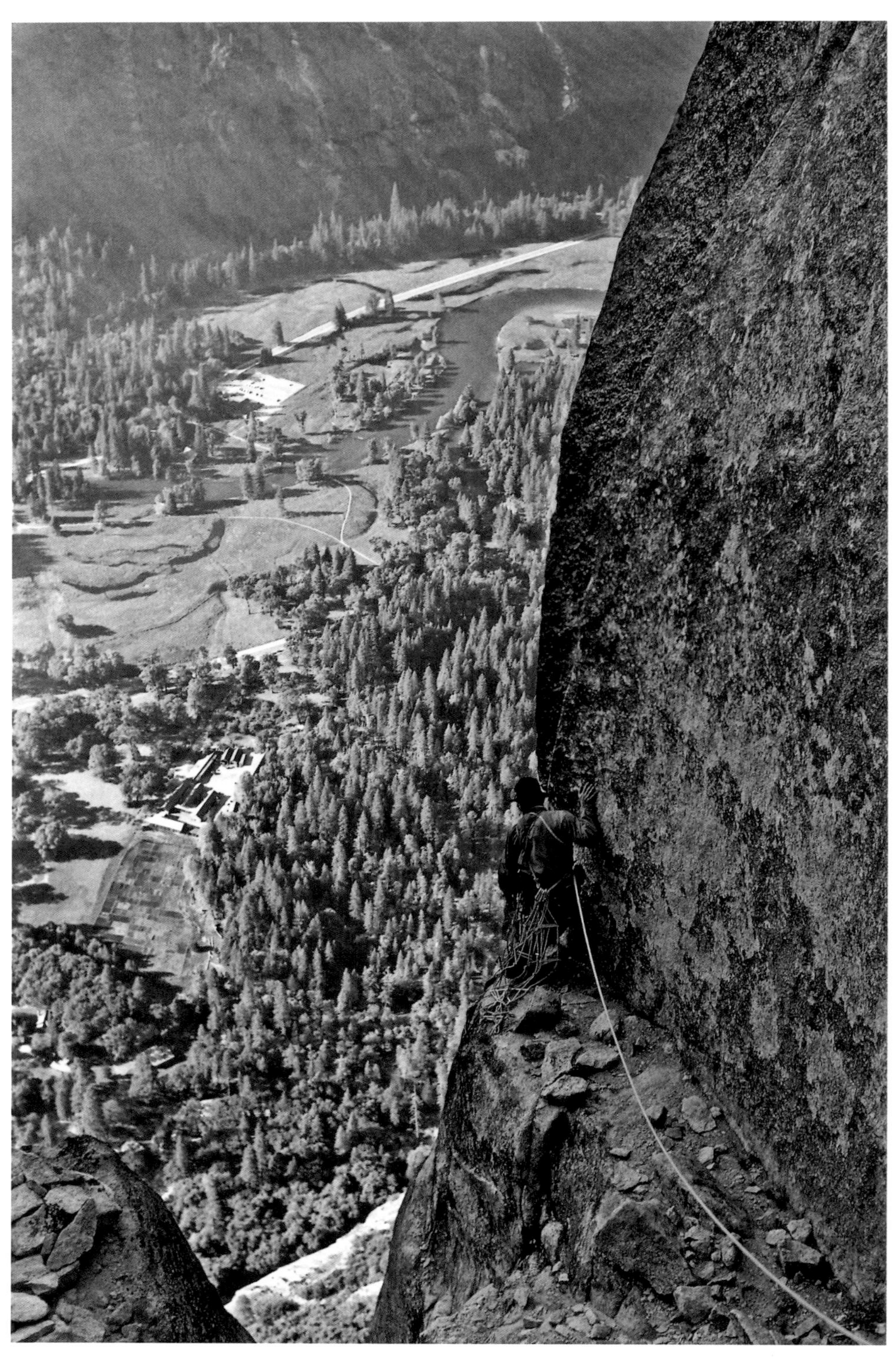

Hobey De Stabeler creeps out toward the first pitch of the Lost Arrow Spire, 1958.
Photo: Henry Kendall, courtesy Archive of the Norfolk Charitable Trust

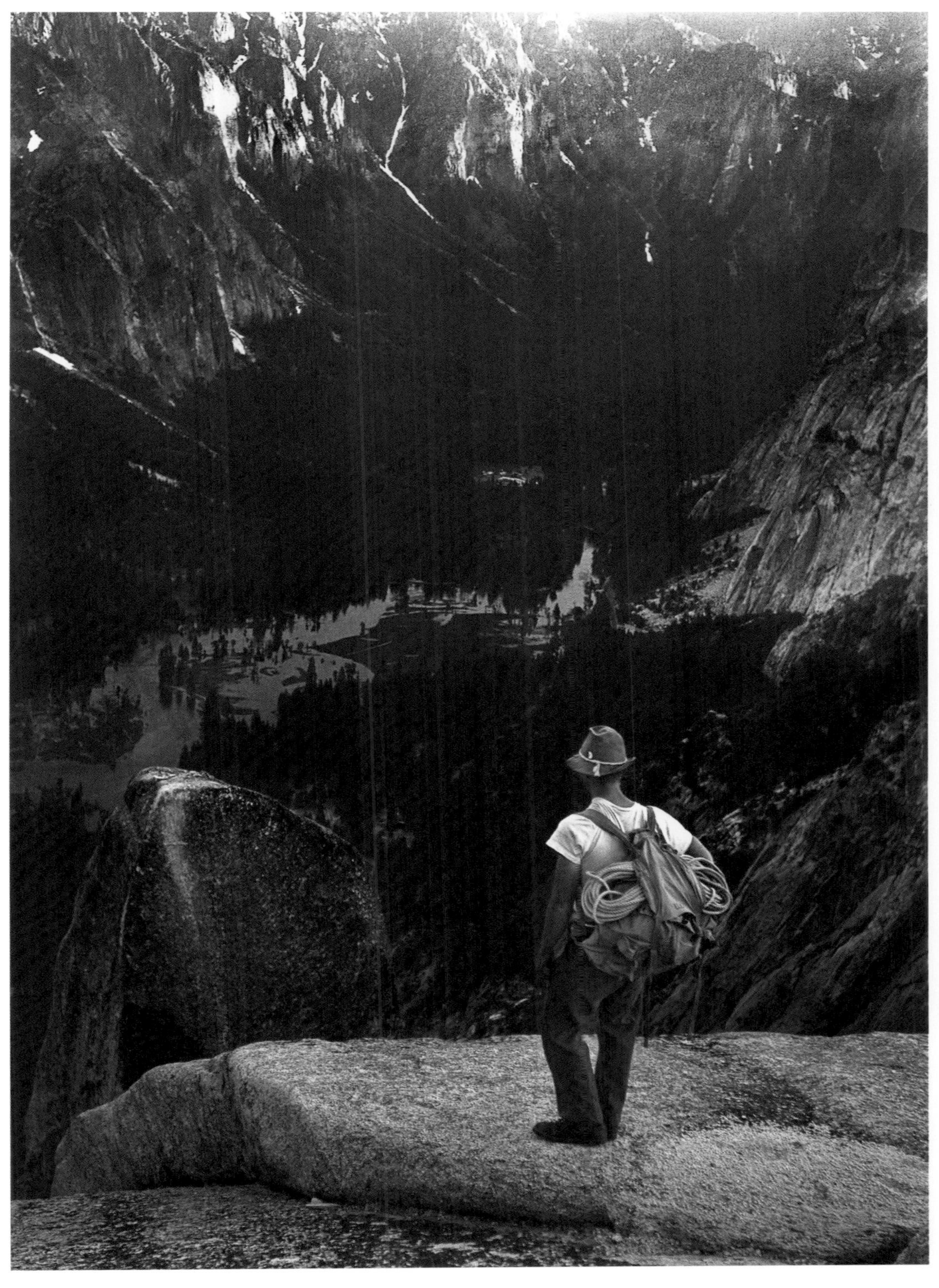

A climber gazes at the very top of the Lost Arrow Spire. Photo: Bob Swift

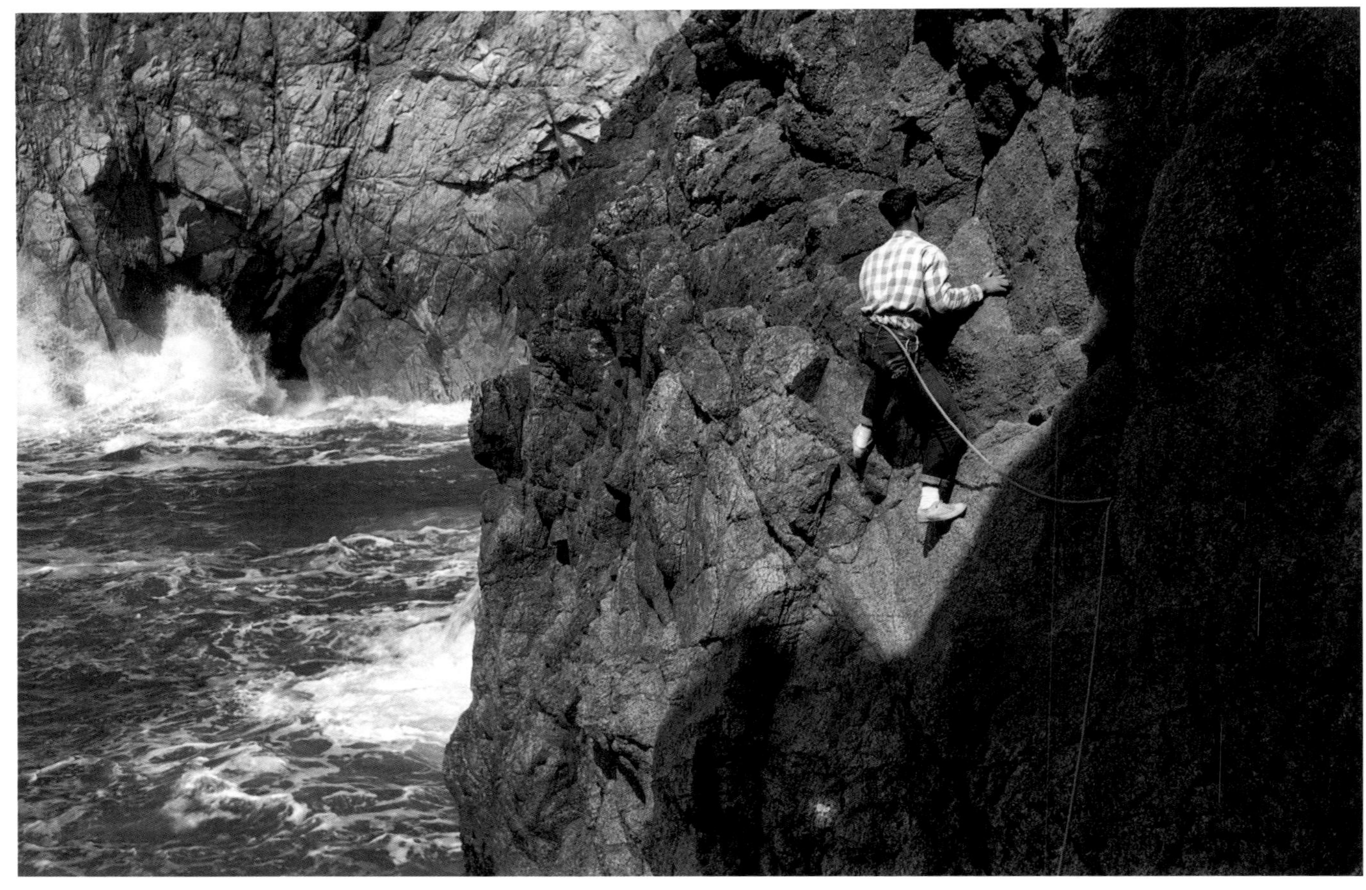

Don Evers at Devil's Slide, a seaside climbing area just south of San Francisco. Photo: Bob Swift

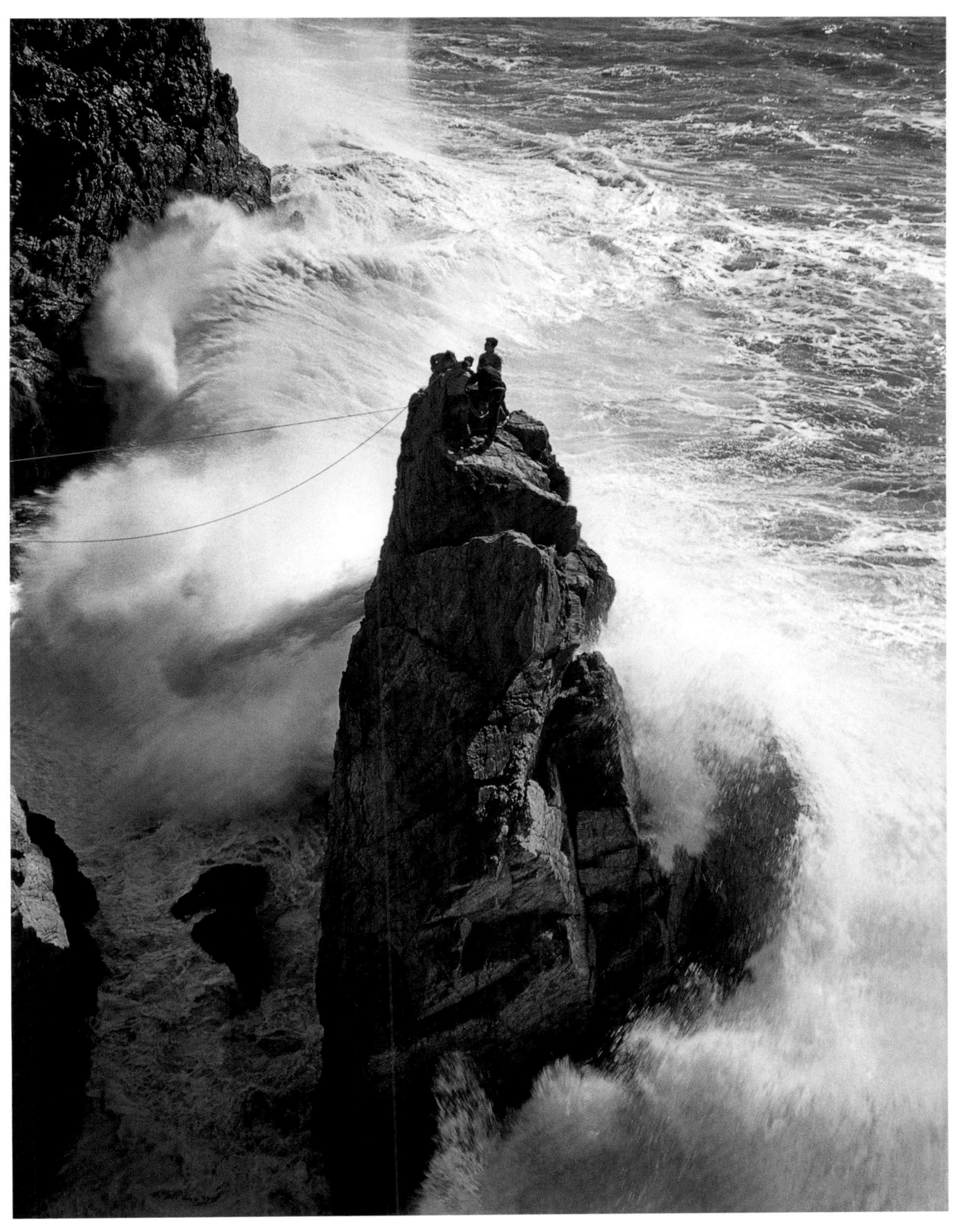

Climbers rig a Tyrolean Traverse at Devil's Slide. Photo: Bob Swift

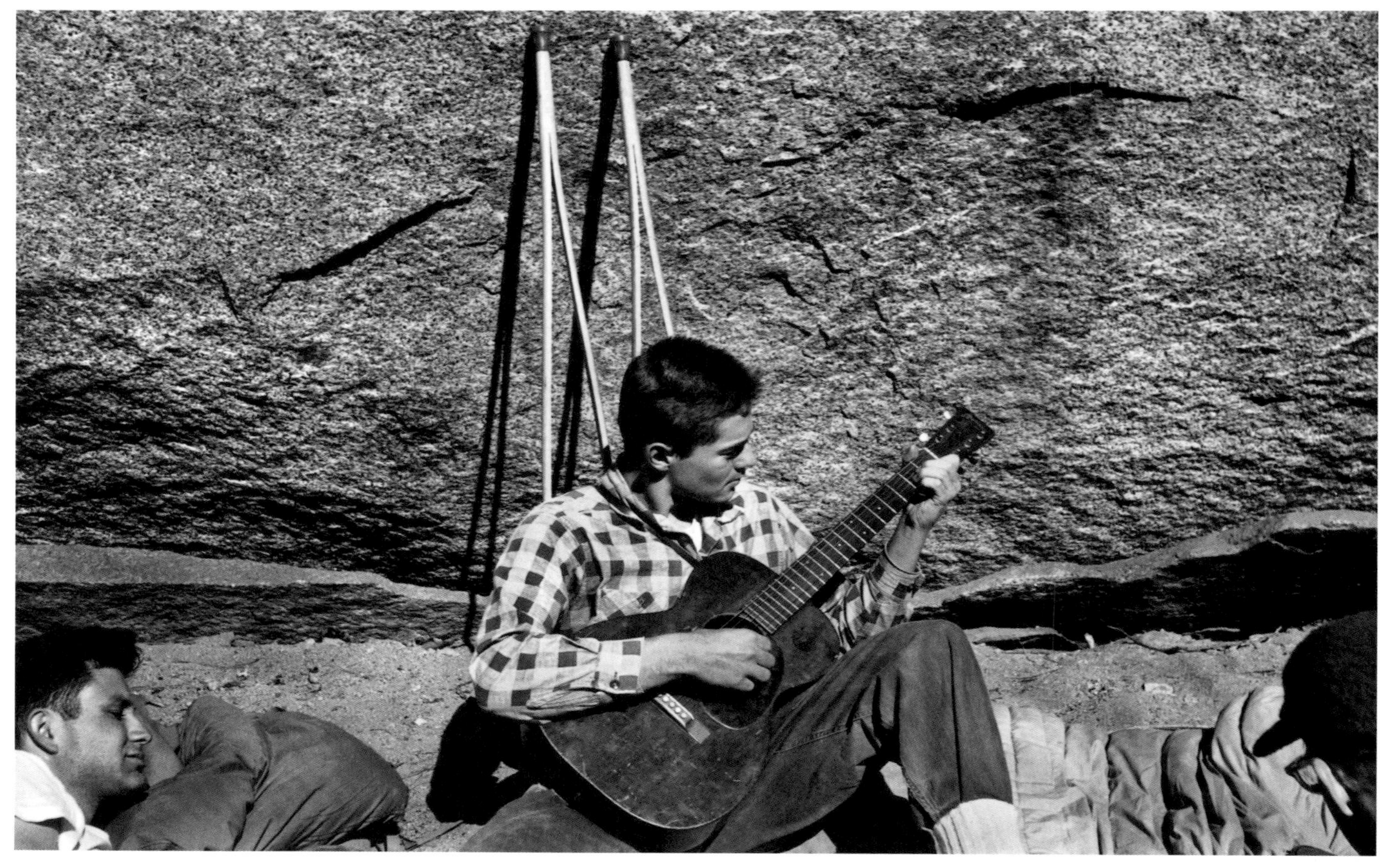

Mike Sherrick strumming his guitar, Yosemite Valley, Memorial Day weekend, 1955.
Earlier that year, he broke his leg skiing at Mammoth. Photo: Frank Hoover

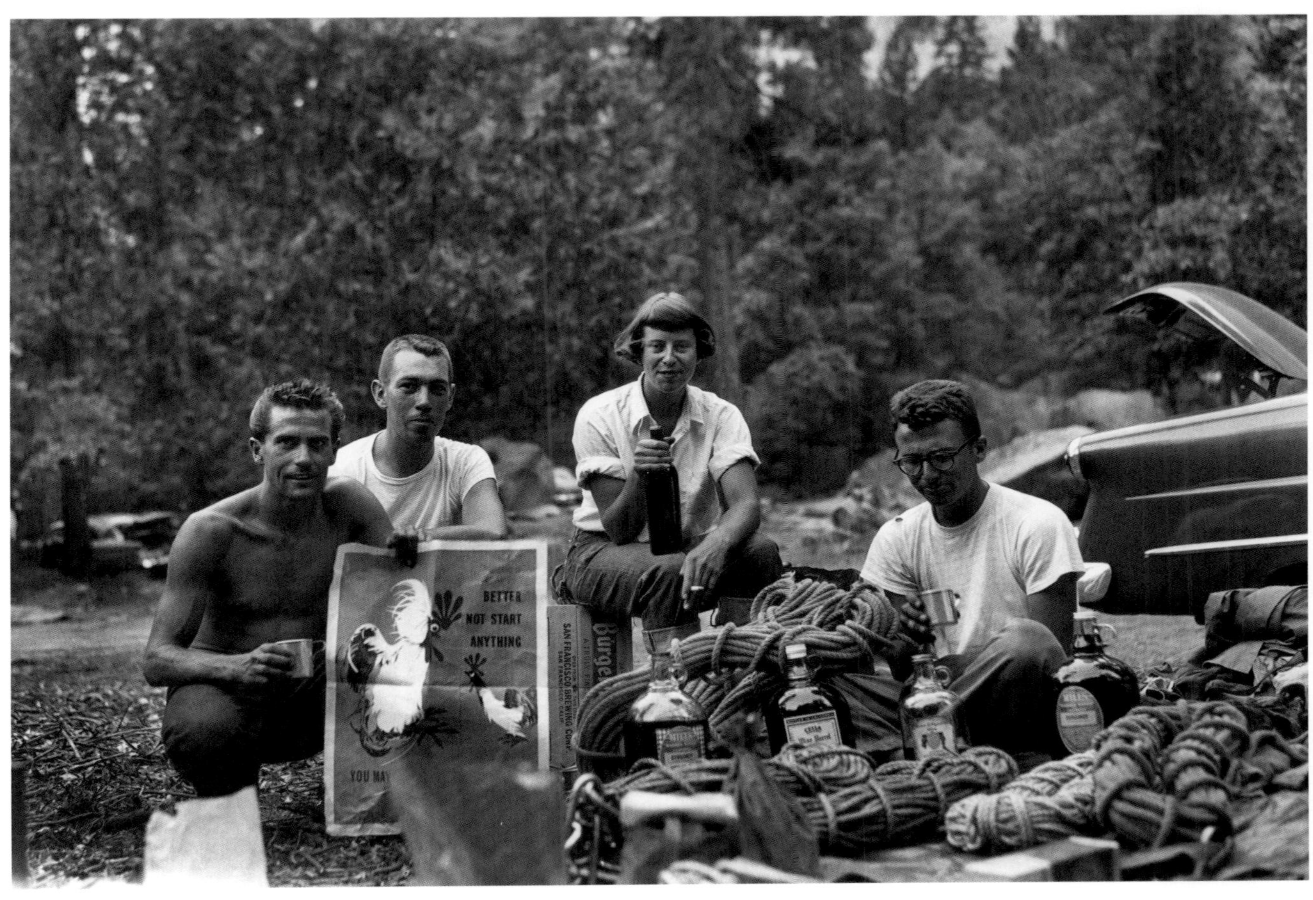

Warren Harding, Bob Swift, Mary Ann ("Corky") Corthell, and Frank Tarver at Camp 4, Yosemite Valley, 1954.
Photo: Bob Swift (taken on tripod with delay release)

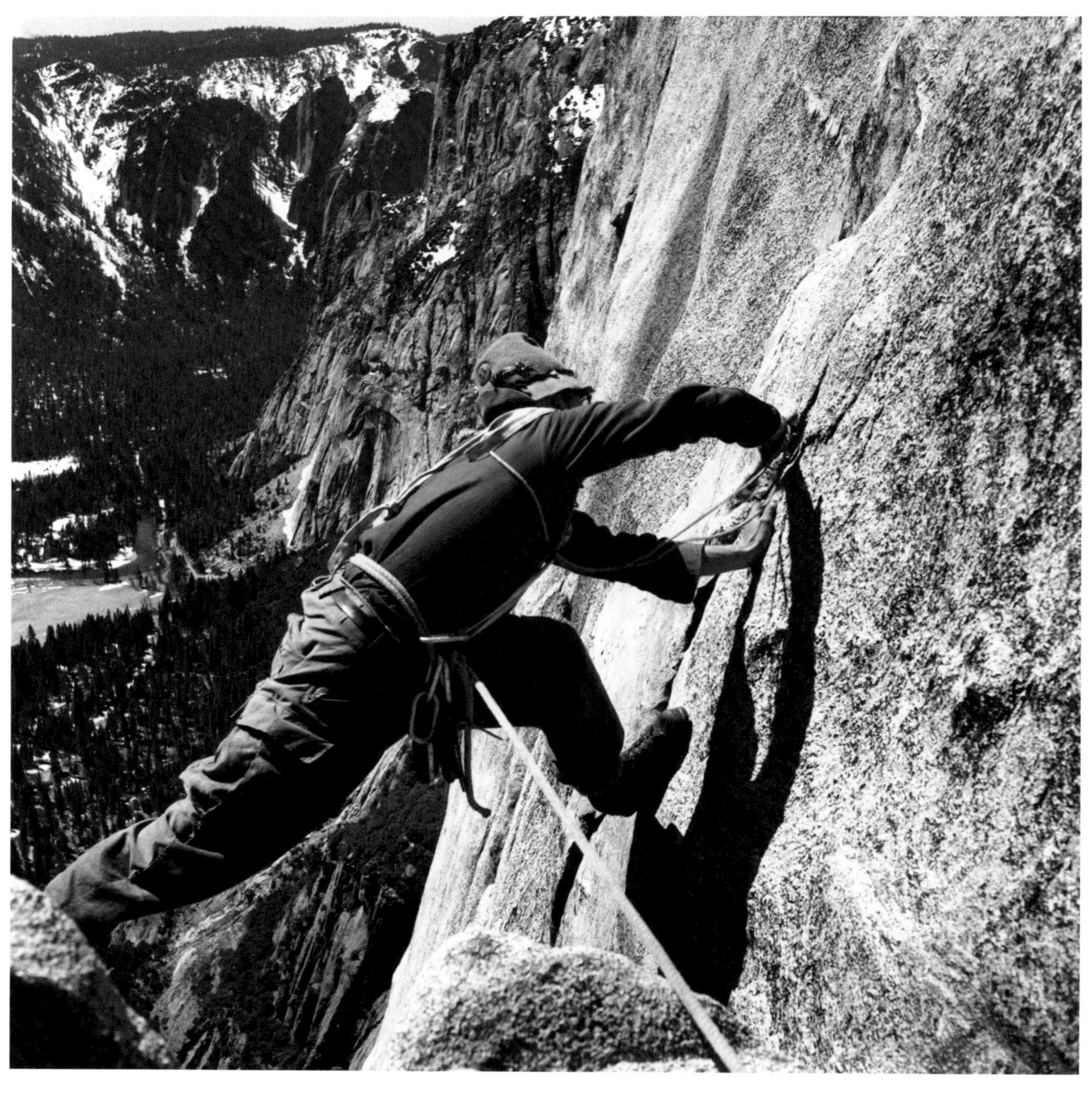

Allen Steck begins the lead off the Pedestal, high on Yosemite Point Buttress, during the first ascent, 1952. Photo: Bob Swift

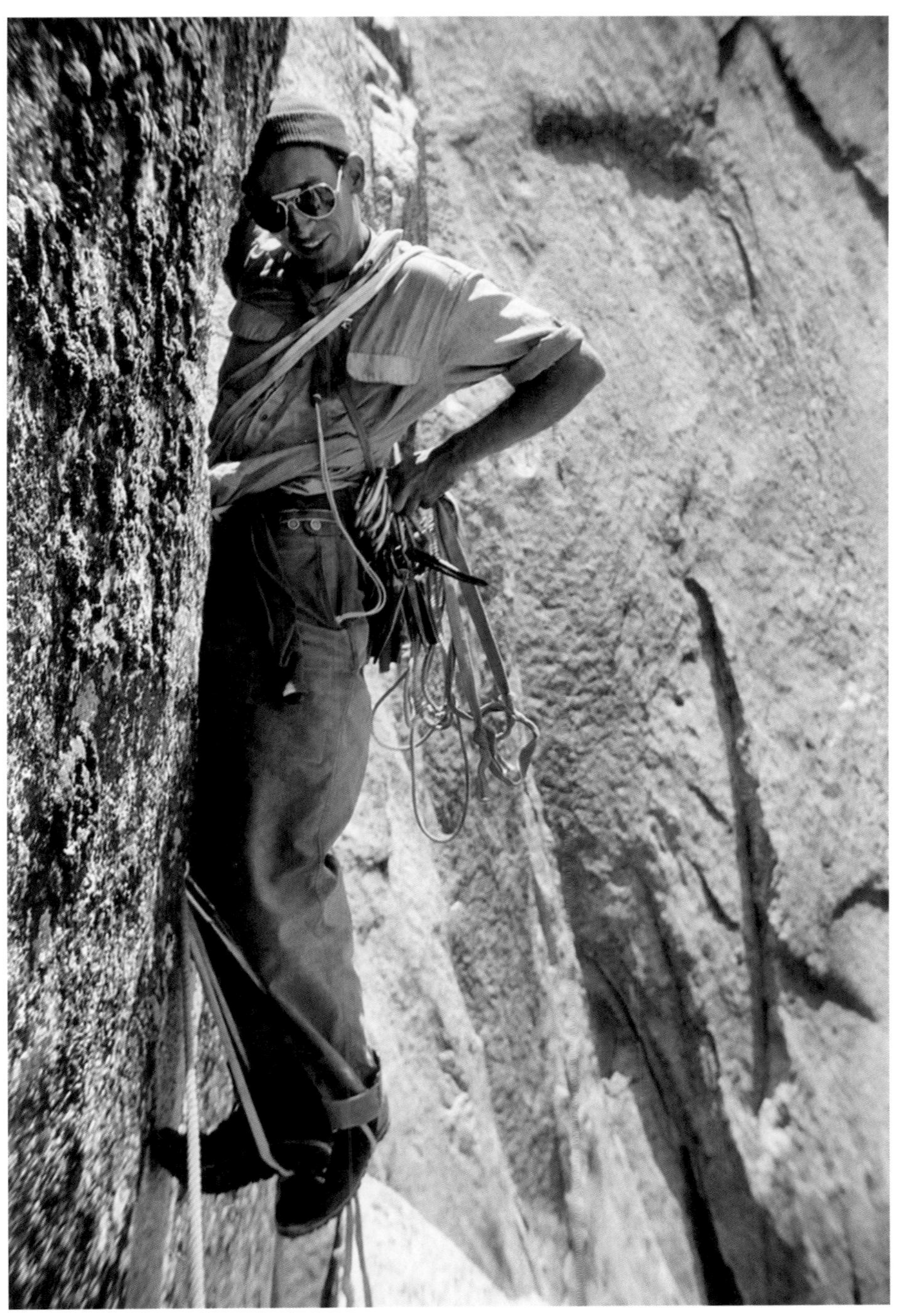

Royal Robbins leads during the first ascent of Half Dome's great Northwest face, 1957. Photo: Mike Sherrick

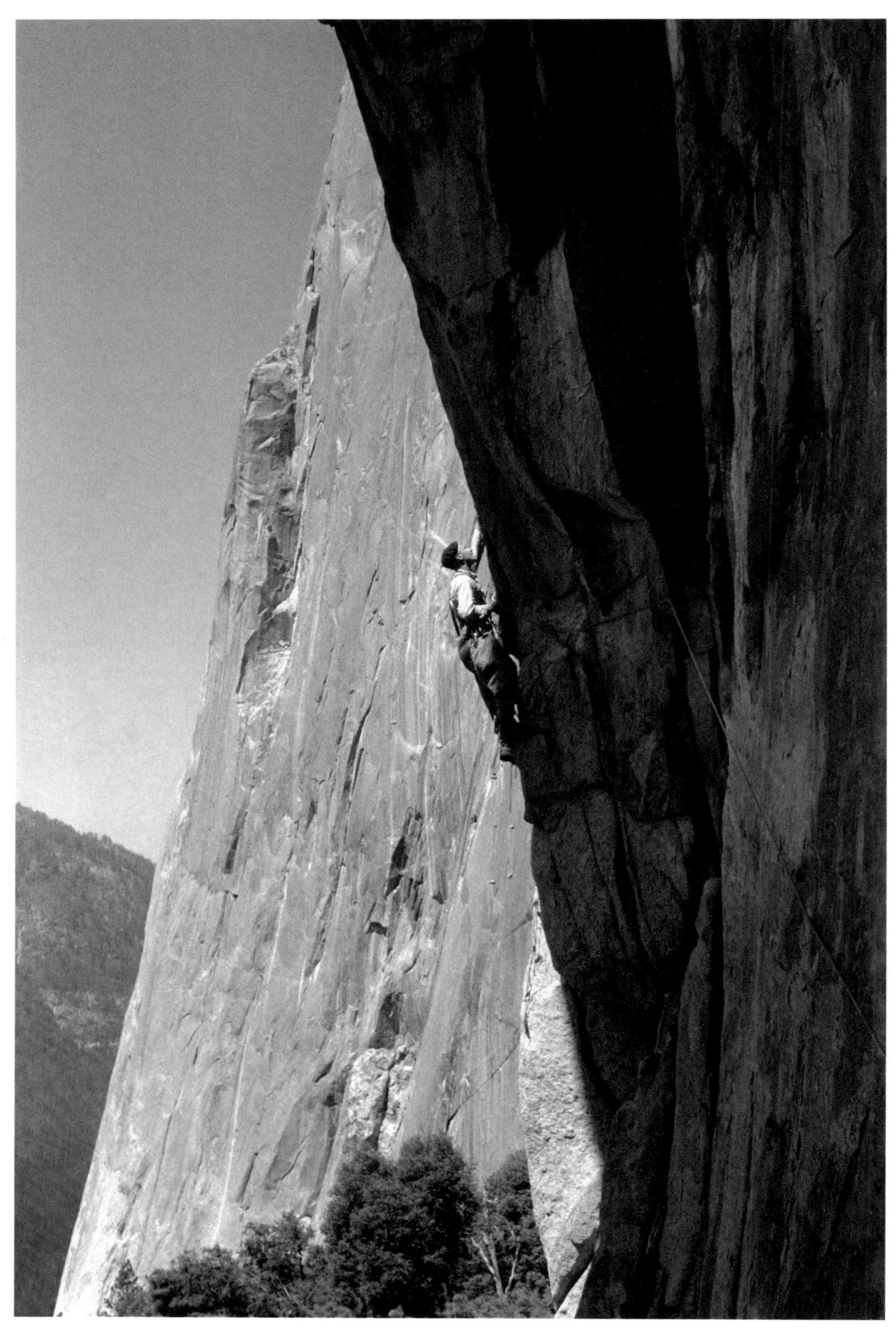

Dave Sowles leads the first pitch of the El Cap Tree Route, a short but stiff climb low on El Capitan.
Photo: Henry Kendall, courtesy Archive of the Norfolk Charitable Trust

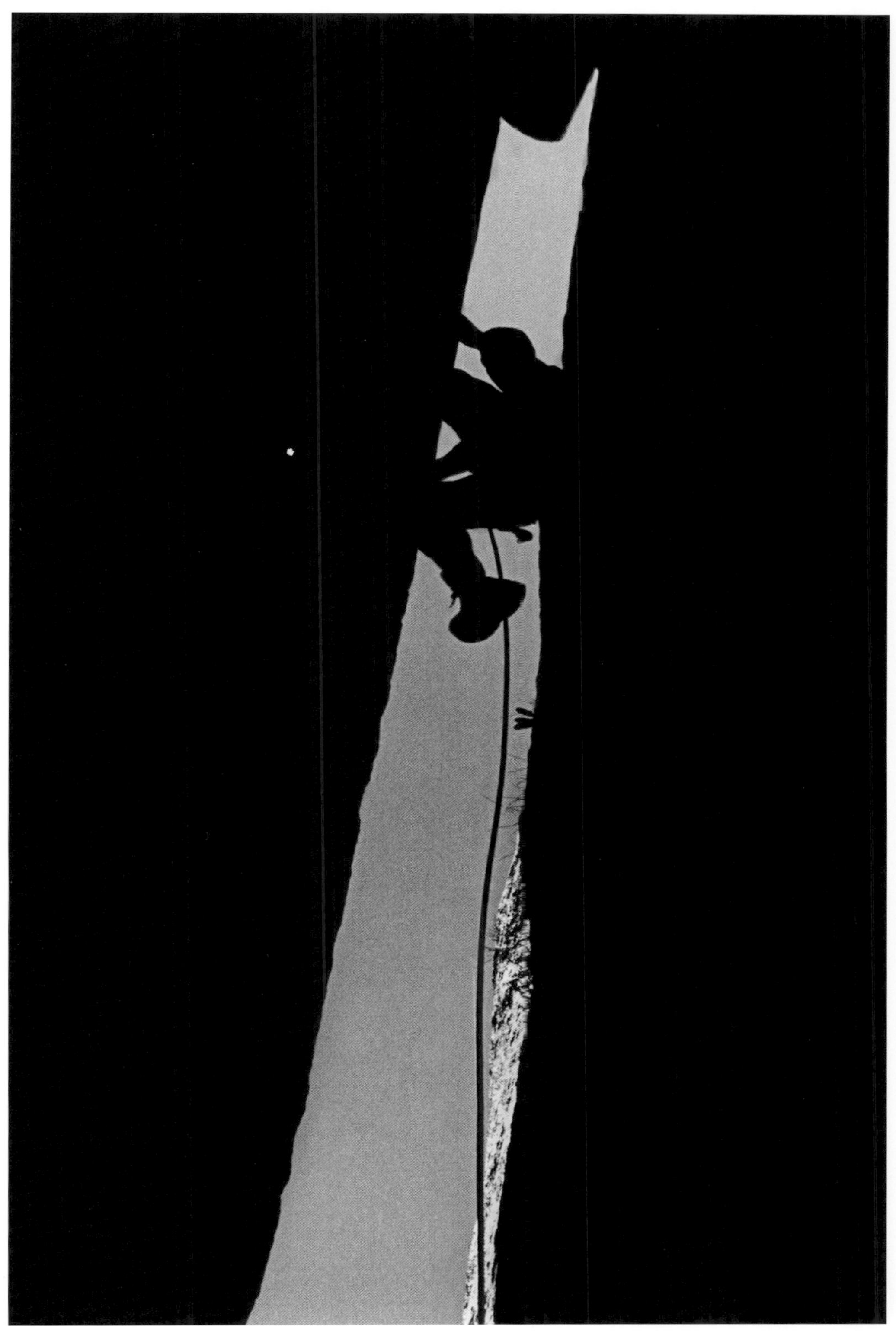

Tom Frost moves up in the Great Chimney, a claustrophobic slot high on the Washington Column, Yosemite Valley, 1958.
Photo: Henry Kendall, courtesy Archive of the Norfolk Charitable Trust

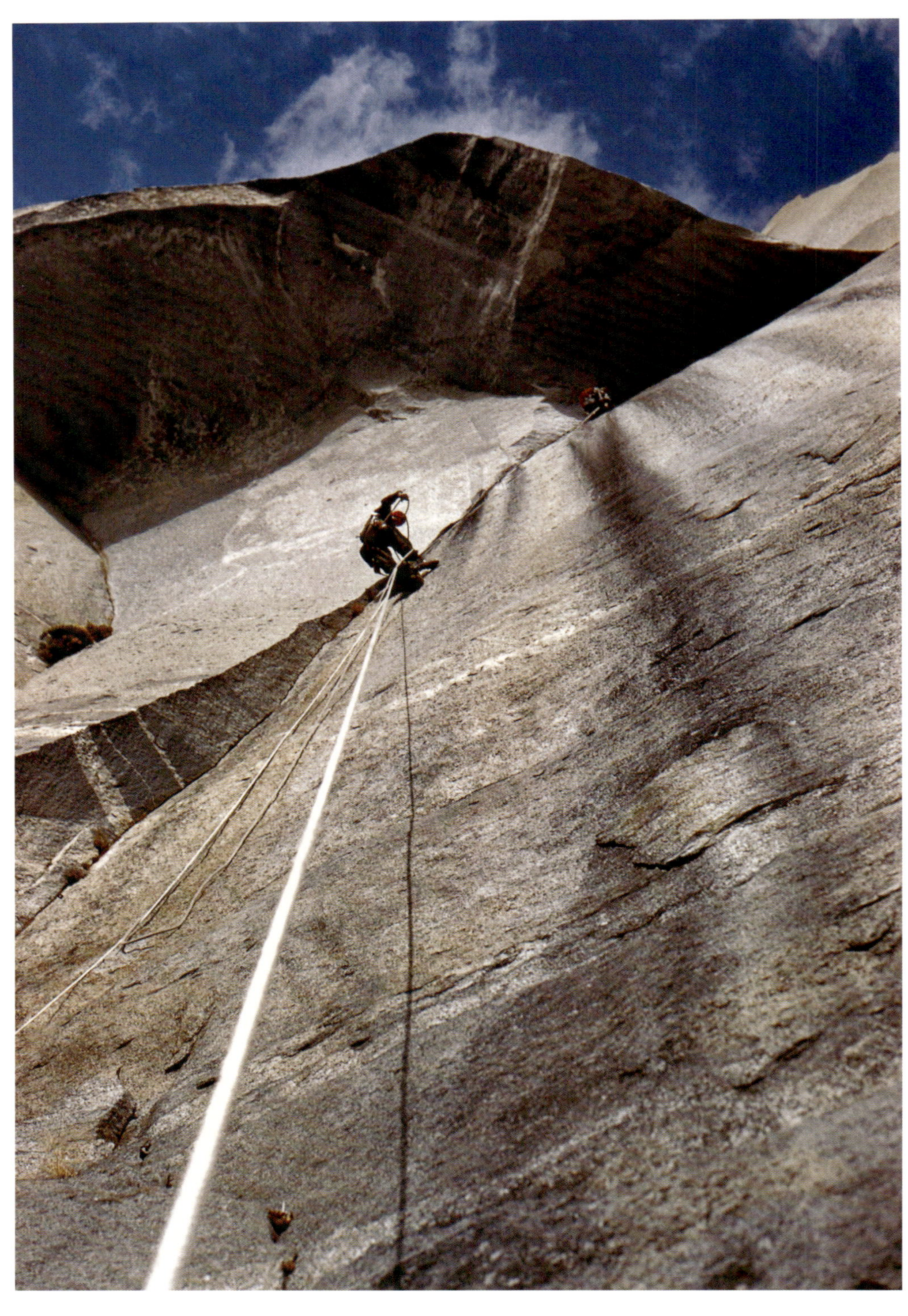

George Whitmore belays Warren Harding on the Great Roof Pitch on the Nose Route of El Capitan. Photo: Wayne Merry

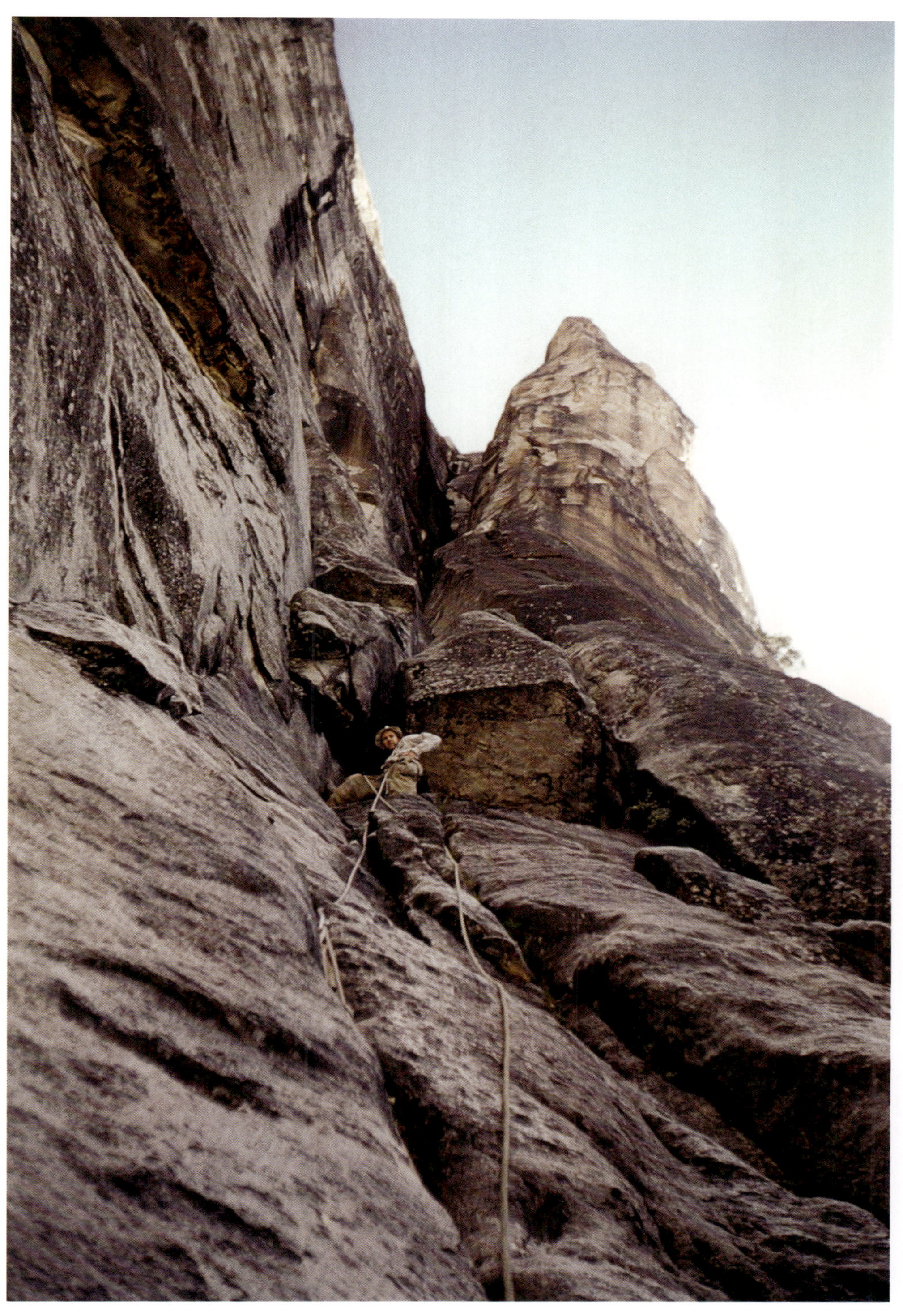

Chuck Wilts low on the Lost Arrow Chimney Route, Yosemite Valley, 1955. Photo: Jerry Gallwas

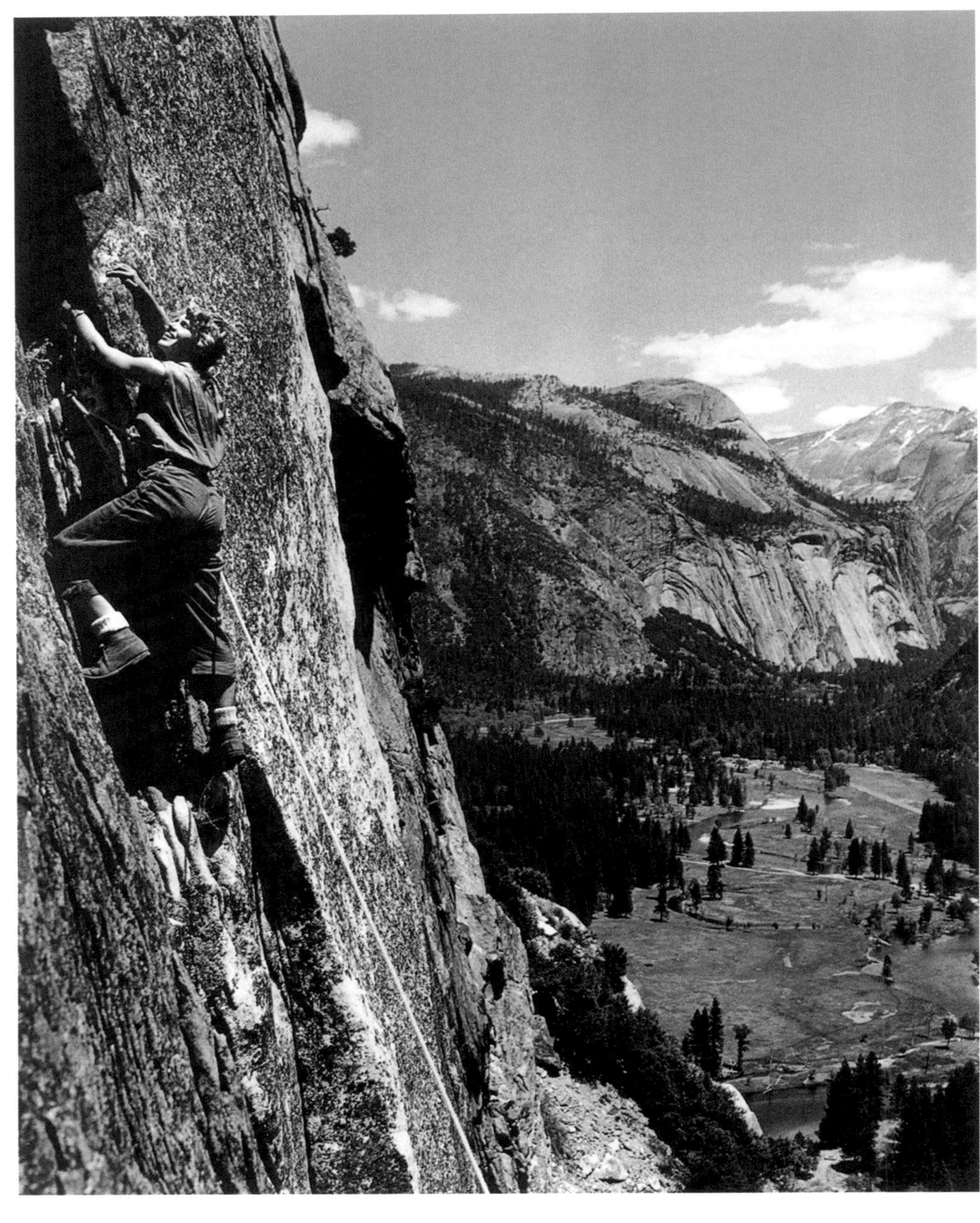

Nancy Bickford Miller leading on the Southwest Arete of Lower Brother, Yosemite 1955.
Photo: Bob & Ira Spring, Spring Trust for Trails

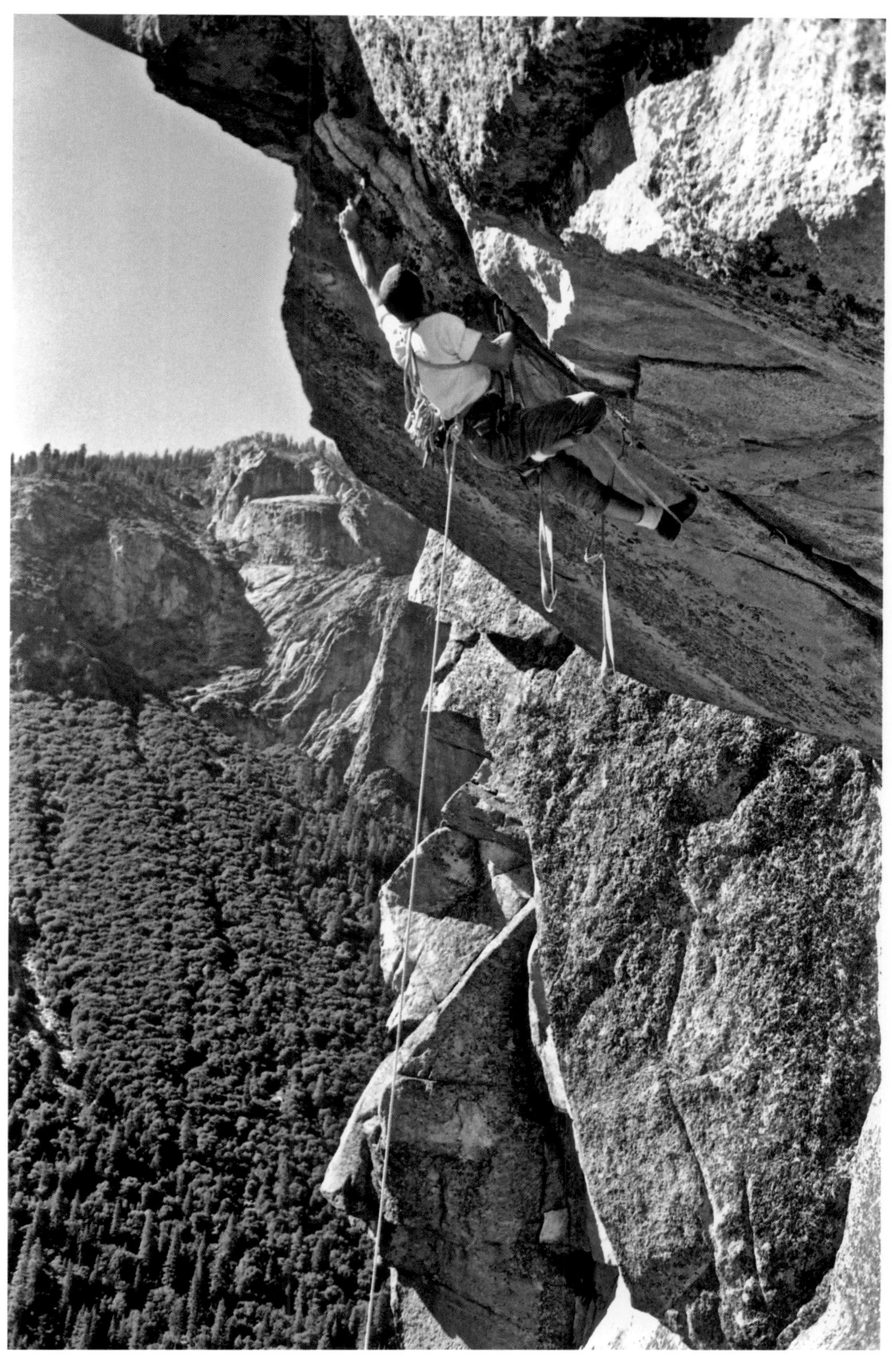

Tom Frost on first ascent of the Roof, Lower Cathedral Rock, Yosemite 1958.
Photo: Henry Kendall, courtesy Archive of the Norfolk Charitable Trust

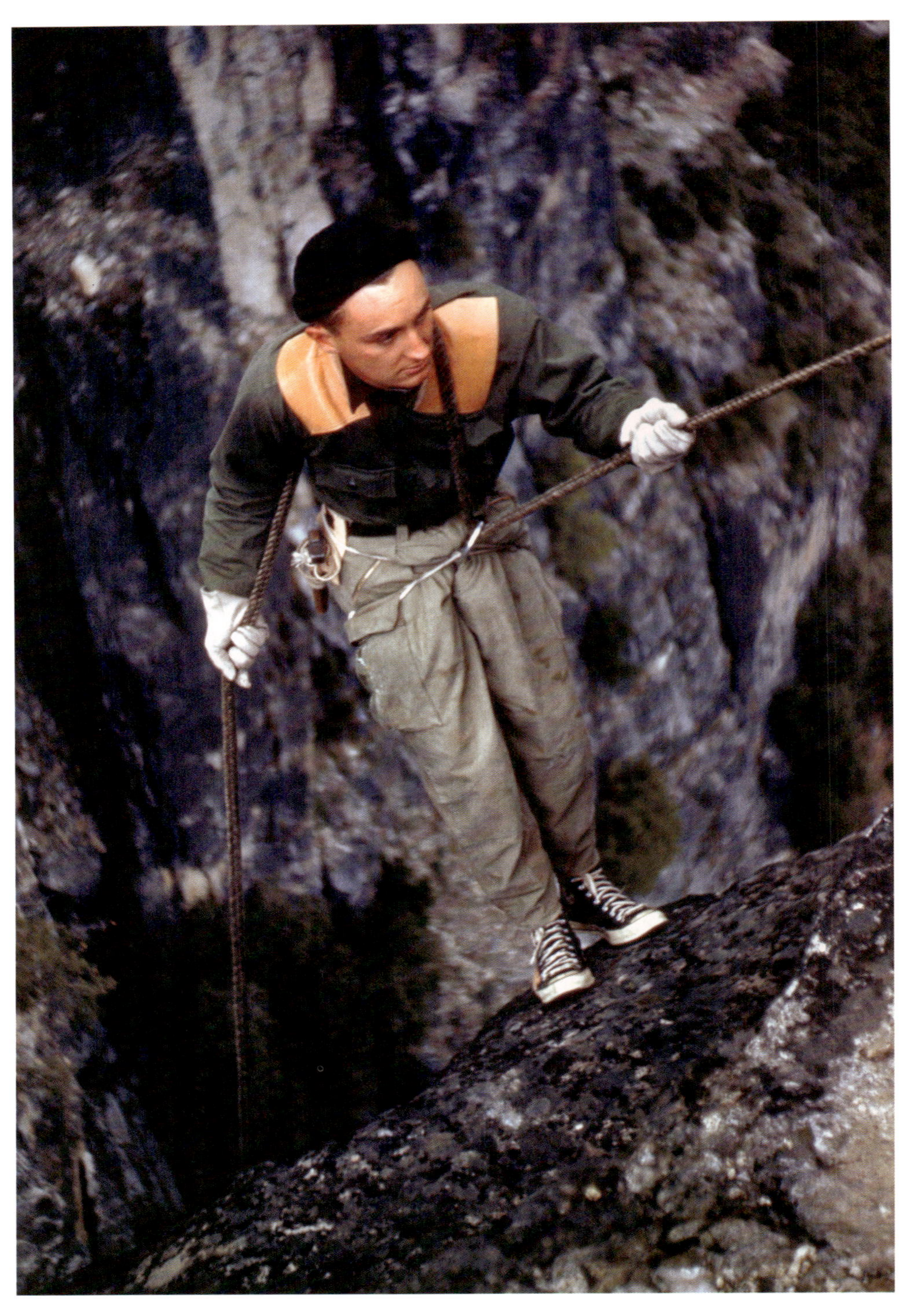

Wayne Merry rappels from Arrowhead Spire, Yosemite Valley, 1953.
Note the leather shoulder patches to protect the neck and shoulder from rope burns while rappelling. Photo: Jerry Gallwas

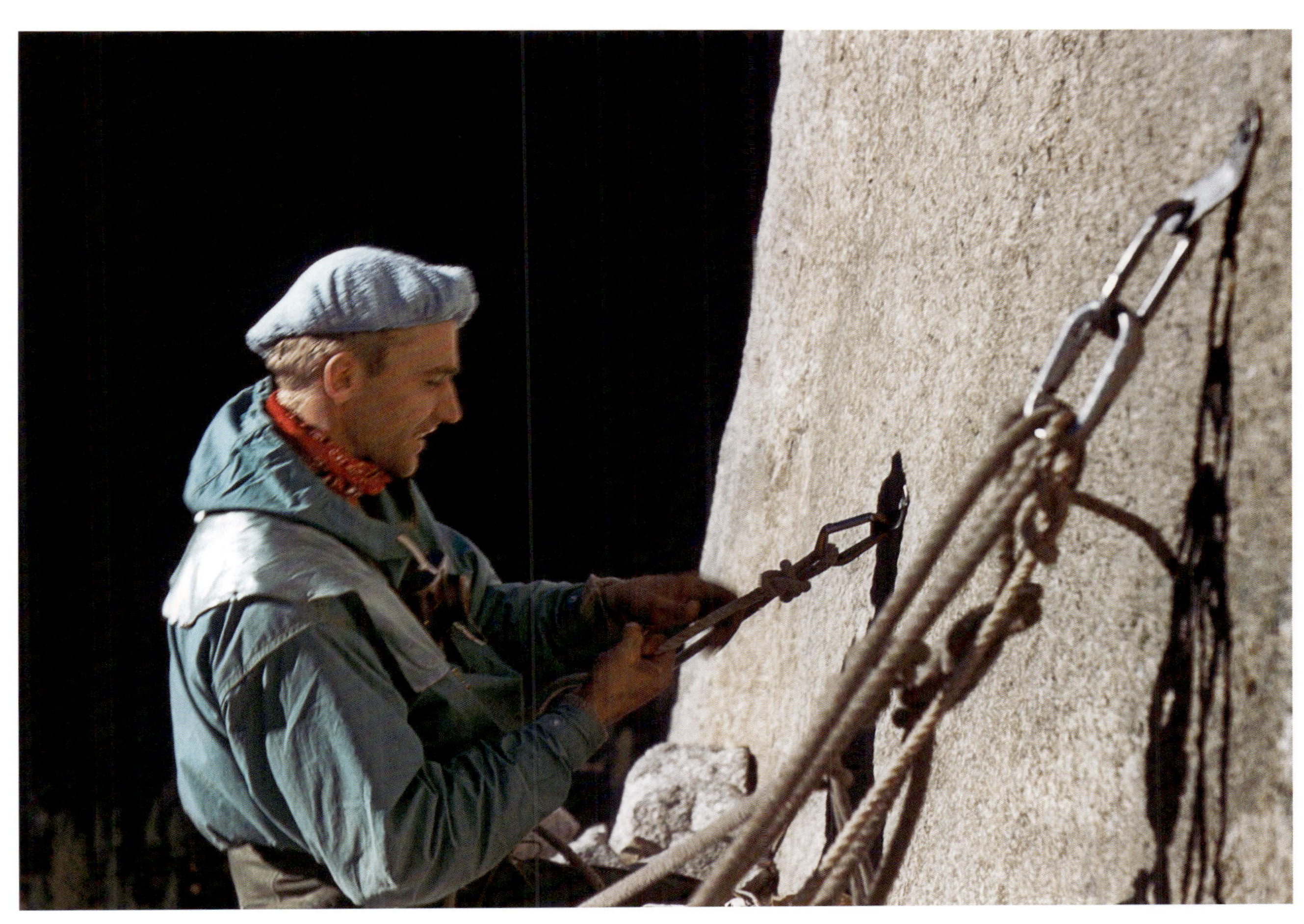

Bill ("Dolt") Feuerer. Photo: Allen Steck

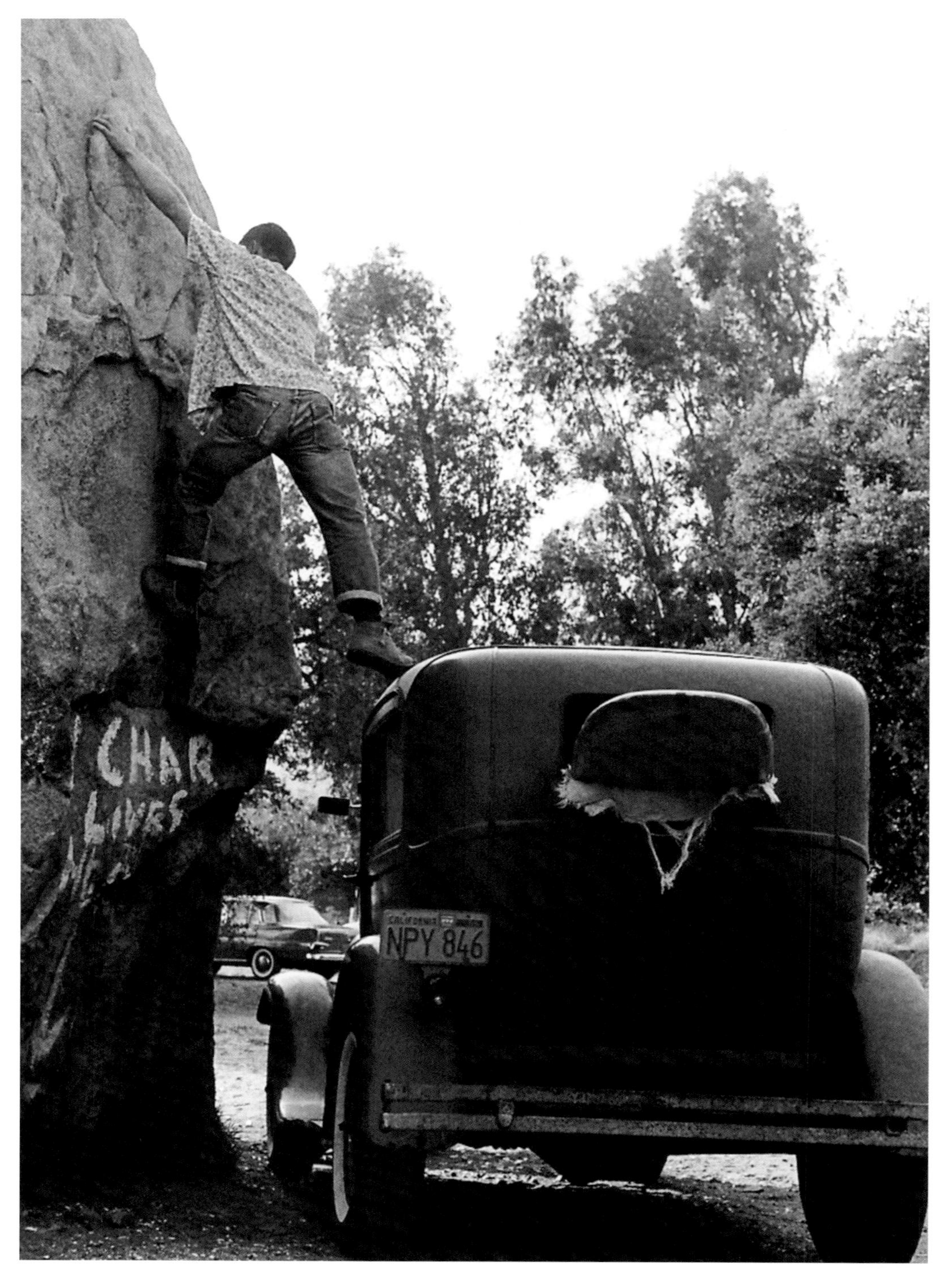

With surfboard in tow, Yvon Chouinard gaining height advantage on a boulder at Stoney Point, a climbing area near Los Angeles, late '50s. Photo: Roger Cotton Brown

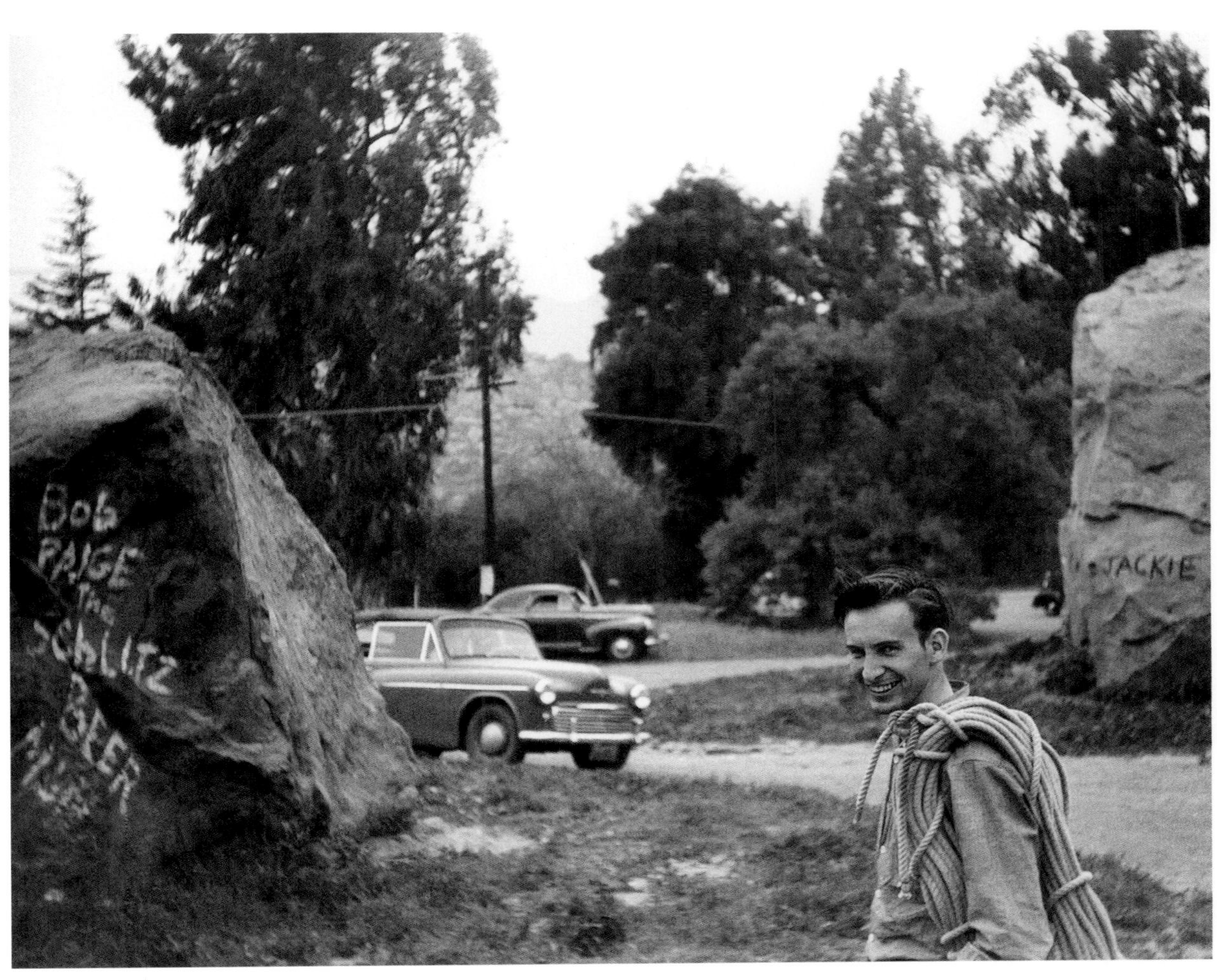

Royal Robbins approaching "Beer Man Rock" at Stoney Point, 1954. Photo: Frank Hoover

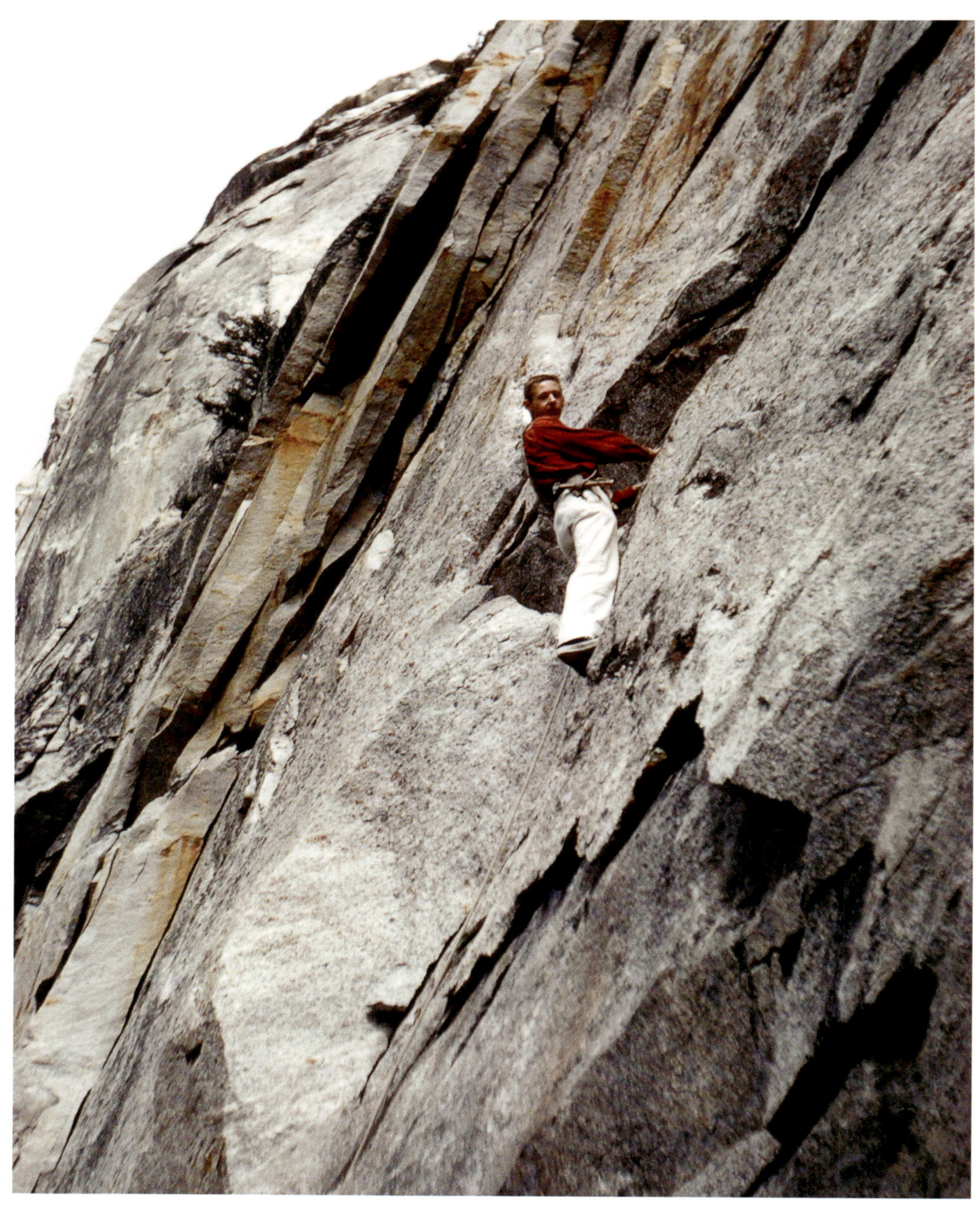

Don Wilson leads at Tahquitz Rock, a major Southern California climbing area. Photo: Jerry Gallwas collection

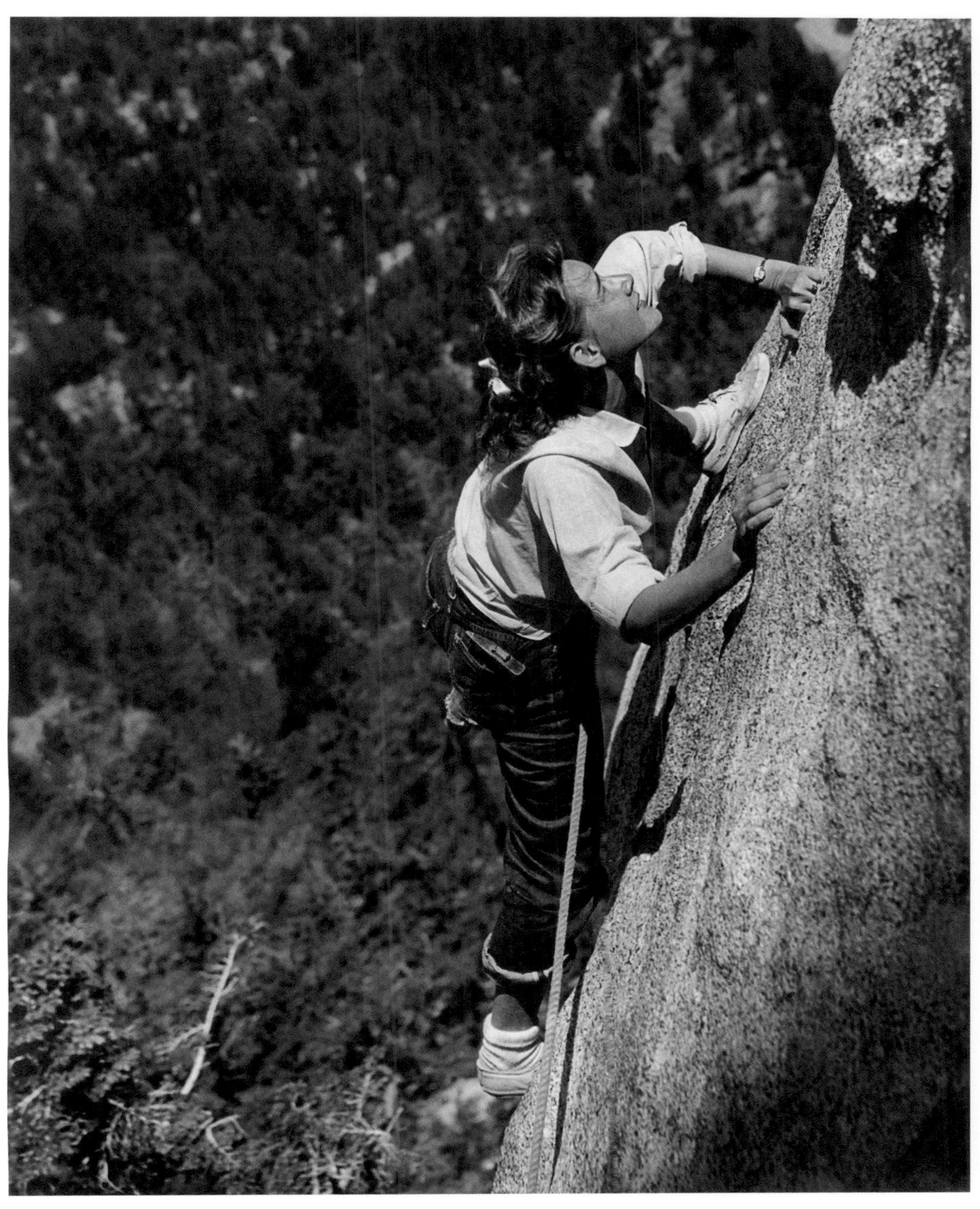

Natalie Sherrick ponders her next move at Tahquitz Rock, Southern California. Photo: Frank Hoover

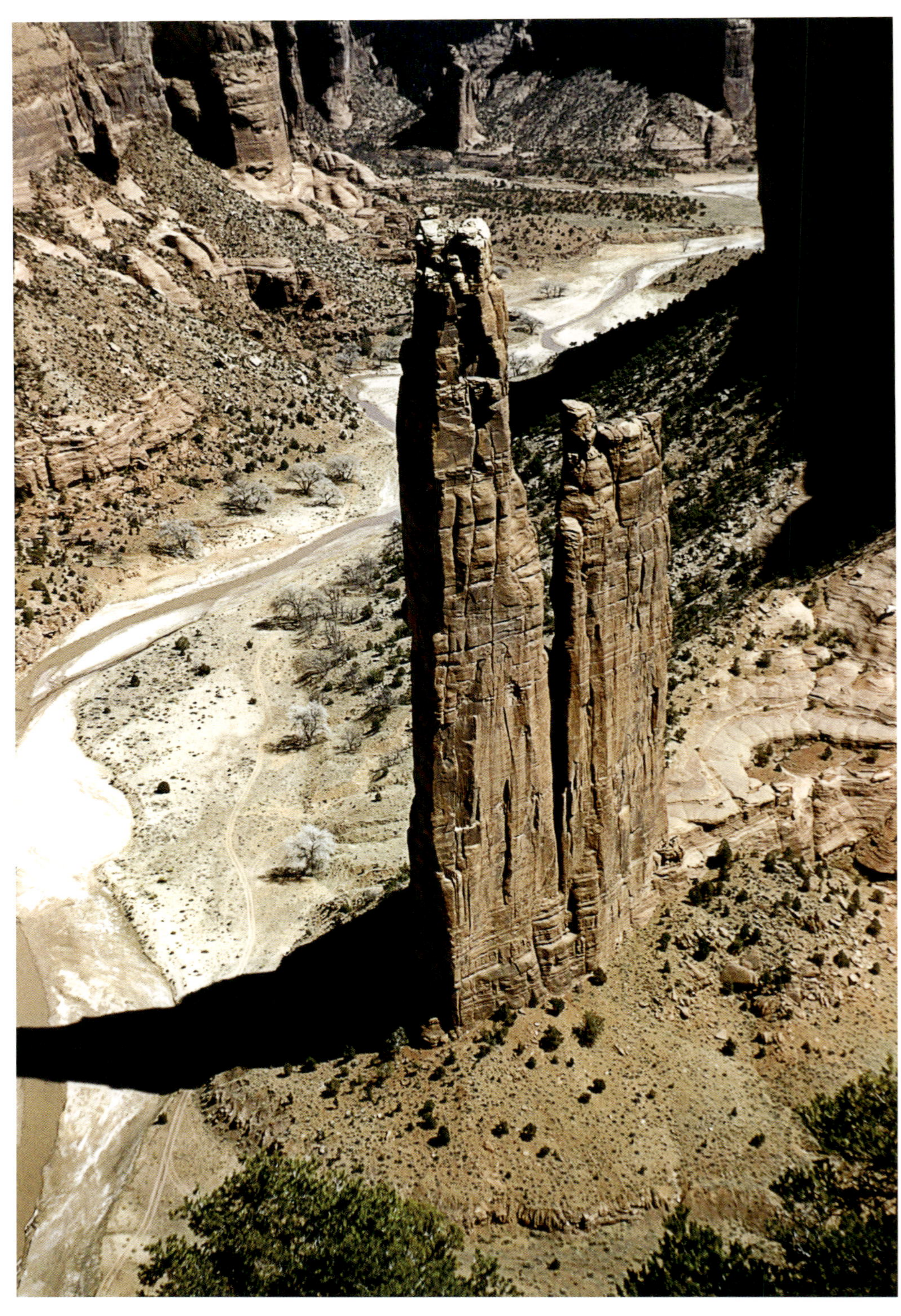

Spider Rock, a striking tower in Canyon de Chelly National Monument, Arizona, 1956. Photo: Jerry Gallwas

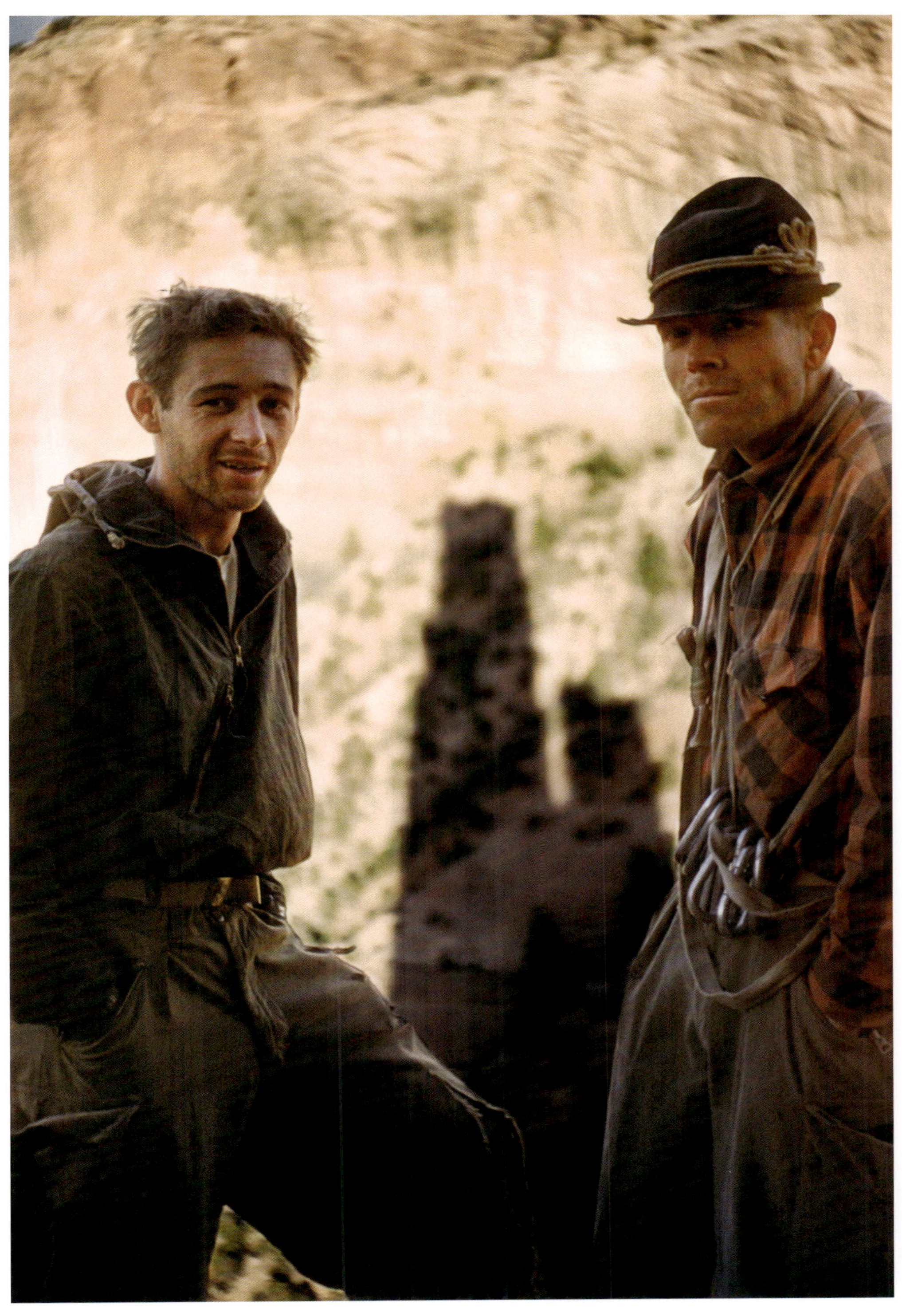

Don Wilson and Mark Powell on the summit after first ascent, with the shadow of Spider Rock in the background, 1956. Photo: Jerry Gallwas

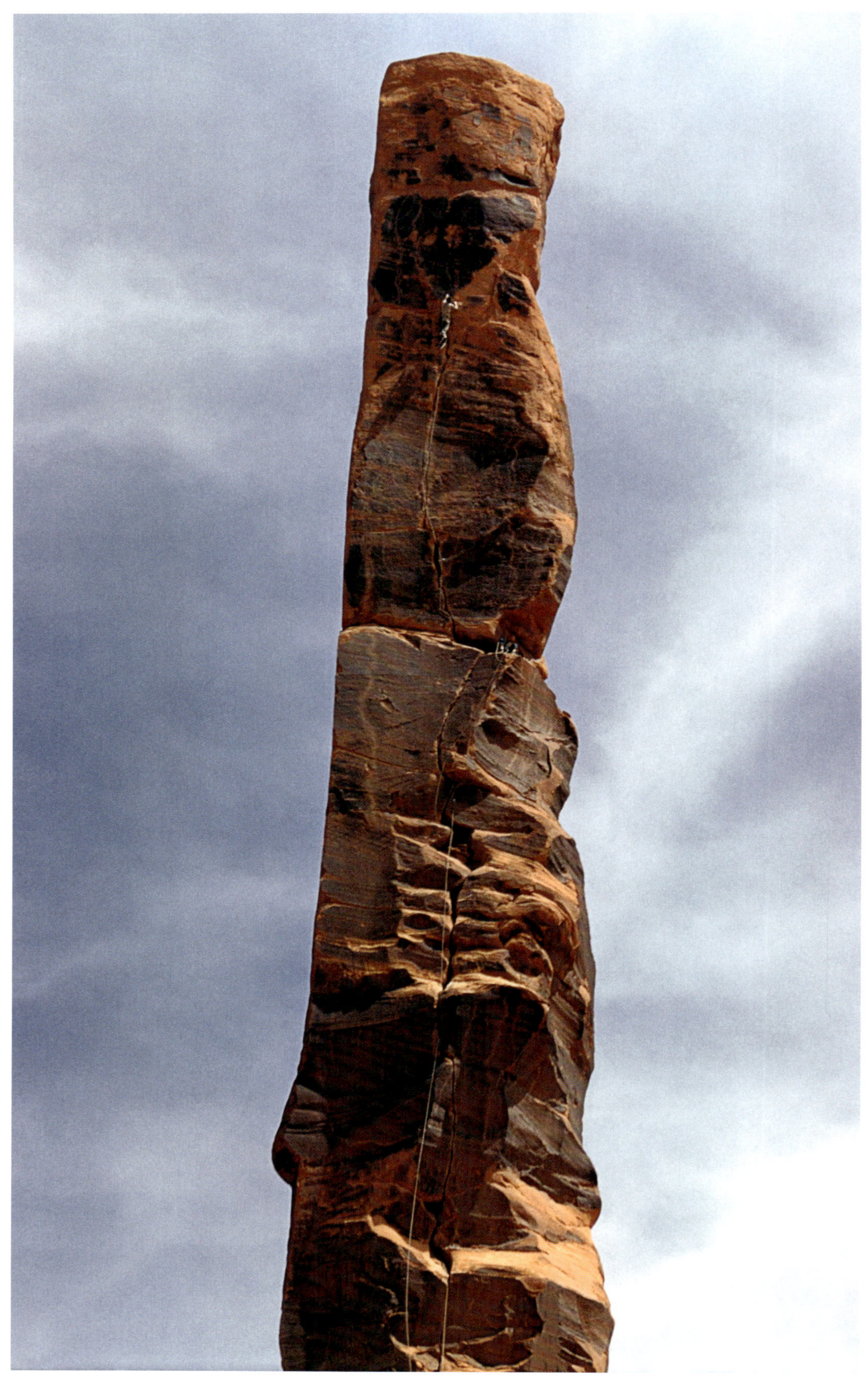

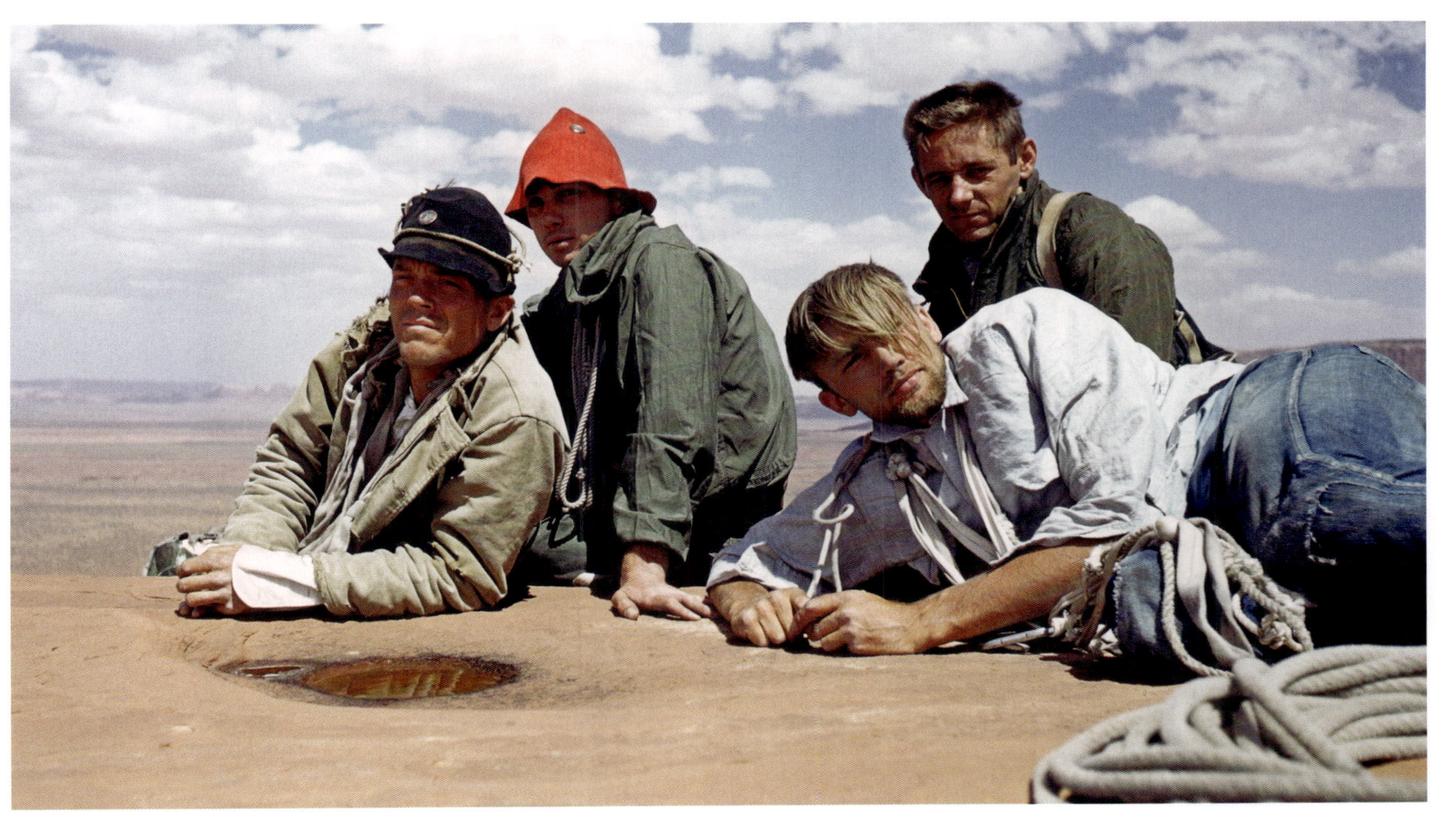

(L): Mark Powell leading and Don Wilson belaying high on the Totem Pole, Monument Valley, Arizona. Photo: Bill Feuerer
(R): Mark Powell, Jerry Gallwas, Bill Feuerer, and Don Wilson atop the Totem Pole after their first ascent, 1957. Photo: Bill Feuerer

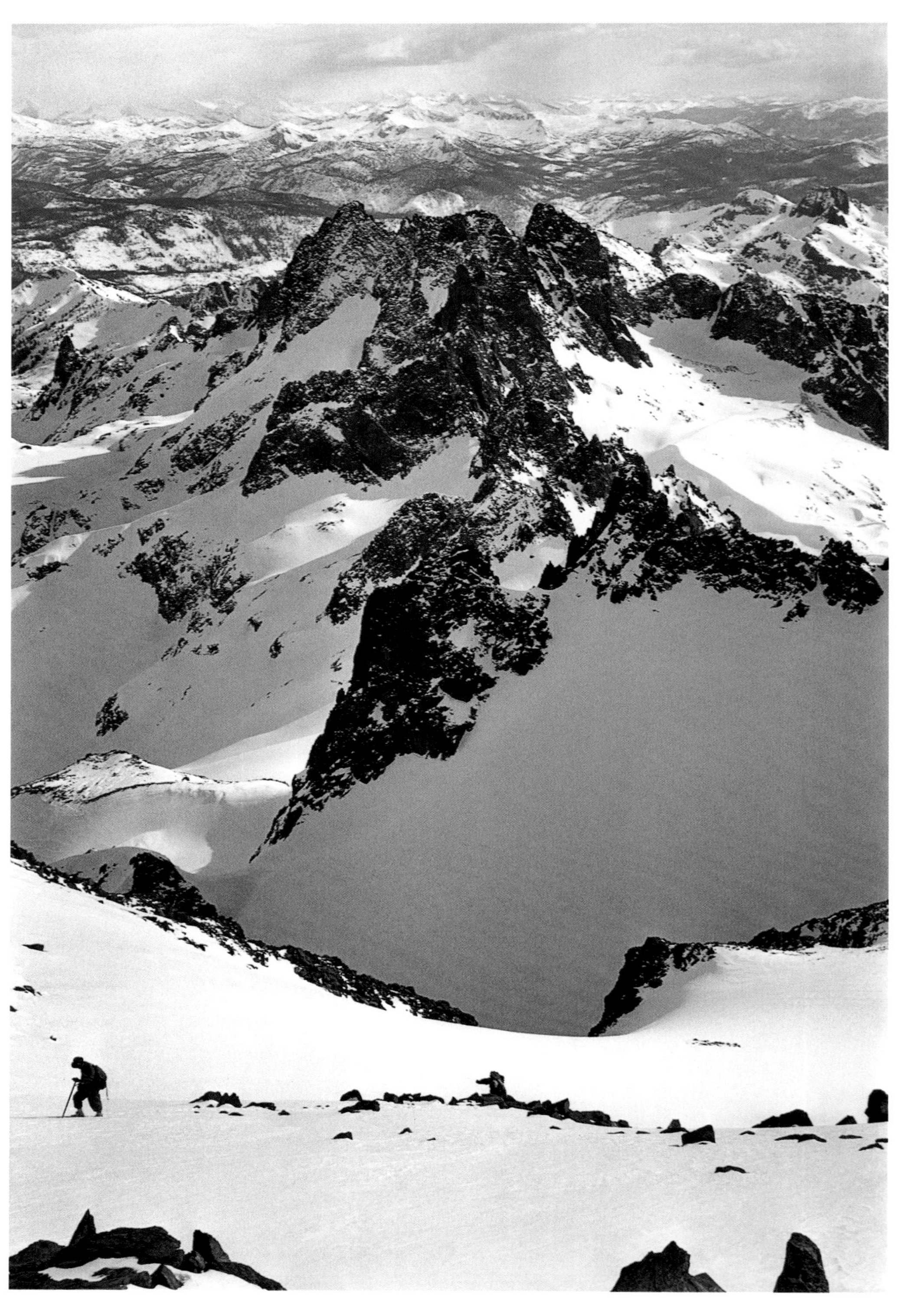

First Winter ascent in the High Sierra, with the Minarets seen from the slopes of Mount Ritter. Photo: Bob Swift

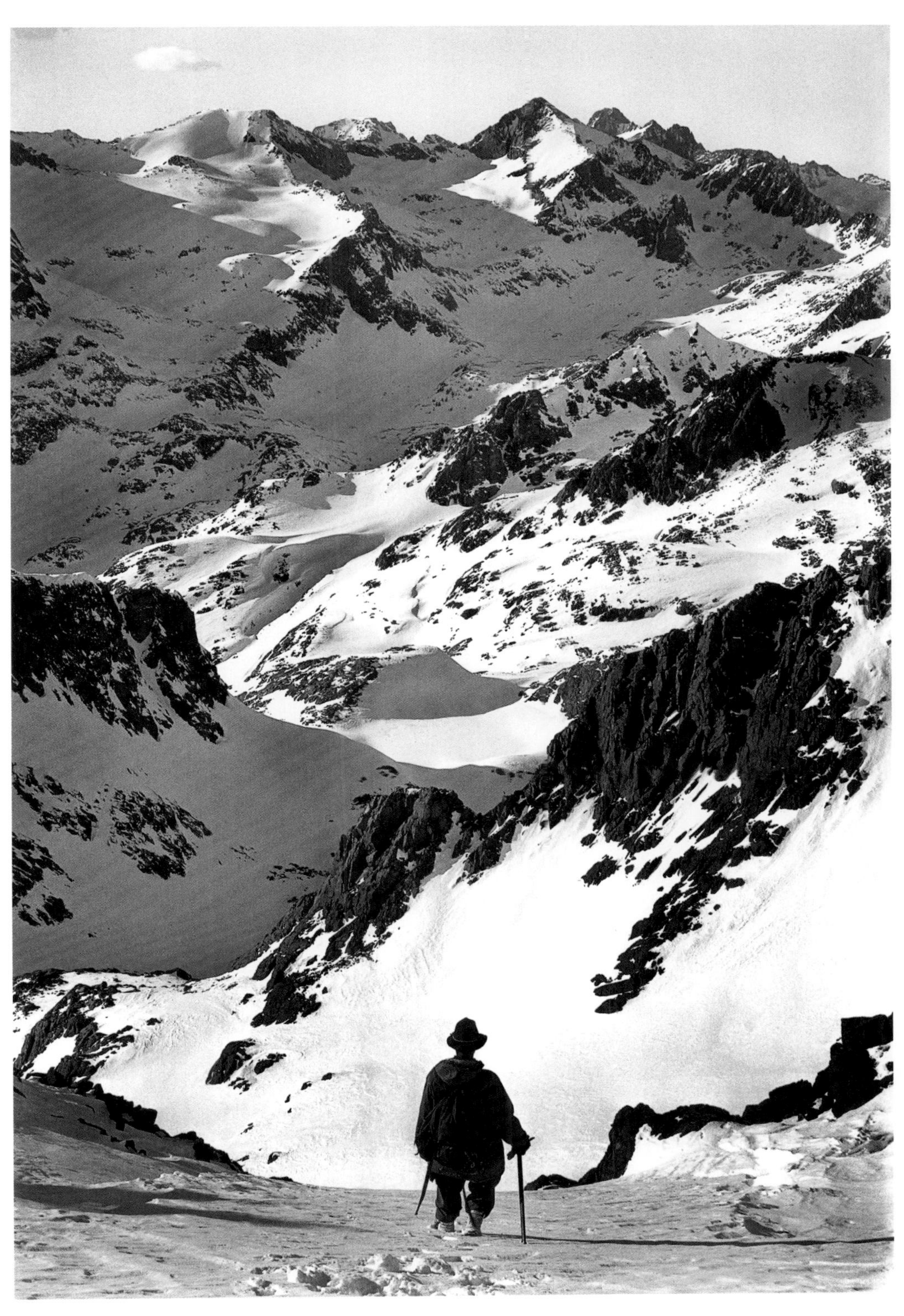

George Bloom gazes north from Mount Ritter toward the high point of Yosemite National Park, Mount Lyell. Photo: Bob Swift

T. Adler Books (tadlerbooks.com) Distributed Art Publishers (artbook.com)
Printed in China by Oceanic Graphic International
ISBN #9781938922268

Loomis Dean photos from Time and Life Pictures/Getty images
Ansel Adams photograph courtesy of The Ansel Adams Publishing Rights Trust

Very special thanks to Evan Backes, Dean Fidelman, Steve Wilkings, Steve Pezman, Jeff Divine, Steve Roper, Glen Denny, Yvon Chouinard, Jerry Gallwas, Rick Ridgeway, Todd Bradway, Ben Hoy, Jeanene Van Zandt, and Kat Borchart. Also, Surfing Heritage & Culture Center, Bev Morgan, Joe Quigg, Aggie Quigg, John Severson (surferart.com), George Greenough, Dana Brown, Dick Metz, Dick Perry, Bob Swift, Allen Steck, Frank Hoover, Mike Sherrick, Mark Powell, Barbara Lilley, John Rawlings and Stanford University Libraries, Ken Yager/Yosemite Climbing Association, Lowell Skoog, John E. Spring, Vicky Spring, Margaret Denny, Roger Cotton Brown, Liz Robbins, Suzy Bennitt and Pink Moment Press, Claudia Rice, Audrey Todd Borisov, Don Lauria, Denise Gose, Spring Trust for Trails, Trip Aldredge, Jim Galoon, Richard K. Irvin/Stanford University Libraries' Department of Special Collections and University Archives, John Dutton, Henry P. Kendall Foundation, Norfolk Charitable Trust, Elizabeth Mcgregor, Michel Ziberstein, Jeff Johnson, Chris Malloy, Luke Adler, Dibi Fletcher, Walter Hoffman, Center for Creative Photography, University of Arizona, The Ansel Adams Publishing Rights Trust, Chris Rohloff (grantrohloff.com), Doug Bunting, Jeff Hollenbeck, Peter Kersten (Getty Images), Jeff Alter, Yvonne Puffer, Pauline Luton Hops, Steve Barlotti, Scott Hulet, Allan Seymour, Steve Hops, Jerry Anderson, Bruce Perkins, Troy Hamilton, Guillermo Valdez, Bob Cornelius, Brie Jones, Harold Ward, Melissa Dickerson, Dustin Lee, Karla Olson, Kevin Blachly & Jason Rys / Wixen Music.

Cover Photographs: (L) Matt Kivlin at Malibu. Photo: Joe Quigg (R): Tom Frost on the East Buttress of Middle Cathedral Rock, Yosemite Valley, California, 1958. Photo: Henry Kendall courtesy Archive of the Norfolk Charitable Trust